Adams and Jefferson
THE STORY OF A FRIENDSHIP

Adams and Jefferson

THE STORY OF A FRIENDSHIP

·

John Murray Allison

UNIVERSITY OF OKLAHOMA PRESS

NORMAN

Library of Congress Catalog Card Number 66–13419

Copyright 1966 by the University of Oklahoma Press, Publishing Division of the University. Composed and printed at Norman, Oklahoma, U.S.A., by the University of Oklahoma Press. First edition.

To Elizabeth
Who stays young along with me

Preface

ANYONE WHO VENTURES to write about the past or people who lived in the past is necessarily under obligation to all those who have covered the ground before him, to all who have investigated the period and written about it or have collected and edited documents from the period. He is also indebted to those who have written biographies of the principals or volumes dealing with a particular phase of their lives. Just as definite, if not as apparent, is his obligation to authors who have written biographies of other persons who appear prominently in the narrative or vignettes which add to knowledge of the men or their contemporaries.

For both Adams and Jefferson the pen was an instrument seldom neglected during their long years of activity. The former began a diary at the age of twenty, and while there are many gaps in that intimate record and it was eventually and permanently discontinued, the aggregate of these entries is imposing, and they are most revealing regarding the man and, in considerable measure also, the history of the period leading up to, continuing through, and following the American Revolution. Jefferson was not inclined to such a practice, but he wrote down all kinds of data of special value to him; more important, from the point of view of later generations, he was one of the most prolific letter writers of his time. His Massachusetts contemporary also wrote much more for correspondents than he did for his own personal perusal.

Moreover, neither Adams nor Jefferson could resist the autobiographical urge. The result of this inner compulsion was, in each case, fragmentary and of limited value for historical purposes. In getting the background for this narrative, however, one of the guiding principles has been that nothing which such men wrote about themselves and their respective parts in making history should be overlooked.

Undoubtedly much that they committed to paper has been destroyed by the ravages of time, but an immense bulk has been preserved and, most fortunately, is being made generally available. The *Adams Papers* are now being published under sponsorship of the Massachusetts Historical Society; and the *Papers of Thomas Jefferson* are also in the process of publication, a project initiated by the Thomas Jefferson Bicentennial Commission. The splendid editing of the Adams collection by L. H. Butterfield and of the Jefferson manuscripts by Julian P. Boyd increases the value of these ventures, which supersede all previous ones of this kind and are of such magnitude as to require many years for fulfilment. The volumes that have already appeared in each of these series have been of inestimable value to this writer, as they will be, along with the ones that follow, to all who in time to come wish to make use of this material.

Every personal relationship is set within a framework of circumstances for which there is no exact parallel. That which existed between Adams and Jefferson was surrounded, and to a great extent fashioned, by events of unusual historical significance. The American Revolution and the scarcely less critical developments that followed as the new nation advanced through adolescence constituted the environment within which their tie of friendship was formed, then broken, to be restored some years later with more than its original strength. Both men were heads of families before they were recognized statesmen and on throughout the many years in which they held the latter distinction. Therefore to tell the story of their friendship without bringing them frequently into focus as men fortunately bound by ties of home and kindred would be as unrealistic as it would be to narrate events leading up to the siege and sack of Troy without reference to the lady whose beauty "launched a thousand ships."

The vicissitudes of life which kept John and Abigail Adams apart, in a geographical sense, for months, even years, at a time over a quarter of a century made their situation something less than ideal.

But if they had spent all the days of those years together, or if Abigail and her sisters and other close relatives had never been separated by thousands of sea miles or long land distances, posterity would have been the loser. In the *Familiar Letters of John Adams and His Wife Abigail Adams, During the Revolution,* the *Letters of John Adams, Addressed to His Wife,* the *Letters of Mrs. Adams,* and the *New Letters of Abigail Adams* are many examples of excellence in the epistolary art; more than that, from these collections the careful reader gets flashes of insight into that cluster of movements and events with which Adams and Jefferson were closely associated and by which the course of their lives was directly affected.

Of less importance historically, but not without interest and value, is a number of letters written by the younger Abigail Adams, composed with filial devotion. These have been made available to the public by the efforts of some of her descendants and, incidentally, in a few volumes under the imprimatur of various editors. Further, her "Journal," limited in scope and outlook as it is, fills some gaps in our knowledge of the remarkable family into which Jefferson was introduced as a comparatively young widower. Her fragmentary diary entries and even the more numerous ones made by her father are dwarfed in comparison with those of her older brother, the American Pepys, who throughout most of his lifetime recorded, with an almost incredible variety of facts and comments, his day-by-day experiences. From the Jefferson side there has come down to us a much smaller amount of personal memorabilia. Except for the material of this nature, abundant as it is, in Jefferson's output as a correspondent, we have only those letters which he received from his daughters (not nearly as many as he desired), which because of his eminence have escaped the oblivion to which most family correspondence is consigned.

The publication a little more than forty years ago of the *Correspondence of John Adams and Thomas Jefferson, 1812–1826,* with informative and sparkling comments by the editor, Paul Wilstach, brought these two great Americans into juxtaposition for twentieth-century readers—an accomplishment without parallel in the century that had elapsed since their death. But the appearance in 1959 of the *Adams-Jefferson Letters*, with ample and scholarly notes by the editor, Lester J. Cappon, was the culmination of a project complete in its scope and an event of major importance in this field. Without the aid of these volumes, the difficulties involved in writing this one might have seemed insurmountable.

The reader will observe that in the use of borrowed material the practice has been to avoid lengthy quotations from any of the original sources and to retain the peculiarities of capitalization and punctuation, even the frequent mistakes in spelling and occasional grammatical errors, as they have been copied in the *Adams Papers*, the *Papers of Thomas Jefferson*, and the *New Letters of Abigail Adams*. If the unrevised letters of either one of the Adams couple were submitted today to an English teacher for correction, red marks would be made on almost every page. There may have been some rule or pattern which they followed in the matter of capitalization, but it is not discernible; apparently their choice of the big initial letter was made at random. Moreover, their spelling was erratic.

In the mechanics of written language, Jefferson conformed more closely to our accepted standards, but he, too, was far from being a champion speller. The author of the Declaration of Independence usually wrote the last word of that title "independance." In other places, however brilliant his ideas may have been, his orthography was deficient. The main purpose of language, however, is not to please the pedant, but to communicate ideas; and the fact is indisputable that Jefferson and the Adams pair surpassed in the art of written communication. It seems fitting to present brief selections from these eighteenth- and early nineteenth-century letters clothed in the same language garb as that in which they first appeared, with only such minor concessions as the capitalization of the first words of sentences, the omission of words and phrases repeated evidently by mistake, and the like.

Paul Leicester Ford's edition of Jefferson's writings has been helpful in the preparation of this work, especially for the three and one-half decades not covered by the volumes that have so far appeared in the *Papers of Thomas Jefferson.* More frequently than the notes indicate, use has also been made of the Memorial Edition (A. A. Lipscomb and A. E. Bergh, editors). Obligation of a similar kind is acknowledged to Charles Francis Adams, who more than one hundred years ago compiled for publication the works of his grandfather, and afterwards carried to completion a task begun by his father—a biography of their eminent forebear. Since that time a few others have taken our second President as a subject for extensive biographical study, most recent among them Page Smith, whose distinctive two-volume contribution clarifies for modern readers the image of a great but complex character.

Jefferson has appealed to a greater number of biographers, beginning, if we include only the large-scale productions, with the work of Henry S. Randall, and continuing to the comparatively recent and masterly accomplishments of Mrs. Marie Kimball, Nathan Schachner, and Dumas Malone. To all of these and to many others, not specifically mentioned in this introduction, who have helped to cast light upon the character and services of one or the other or both of the principals in this friendship (or have merely provided a sidelight), there is due an expression, inadequate as it must be, of gratitude. Coupled with this feeling is one of near-trepidation induced by entering into a field where many others have labored so fruitfully.

Also, a most appreciative recognition is herewith extended to all who have given immediate and face-to-face assistance along the lengthy way leading to publication; first of all, to Gilbert Chinard. In addition to being the source of many benefits as the author of twin biographies—one of Adams and one of Jefferson—he was generous with initial encouragement in this venture. The help of many librarians and their staffs of workers has been immeasurable. Special mention should be made of facilities rendered available, often in second-mile fashion, by personnel of the Library of Congress, the Public Library of Cleveland, Ohio, the New York City Public Library, and the various public libraries of Albany, New York.; and by those in charge of the vast collection of books and bound newspapers in the New York State Library. Last to be mentioned, but far from the least among those helping directly to make this book possible, is my wife, who has made the home where it has been written a haven with a minimum of interruptions and a maximum of opportunities to do one's best work.

This final introductory word seems necessary: the writer makes no claim to be a professional historian. What is presented between these covers is the product of an avocation. But no effort has been spared and an incalculable amount of time has been spent in compliance with a constraint to make the narrative as accurate and informative and interesting as possible.

John Murray Allison

Albany, New York
January 5, 1966.

Contents

❧

Adams and Jefferson
THE STORY OF A FRIENDSHIP

"I find friendship to be like wine, raw when new, ripened with age, the true old man's milk and restorative cordial."
—THOMAS JEFFERSON

CHAPTER I

Birth of a Nation and of a Friendship

PHILADELPHIA, 1775–76

꼬ᴖᴗᴗ꼬

O N A JUNE MORNING in the next to the last year of the American colonies' formal dependence upon Great Britain, Philadelphia breadwinners went about their tasks in the usual manner. Over their way of life coming events were casting premonitory shadows, but, just as in less anxious times, there was a day's work to be done.

At the regular hour, offices and stores and shops and taverns were opened, and within preparations were made to receive clients and customers. Housewives and servants, carrying bulky containers, began to cluster about long rows of stalls on High Street and to inspect food supplies, for this was a market day, and great quantities of vegetables and fruit and other farm products, having been unloaded from Conestoga wagons, were being offered for sale. Beyond the wharves that lined the Philadelphia water front, on the rippling surface of the river, packets, lumber rafts, ferryboats, sloops, and schooners were riding at anchor or threading their separate cautious way through the maze of the busy harbor. In the State House, delegates to the Second Continental Congress assembled to "consider the state of America."

At nine o'clock John Hancock, who had been elected president of the Congress four weeks before, started proceedings in regular form. Urbane and diplomatic in manner and singularly devoted, for one of his class and station, to the movement that was to result in independence, this merchant from the elite district of Boston had been the unanimous choice of his fellow delegates as Peyton Randolph's successor after the latter resigned to take up his former duties as speaker of the Virginia House of Burgesses. On this particular morning Hancock's features and actions betokened a mild excitement.

In fact, most of the members of this assembly were showing more than routine interest in the business immediately before them, for Thomas Jefferson, a man of whom they had heard much, Randolph's replacement, was making his first appearance as a delegate. He would present his credentials and, presumably, would be duly seated. He had arrived in the city the preceding day, having traveled the 325 miles from Williamsburg at a rate averaging more than 30 miles a day.

There was no hitch in the formalities. Within a few minutes Jefferson entered officially another phase of his public career.[1]

The way now clear for other business, Patrick Henry arose and received recognition. He had recently been in consultation with General Washington who, not without reason, was awed and mystified by his new responsibilities as commander of the colonial army. On the day before, he had written to his stepbrother: "I am embarked on a wide ocean, boundless in its prospects, and from whence, perhaps, no safe harbor is to be found."[2]

Acting now in liaison capacity, Henry announced that the General had "sundry queries" to make of Congress and desired to have a prompt answer to them. The "queries" were read, and as the forenoon advanced, there was debate regarding the reply.[3] Other matters pressed upon the attention of the delegates, who were themselves steering a hazardous course, very much like sailors on an uncharted ocean. For most of them there was little time, that long summer day, for anything except the business which had brought them together.

The new delegate was not unfamiliar with legislative assemblies, but never before had he rubbed shoulders with so many men of such moral and intellectual stature. His keen eyes, accustomed to wide mountain and valley vistas, ranged repeatedly over the occupants of

---

[1] *Journals of the Continental Congress*, edited by Worthington C. Ford (34 vols., Washington, 1904–37), II, 101–102 (cited hereafter as *Journals*).

[2] Washington to John Augustine Washington, June 20, 1775, *Letters of Members of the Continental Congress*, edited by Edmund C. Burnett (8 vols., Washington, 1921–36), I, 138 (cited hereafter as Burnett, *Letters*).

[3] *Journals*, II, 102. See also *Patrick Henry, the Voice of Freedom*, by Jacob Axelrad (New York, 1947), 123.

this walled-in space and flashed their respective images to his inquisitive mind. Of several in the group, impressions previously made by correspondence or by general report were now confirmed or revised. Among those whom he had looked forward to meeting for the first time was a man prominent in the cause already designated as "American"—John Adams of Massachusetts.

Brought together in this fashion by an unusual surge of events, these two men began to estimate one another along lines different from those they would have followed if their first meeting had been more casual and the circumstances surrounding it less portentous. Both were accustomed to evaluating men according to their actual or possible usefulness to the "American" cause.

The staid old city in which that cause was being directed had rarely, if ever, experienced a week as crowded with thrilling happenings as that third one of June, 1775. Every day infantry battalions and artillery companies were drilling in the State House square and other open spaces about the city, each potential soldier arrayed in a striking uniform. On the very morning Jefferson assumed his new duties these units maneuvered in formal review before the designated commander-in-chief, about to start northward to make contact with his army. For his actual departure on Friday morning there was an escorting cavalcade, with martial music and, in general, éclat usually reserved for returning conquerors. Adams and a number of other members of the Congress rode in the procession for five miles. In places the road was dusty, at times there were threats of a downpour of rain, and the summer heat was enervating. But these circumstances detracted only slightly from the attention given by Adams and his fellow members to the mounted central figure, who appeared every inch a hero.

That night, in the privacy of his room, this delegate from Massachusetts indulged in a mood of self-pity. In a letter to his wife, he contrasted the "pride and pomp" of war with his own poor estate, as one "worn out with scribbling" for his bread and liberty.[4]

---

[4] Adams to Mrs. Adams, June 23, 1775, *Familiar Letters of John Adams and his Wife Abigail Adams During the Revolution,* edited by Charles Francis Adams (Boston, 1875), 70 (cited hereafter as Adams, *Familiar Letters*).

But it was to his lodgings that a "hundred Gentlemen" came (or "flocked," as Adams himself put it) the next night. Instead of the normal Sabbath-eve calm, there was city-wide excitement over news of a military defeat at Bunker Hill. Never since the beginning of the crisis had "war's alarums" been more ominous. Instinctively many of his fellow delegates were turning to this intrepid Yankee for leadership.

After a long consultation, the company designated John and Samuel Adams and John Hancock an informal committee to investigate the possibility of rounding up a supply of a commodity which, under the circumstances, was more precious than gold—gunpowder—and having it transported to the army. These three men lost no time in carrying out the mission entrusted to them. In the dim light which the city lanterns provided they fared forth and before they slept made arrangements with local authorities to have ninety "quarter casks" of the essential explosive sent to the troops.

As the summer advanced, Adams did everything he could to counteract the influence of the Pennsylvania farmer and lawyer, John Dickinson, and others who favored a course of moderation in dealing with the mother country. The tasks assigned him were time-consuming and onerous. During the first Congress he had lingered frequently with fellow-delegates over glasses of Madeira and Burgundy; in this second session there was less leisure for doing so. It appears also that there were no more gastronomic adventures such as those which were part of his earlier experiences in Philadelphia, in the course of which he indulged, as he confessed, in "ten thousand delicacies." He adhered now, with but little deviation, to a Spartan way of life. He was willing, he declared, if necessity should arise, to be reduced to a regimen of potatoes and water.[5]

He fretted over the state of his health. Naturally inclined to hypochondria, during those tense weeks he kept exaggerating his physical ailments. One of them, however, was apparently more real than imaginary. A persisting eye malady not only interfered with his

---

[5] Adams to James Warren, June 27, 1775, Burnett, *Letters*, I, 145.

correspondence and his duties at the State House, but also helped to induce recurring moods of depression.

Still worse in its effect upon him than bodily ills actual or fancied was an apparent lack of momentum in the spirit of rebellion. He did join most of the other members of Congress in signing a "humble petition" to their "gracious sovereign," George III, begging for the redress of grievances, but he made this gesture of obeisance with reluctance. His real feeling was set down in a letter written when the ink was scarcely dry on the signatures to the document addressed to the King. Sycophancy, he maintained in the letter, did not belong to his nature. Such "Prettynesses," "Juvenilities," and "Puerilities" as the petition contained were unworthy of an assembly representing a "great People."[6]

With a devotion appropriate to one of his background and training he faithfully observed the "Fast Day" appointed by Congress. For that day at least the oppressive blanket of heat which had been covering the city was lifted. In cool, clear sunshine Adams and his compatriots made their way to the sanctuary of Christ Church. Under the multi-branched chandelier they sat solemnly as invocations to Providence were mingled, in what was regarded as proper balance, with exhortations to citizens to meet with resolution and courage the crisis that was thrust upon them.

Indeed it was a time calling not only for prayers but also for more flesh-and-blood leadership, for the spirit of determination on the part of men of varied talents, to see the cause of liberty through to the bitter or glorious end. The new delegate from Virginia had heard the summons, and his response to it was ready.

Two days after the "Fast" the Congress put Jefferson on a committee with Benjamin Franklin, Richard Henry Lee, and John Adams to draft a reply to the so-called "Conciliatory Proposals" which Lord North, the British prime minister, had made a few months before. Jefferson's masterly marshaling of the arguments against the acceptance of these proposals, a task which he had recently

[6] Adams to James Warren, July 11, 1775, *ibid.*, I, 162.

performed as spokesman for the Virginia House of Burgesses, earned for him a literary reputation which extended as far north as Massachusetts. This accounted in large part for his being given, along with an already distinguished triumvirate, a very important assignment. It was a procedure unusual in the case of a member whose service in the assembly had been of such short duration.

Within this framework of events Adams and Jefferson began a long series of joint labors for their country. In the short period that had elapsed since the arrival of the new member of the Virginia delegation, he had been the object of an informal appraisal on the part of the staunch leader from New England. Now there was opportunity for closer inspection.

The first business before the committee was to choose one of its number to make a preliminary draft of the document desired. There was quick agreement on this matter. Neither Adams nor Franklin had any liking for such a labor. Lee, who could have performed the task with distinction, was well satisfied to let his younger colleague from Virginia assume the responsibility. Jefferson accepted. Shortly after their first meeting, the committee reassembled and gave hearty approval, without any substantial change, to Jefferson's paper. It brilliantly unmasked the "conciliatory" approaches of Lord North and stated the case for the rebelling colonists in such sentences as these:

"We conceive that the British Parliament has no right to intermeddle with provisions for the support of civil government"; "The provisions we have made [for local administration] are such as please ourselves"; and this bull's-eye shot at the close: "Nothing but our own exertions may defeat the ministerial sentence of death or abject submission."[7]

It could not be foreseen that in less than a year a similar committee, with Jefferson as its instrument of expression, would follow the same general pattern of procedure, leading directly to one of the great events of history. But at this juncture his words were worth more than powder. From them Adams himself, and all the "forward" members of Congress, acquired new courage for the struggle ahead. Here was

[7] *Journals*, II, 230, 234.

no trace of "Prettynesses" and "Juvenilities." Here was an answer to prayer.

On July 31 the statement penned by the newcomer from Virginia became by formal vote the colonies' answer to the British Prime Minister's invitation to appeasement.

It appears that in his correspondence that summer Adams made no mention of Jefferson, but within the matrix of incipient revolution there was the beginning of a most singular relationship. Long afterward, in the mellow calm of old age, a man whose memory of dates and places and the sequence of events was sometimes faulty but whose recollection of human association was, in the main, trustworthy, he wrote of the part played by himself and by others on the threshold of the American Revolution. Referring to his fellow patriot who did the composition work for this committee, he declared, "He soon seized upon my heart."[8]

Whether sitting together in committee session or in an interval of leisure standing near to each other in the State House, these two men would have provided, even for a very casual observer, a study in contrast. Jefferson, over six feet in height and "straight as a gun barrel," was in those physical characteristics like the Lombardy poplars that lined certain Philadelphia streets. Adams, inclining already to corpulence, in the same type of comparison roughly resembled a full-grown elm in his native colony. In the matter of age, the disparity between them, while not great, was outwardly apparent. Adams was well advanced in his fortieth year; Jefferson was only thirty-three.

There were differences, too—likewise similarities—in the backgrounds, far and near, from which they emerged on this historic scene. Each of them traced his ancestry back through several generations of men and women who had eked out a living or acquired a competence as colonial subjects of English sovereigns. Henry Adams, first of his line to come to the New World, settled in Braintree, Massachusetts, almost exactly one hundred years before the birth of

---

[8] Adams to Timothy Pickering, August 6, 1822, *The Works of John Adams with Life of the Author*, edited by Charles Francis Adams (10 vols., Boston, 1850–56), II, 514n. (cited hereafter as Adams, *Works*).

the first of his descendants to become famous. The tangible part of his legacy to posterity consisted of little more than a house and a barn, a cow and a calf, and some pigs, some pots and pans, a minimum of household furniture, and one silver spoon.[9] His grandson Joseph married, on one of his three ventures of the kind, a granddaughter of John and Priscilla Alden, and lived long enough to see his grandson, baby John Adams.

Just who Jefferson's first colonial progenitor was remains an unanswered question. The tradition is that at a time when settlers in Virginia were not numerous, he came there from the vicinity of Mount Snowden in Wales. At any rate, three generations of the family had lived out their time in that colony when the Thomas whom we know was born in 1743. Some written records about them, certifying to ownership of land or to the dates of such elemental events as birth, marriage, and death, are still preserved. Along both the Adams and the Jefferson line of descent there was a succession of hard-working, frugal, industrious, respectable men and women. A few were honored locally by being chosen to fill offices of public trust, but none rose very far above the level of mediocrity.

It is worth noting that after the long migrations which established the two families on American soil, one of them remained fairly near to the seaboard, while the other produced a few more pioneers who kept pushing out toward the vast hinterland. Adams' colonial forebears lived and died within or near the sound of the sea. But Jefferson's father, a land speculator and tobacco grower, like many other Virginia planters, came to need virgin soil for his crops and staked out claims in the Piedmont area. Eventually he made his home within the shadow of the mountains, and their long, forest-covered ridges were as much a part of young Jefferson's physical environment as the ocean was for the Braintree lad. It was in line with their early surroundings that the former should negotiate the acquisition of the vast Louisiana Territory and the latter should take the initiative that earned for him the title of "Father of the American Navy."

Twenty years before the time when this account begins, Adams had

[9] James Truslow Adams, *The Adams Family* (Boston, 1931), 5.

graduated from Harvard College. Among the proud witnesses of the elaborate commencement exercises were his father, "Deacon John" Adams, and his mother, *née* Susanna Boylston. Both of them were eager for this son, their first-born, to become a minister. Five years later Jefferson, who was then fatherless and apparently without much guidance from his mother, rode horseback into Williamsburg and enrolled in William and Mary College. Following two years of study there, he entered the law office of George Wythe. Under his tutelage, the young man's native talents flowered. In the years that followed, Jefferson often referred to this older master of jurisprudence as his "beloved mentor."

In due time, the lean, tall student from the upper Piedmont became a full-fledged lawyer. When he begin riding a circuit that took him to most of the counties into which Virginia was then divided, his Massachusetts contemporary was well settled in the same vocational groove. Adams was appearing in county courts all the way from the Kennebec Valley to Martha's Vineyard, traveling most of the time in a metal-tired sulky. His own youthful plans to be a farmer were partially fulfilled in such intervals as he could spare from the service of his clients, but his parents' ambition for him was completely thwarted. The "holy office," he had decided, was not for him. Unlike him, Jefferson, it seems, was not subjected to pressure, inner or outer, in that direction; like him, however, he spent all the time he could as a "gentleman farmer." But it was by way of courts of law that each came to a place in the Continental Congress and eventually to full stature as a statesman.

Beyond the orbits which they followed in pursuit of the legal profession, neither of them had traveled extensively prior to their first meeting in Philadephia. When Adams went for a brief stay to Stafford Springs in Connecticut shortly before the outbreak of the Revolution, he declared that the place seemed as far away as China. For an ailment which the family doctor diagnosed as a "serious irritability of the spleen," the chalybeate waters of which the Connecticut village boasted had been recommended. But the patient, having tested the curative properties of this colonial spa, concluded that, in his case at least, they were something less than phenomenal. However, the change in his surroundings was interesting, and as he rode back to Braintree from the "west," the splenetic "irritability" was at least no worse.

It was not in search of a cure for sickness but for the purpose of preventing, if possible, a certain offensive disease that Jefferson traveled to Philadelphia several years before going there as a public servant. In the spring of 1766 a leading physician in the city inoculated him against smallpox. Not long after he submitted to vaccination the Virginia House of Burgesses passed legislation forbidding such tampering with the processes of nature. In Massachusetts, Adams' great-uncle, Dr. Zabdiel Boylston, encountering some opposition, introduced the practice. Young Adams was one of the few to take the preventive treatment. While his bride-to-be shivered at the thought of "poison passing through his veins," he spent several days in quarantine in a Boston hospital.

Thus these two men, long before they knew each other, separately defied the mores of their time. Even then they possessed a spirit of independence which was to become more pronounced when linked definitely with the destiny of America.

Jefferson's first and only trip to Philadelphia in those pre-Revolution years brought him much more than comparative immunity from a dread disease. There were stimulating contacts with Dr. John Morgan, a well-known physician and patron of the arts, with Robert Smith, the eminent Scottish architect, who at the time had for one of his projects a new house for Benjamin Franklin, and with other men of high professional standing. There was time also for sight-seeing trips about this urban center, in which he gave special attention to ornate mansions, to Christ Church with its stately steeple lately brought from London, and to the State House, interesting architecturally if not yet important historically. One natural effect of these new experiences was expansion of his already abundant store of ideas.

Included in this journey was a stay in the city of New York, with attractions for the young traveler only a little less varied than those of the city on the Delaware. In a letter written soon after his return to Virginia he referred to this excursion as a "long but agreeable trip."[10] But this was the extent, at the time he began making history on a large scale, of his direct contact with the world outside the borders of his own colony. Neither he nor Adams, when their paths first crossed, was a narrow provincial with a shuttered mind; but Jefferson had never gotten as far away from home as New England, and Adams had never set foot in any place as far distant from Braintree as Virginia.

By way of contrast, both of them had become familiar, through reading, with wide ranges of history, philosophy, and poetry. In Adams' case there was acquaintance with a fair expanse of theology. His great-great-grandfather who had begun the Adams saga on this side of the Atlantic had, as he boasted, at least as many books as children. His own father was another member of the family the number of whose books equaled that of his offspring. But that meant only three, one of which was a well-used Bible. From this parent and others of his progenitors who had a greater than average eagerness for knowledge, young John may have inherited an inclination to seek truth contained in bound volumes. Certainly such a trait manifested itself at an early period in his life.

When he entered Harvard College, he pounced on the contents of the library there somewhat in the fashion of a half-starved man at a banquet. He helped himself liberally to many of the items on that literary menu. Later, when he had a few shillings to spare, and sometimes when his intellectual appetite was out of proportion to his financial means, he kept adding to his shelves informative and inspirational volumes. He would have been far more prolific than any of his ancestors if he could have begotten sons and daughters at the same rate as he added to his library.

In the matter of access to literary treasures, Jefferson as a boy was more fortunate than Adams before the latter's years at Harvard. In the former's cherry-wood bookcase, bequeathed to him later by his father, were some standard histories, a few legal tomes and treatises,

[10] *The Papers of Thomas Jefferson*, edited by Julian P. Boyd (Princeton), 1950–), I, 21 (cited hereafter as Jefferson *Papers*).

13

and also a row of bound volumes of *The Spectator*, *The Tatler*, and *The Guardian*. Most of these and numerous additions for which the inherited bookcase had become inadequate went up in flames on a winter night in 1770, when the house at Jefferson's birthplace caught fire and burned to the ground. He calculated that the volumes destroyed were worth £200, but the actual loss could not be measured completely in financial terms. Although the benefit he had received from the books was beyond the reach of flames, he considered a personal library an absolute necessity. Ere long he was sending orders of considerable size to London booksellers. In less than four years he could count 1,250 books in his possession—one of the most valuable collections of its kind in the American colonies.

Neither Jefferson nor Adams was lacking in the sterner virtues, and of those none was practiced more conscientiously in both cases than diligence in the husbandry of time. Near the beginning of his public career the Virginian drew up for friends expecting to study law a daily agenda of reading and writing which almost ruled out such activities as eating and sleeping. He did not follow rigorously the schedule which he prepared for others, but not many have allowed fewer hours to slip out of their grasp unutilized. Adams was equally concerned as a youth to make every unit of his time yield a maximum of profit. At the age of twenty he wrote in his diary: "May I blush whenever I suffer one hour to pass unimproved."[11] Later there were, of course, occasions when, in accordance with this self-imposed regulation, blushing would have been in order. But in general both he and Jefferson, unlike some men with unusual natural abilities, made good use of the opportunities open to all men in the form of time.

The range of Jefferson's active interests was much wider than that of Adams. Indeed, of all the contemporaries of this new addition to the roster of delegates in the Continental Congress, only Franklin was his equal in versatility. At home, Adams could have been seen at times, pruning apple trees in his orchard, carting away stones from

---

[11] *The Adams Papers, Series I: Diary and Autobiography of John Adams*, edited by L. H. Butterfield (4 vols., Cambridge, Mass., 1961), I, 35, (cited hereafter as Adams, *Diary and Autobiography*).

his pasture lands, or plowing with yoked oxen some of his arable acres. But playing a violin, calculating an eclipse, surveying an estate, designing a house, evaluating a painting or a piece of statuary—to any of which activities Jefferson could turn his mind or hand—these were not in the line of Adams' aptitudes. One day he visited a Philadelphia museum in which wax figures were displayed, but without such curiosity as prompted Jefferson to spend some loose shillings in the same city for a look at captive monkeys and elk. The sight of a pet crow with long, scrambling claws, a bird owned by children at a tavern where Adams stayed one night, aroused mild curiosity, but his interest in fauna and flora, in music, painting, and sculpture, was peripheral. One cannot imagine his looking more than once at many objects of nature or art which frequently riveted Jefferson's attention.

Adams was capable of eloquence as a speaker, a talent which he had already exercised on occasion with telling effect. On a cold day in December, 1770, many Boston citizens, assembled in the Supreme Court of Judicature, heard his defense of British soldiers standing trial for their part in the "massacre" of March 5, of that same year. They were treated to an account of what happened at that time which was almost as exciting as the events themselves; also, to as lucid and convincing a summary of relevant points of law as had ever been heard in a Massachusetts court room. At other times Adams had won important cases by presenting facts and arguments with more originality and verbal skill than juries were accustomed to hear. By way of contrast, when he used a pen, the product was sometimes dull and pedantic.

To a great extent, the gifts of expression were portioned out to Jefferson in reverse order. Oratory was not his forte. The longest speech he ever delivered in the Continental Congress, according to a statement made by Adams more than a quarter of a century later, contained not more than two sentences and was, in the opinion of the Puritan Yankee, a "gross insult on Religion." Immediately, as he recalled the occasion, he felt constrained to give the offender the public "Reprehension, which he richly merited."[12]

[12] *Ibid.*, III, 335.

We are obliged to qualify our acceptance of this bit of memoranda with reservations. Adams' faulty memory and the nature of his personal feeling at the time he was writing, along with his persisting tendency to exaggerate, make him to some extent untrustworthy as a factual reporter of Jefferson's part in the 1775–76 proceedings of the Congress. Nevertheless, his recollection of the Virginian's aversion to public debate is in harmony with other evidence that the delegate from Monticello was usually a silent member.

In fact, Jefferson, having little inclination to speak in public himself, was often suspicious of oratory in pulpits, legislative forums, or elsewhere. But lawyers must sometimes address juries and others gathered to hear court trials, and there are reliable reports that when Jefferson did so, he commanded attention by the clarity and force of his arguments. No one knew better than himself, however, that he was not a Demosthenes. And after he sat for a while in the great deliberative body meeting in Philadelphia, he realized that as a master of assemblies he was not in the same class as John Adams. On the other hand, he could at times work a kind of magic with written words. And, as we shall presently see, it was the "elegance of his pen" which Adams himself would give, in the early summer of 1776, as one reason for insisting that this pen should write the Declaration.[13]

When they first met, both Adams and Jefferson had been married for some time, Adams for a longer period than Jefferson. Each was a father as well as a husband and unaccustomed to being away from home as long as present duties now required.

During his boyhood Adams often played in the cherry orchard adjoining the parsonage in Weymouth and came to show more than passing interest in Abigail, the second of the daughters of the Reverend William Smith, the village minister. Not long after she reached marriageable age, an engagement was entered into which continued for more than two years. Then, on an October day in 1764, in a setting of autumn foliage such as had never been seen before in the old parsonage, brown-eyed Abigail and the young lawyer exchanged vows. Long afterwards, writing tersely about this event, Adams packed into

[13] *Ibid.*, III, 336.

one revealing sentence what he had to say about it in his autobiography: "I was married to Miss Smith a Daughter of the Reverend Mr. William Smith a minister of Weymouth, granddaughter of the Honourable John Quincy Esquire of Braintree, a Connection which has been the Source of all my felicity."[14]

Now she was writing to him frequently, addressing him sometimes as "My Dearest Friend" and occasionally signing her letter with one of her pet names, "Portia." Adams himself had bestowed this cognomen upon her with admiration as well as affection. He believed that before a public tribunal she could have argued as well as the heiress of Venice.

During those summer weeks of 1775, Jefferson seldom, if ever, received a letter from his wife. This misfortune, a very real one, was certainly not due to any aversion toward himself, but apparently toward writing of any sort. It seems that only two brief notes from her have been handed down through the generations—an indication that she rarely communicated with anyone in this fashion. But she was a diligent and thrifty homekeeper, naturally sunny and gracious in disposition, and known for her proficiency in instrumental music. Tradition has it that Jefferson's violin playing had something to do with his winning out over two rivals for the affections of this young widow. They were married on New Years' Day, 1772.

With this ceremony there was no association of bright autumn leaves, but as long as life lasted, each of them vividly remembered riding on horseback late at night through two feet of snow to their mountaintop home, thus ending their wedding journey in the middle of a fantastic Virginia winter.

Now, as the budding statesman came to grips with weighty problems in the distant city, young Martha (named after her mother) was toddling about the rooms of the comparatively new house, sometimes tugging at her mother's skirts with the insistence of a three-year-old. Her sister Jane, not yet far advanced in her second year, kept holding on to life rather precariously. And over in the cottage which fronted on Braintree's main street, a structure which to the

14 *Ibid.*, III, 280.

bride who went there to live seemed too much like a doll's house, Abby, aged ten, John Quincy, eight, and Charles and Tommy, five and three respectively, kept "Portia's" time well occupied. She often told herself that the nest was too small for the brood.

On the whole, there were more likenesses than differences in the background of training and habits and environment from which these two family men were brought into daily contact by the exigencies of colonial revolt. Some of the differences even favored rather than retarded an acquaintance that was to ripen slowly into friendship. But more than the other contributing factors was one shared passion which helped this maturing process. Neither spoke very openly as yet of political independence, but both were ready for any sacrifice necessary in the effort to preserve the civil rights of their cultural heritage.

John Adams wrote in his old age that the "child Independence was born" on a winter day in 1761 when James Otis argued impressively for hours in the Boston Council Chamber against the "writs of assistance."[15] If in this reading of events a birth pang was mistaken for an actual delivery, there was undoubtedly on that occasion the beginning of a genuine dedication on the part of Adams himself to the cause of liberty. In the intervening years there had been, deep within his nature, a growth of the spirit evoked by the performance of his friend Otis. So sturdy did that spirit become that about a month before he left home to take his place in the First Continental Congress, it impelled him to break off relationship with Jonathan Sewall, who for years had been one of his closest friends. Indeed, at times their feeling towards each other had been comparable to that existing between the Biblical Jonathan and young David.

On the day of their separation, the two had been sitting together on a hilltop near Falmouth, which was Sewall's home.[16] In an effort to dissuade Adams from his purpose of taking the part delegated to him in the fateful deliberations that were soon to begin, his friend used every possible argument. Most men of property and of profes-

[15] Adams to William Tudor, March 29, 1817, Adams, *Works*, X, 248.
[16] In colonial times Falmouth was the name of the town which later became the city of Portland, Maine.

sional standing, he contended, were not in favor of complicating further the relations with the mother country. Adams was running the grave risk, if he persisted, of ruining his career, even of putting his family as well as himself in jeopardy. More to the point—he knew Adams well enough to realize that these were not the most forceful considerations—the cause of the so-called patriots was hopeless. For ten years Great Britain had not made any concessions worth mentioning. There was no possibility that she would do so. Rather than bringing about an improvement in the condition of the colonists, such measures as Adams and like-minded men were contemplating might well result in tightening of control on the part of the King and his ministers.

Adams heard him out and then delivered his predetermined answer. His own purpose in this matter was as fixed as that of George III and his policy-makers. Perhaps the alternatives historically associated with his name first came to utterance at that time: "Sink or swim, live or die, survive or perish, I am with my country from this day on."[17] At any rate, Jonathan and John came that day to a parting of the ways.

In the case of Jefferson, also, the spirit of seventy-six, as eventually it was called, gathered momentum as he advanced through the years of his early manhood. From the very beginning of the quarrel with England, he felt the stirrings of rebellion against the encroachments of the government of that country. As a law student, he stood in the door of the lobby of the Virginia House of Burgesses and heard Patrick Henry's outburst against the Stamp Act. In spite of his avowed suspicions of oratory, he was affected much as the youthful Yankee lawyer had been by the fiery utterance of James Otis. Seven years later, as a member of his colony's legislative body, he spent a March evening in Williamsburg's Raleigh Tavern with a company in which was Patrick Henry himself, as well as Richard Henry Lee and a few others who believed that the time was ripe for concerted colonial action.

[17] A vivid account of this meeting of Adams and Sewall is given in *John Adams and the American Revolution,* by *Catherine Drinker Bowen* (Boston, 1950), 455–57.

There are as many plausible reasons for giving that early spring-time night as the birth date of the "child Independence" as Adams could have advanced for the earlier date, for out of that nocturnal talk came the proposal for a committee of the burgesses whose business it would be to make contact with legislative bodies and individuals in other colonies on matters of common interest, especially grievances arising from disregard of their "ancient, legal, and constitutional rights." From that proposal came the first Committee of Correspondence; and out of it and similar committees there came, by a kind of parturition, the Continental Congress.

If in respect to the issues which created the occasion for their first meeting, there was any difference in the feelings of these two protagonists for the rights of King George's subjects in America, it was in the form of deeper vexation on the part of the one who could trace his ancestry to Celtic forebears in Wales. When he made his own the maxim of other revolutionists, *fiat justitia ruat caelum*, and proceeded to apply it, he was motivated primarily by a passion for the natural and inalienable rights of man, but he was also influenced by a kind of distaste, which later became more pronounced, for England itself. He, too, in that summer of 1775 had a "sink or swim" attitude in relation to his own fate and fortune, as they might be affected by the turn of events. Beyond that, he was willing, not only for the heavens to fall, but also for the "tight little isle" itself to sink, or be sunk, if nothing but such a catastrophe would bring an end to abridgment of the liberties of Virginians and other colonials. During that summer he wrote to his distant kinsman, John Randolph: "I am one of those ... who, rather than submit to the rights of legislating for us, assumed by the British Parliament, and which late experience has shown they will cruelly exercise, would lend my hand to sink the whole island in the ocean."[18]

Such was the spirit of the man who, without knowing that he was doing so, stepped forward, one year before independence was declared, to fill a gap in the ranks of Adams' friends made by the defection, as Adams himself regarded it, of Jonathan Sewall.

[18] Jefferson to John Randolph, August 25, 1774, Jefferson *Papers*, I, 242.

On the day following the adoption of the reply to Lord North's propositions, this action being regarded as a climactic event in the summer's proceedings, the Congress adjourned until September 5. Most of the delegates were in need of the vacation. Many were inured to discomfort and hardship, but in nearly every case the sticky heat, the long hours of labor, the ceaseless anxiety, and the mounting load of responsibility had made heavy inroads on their capital of endurance.

Adams straightway started north toward Abigail, the children, and the old, narrow, crowded house in which, however, there was always room for him. Jefferson journeyed southward with portly Benjamin Harrison, a fellow delegate from Virginia, as traveling companion. After a stop at the Virginia Convention, then meeting in Richmond, a pause made in the line of duty, he hurried on to the lofty haven which he had named Monticello. Very welcome to him was the sight of its gardens and orchards, its field crops, its horses and stables, and above all, the two Marthas and baby Jane.

In the following months there was for each of these men a succession of anxieties and bereavements. Within a few hours after Adams' arrival in Braintree a plague of dysentery claimed his younger brother, Elihu, as one of its victims. The epidemic was still raging when the time came for him to say good-bye and start back to Philadelphia. Not until the heavy frosts came was there any abatement of the terror.

In the meantime Abigail kept him informed of its ravages. She herself and all the younger members of the household were stricken, but no one of them as severely as many other adults and children. Abigail's mother sickened and soon died in her parsonage home. "So sickly and so mortal a time the oldest man does not remember," his faithful reporter, grief-stricken herself, informed Adams in one of her letters that season.[19]

One day in October, there being nothing in letters from Braintree to lift his spirits except the renewed evidence of Abigail's quiet courage, Adams was almost at the point of calling for his horse and

[19] Mrs. Adams to Adams, September 8, 1775, Adams, *Familiar Letters*, 95.

leaving Congress behind him in a cloud of dust. The snail-like pace of that body and his inability to accelerate it made him wonder if he were not needed at home more than in Philadelphia. But true to a form that had become characteristic of him, he dismissed the idea of even temporary escape as unworthy of one in his position.

On that same day, or one very near to it, Thomas Jefferson presented for the second time his credentials as a delegate to Congress, his colony having honored him again with this appointment. He was four weeks late in arriving—a delay principally due to the death of his younger child. It is not unlikely that the man from Monticello and the one from Braintree had opportunity, as the session continued, to tell each other about these sorrowful experiences and to exchange expressions of sympathy. For each of them, too, there was inevitable concern about the existing conditions in their respective homes.

In Jefferson's case, anxiety was heightened by the fact that, just as in the recent summer months, no one in his home colony, not even his wife, could, or would, write to him. "I have not received the scrip of a pen from any mortal in Virginia since I left it" was the complaint he made as he wrote that fall to his brother-in-law, Francis Eppes.[20] He did learn by the public papers and by contacts with his fellow delegates that events within the borders of Virginia, as elsewhere throughout the colonies, were pointing in the direction of an unprecedented crisis. Nor did he remain in ignorance of the fact that Lord Dunmore, the royal governor, was summoning frigates of war, constructing a fort, and doing everything possible to incite slaves to counterrebellion. He shared vicariously in the alarms being spread through Virginia towns and countrysides.

In general, the "tree of liberty," a very tender sapling at that time, was being threatened as never before. Abroad, agents of the British sovereign hired thousands of professional Hessian and German soldiers to help subdue his rebellious American subjects. While these troops were being assembled, cannon mounted on a British vessel shelled the town of Falmouth, the scene of Adams' "sink or swim" avowal. When the fire that followed died down, 150 buildings had

[20] Jefferson to Francis Eppes, November 7, 1775, Jefferson *Papers*, I, 252.

been destroyed. Very soon frightening rumors spread outward from the smoking ruins left after this attack. The probability was that other coastal towns would be subjected to similar onslaughts. Braintree, just emerging from "so sickly and so mortal a time," like many other normally peaceful New England villages girded itself against an enemy that might work more havoc than a plague. Some of the Bible-reading inhabitants of the area could hear in imagination, if not the approach of the four horsemen of the Apocalypse, that of their sinister equivalents on the paths of the sea.

Prior to that time the strength which comes from union in resistance to oppression had been slow in developing. There were many, indeed, who shared, in adamant fashion, Jonathan Sewall's sentiments. In the very city which served the purposes of a capital for the colonies, Tory sympathizers were numerous and influential enough to hamper seriously the growth of the "tree" being cultivated by such patriots as Adams and Jefferson.

The former, tired out physically and troubled more than ever with nostalgia, early in December sought and procured a leave of absence. On the ninth he rode out of the city, and in about two weeks was at home. Jefferson stayed until the last week of the year. Then slowly, through winter weather and over uncertain roads, he made his way toward a family, a plantation, and a colony much in need of his help. Serious as the general situation was as viewed from the State House, Jefferson thought of himself as "expendable" for the time being. His knowledge of Lord Dunmore's maneuvers and his fears for the safety of Monticello, his family, and many of his long-time friends made imperative, in his judgment, a return to his home and continuance there until the threat became less imminent.

On the way, word came to him that on New Year's Day the city of Norfolk had been shelled by British vessels offshore, much of it being leveled to the ground. Except that the dose was larger, it was a repetition of the treatment given to Falmouth a few weeks before. These attacks, of course, were acts of war, apparently authorized by men in control of the British government. But to Adams and Jefferson and many others they were as barbarous as Indian raids. Lexington and

Concord and Bunker Hill had been fair fighting; but havoc of this kind, many of the patriots insisted, was the work of incendiaries and pillagers heedless of the rules governing "civilized" warfare.

There was much to indicate that the so-called "spirit of '76" was active as the calendar year which designated it began. Within the space of a few weeks the spirit became more formidable than ever. Adams, on his way back to Philadelphia for another session of the Congress, came into possession of a pamphlet entitled *Common Sense*. Written by a hitherto obscure Englishman, Thomas Paine, who had recently come to America virtually an outcast from his native land, it soon was being widely sought and read. It was a stirring combination of fact and propaganda. Adams was mildly critical of it, stating that while he could not have improved upon the style, he flattered himself to the extent of believing that he could have given better substance to the argument. Up to that time not even Jefferson himself had written anything which did as much as this little volume to spark enthusiasm for the cause of liberty. To some it might seem that back of its publication was a sense of timing more than human. Not by mere chance or by human design alone, it could be argued, was such an inflammatory booklet published at such a psychological moment.

It was indeed a time when the shape of things that had recently come and of those then coming was favorable to the efforts of leaders scornful of halfway measures. To persons hesitating between two opinions but leaning toward the patriots, there came indications that, even though the struggle might be long, it was not hopeless. Contrary to fearful expectations following the Falmouth incident, Boston and the surrounding area went through the winter unscathed. Washington's seizure of Dorchester Heights compensated, in some degree, for the near debacle at Bunker Hill. A little later, on March 17, Abigail Adams stood with her great-uncle in the latter's mansion above Wollaston Beach and watched as scores of British vessels carried the enemy troops and some New England Tories out to sea. She and her fellow rebels, in New England and elsewhere, were given new assurance that while the war was not over, it was by no means lost.

Even the unfortunate denouement of the Canadian military expedition led by Montgomery and Arnold strengthened rather than weakened the spirit of aggressiveness in revolution. A common reaction to the attacks on Falmouth and Norfolk, strengthened by Paine's arguments, reflected Patrick Henry's earlier pronouncement regarding the comparative appeals of liberty and of death. For the first time in American history, public pressure was brought upon the Congress to take decisive action. In this initial case the demand was that responsible officials lead in a move toward nationhood. As another springtime came, there was indeed much to spur the initiative of laggards among the chosen representatives of the colonies, and delegates who had set their sights on independence became certain that it was not beyond their reach.

After an absence of four months from Philadelphia, Jefferson made final preparations to resume his duties there, which he might have been accused (and probably was) of neglecting. In the interval between periods of his attendance at the State House, death had once more interfered with his plans. On the last day of March his mother died, apparently from apoplexy. The unavoidable adjustments to be made after her death took some time, but by early May his household was in good running order. Some moves had been made, a few of them by himself, to make life and property safer in his own and surrounding counties. Much less anxious about his estate and family than when he came home in midwinter, he took to the road again, Philadelphia his destination.

Eight days later he rode through the lush farm country east of Lancaster, his journey almost completed. The burgeoning orchards and meadows, the long rows of upthrusting corn and wheat, were giving promise of harvests to come. He thought of his own crops at home, of all he had left behind; but he was also looking forward, his spirit alert with a growing conviction that portentous things were about to take place.

There was no delay at the State House in getting the tardy delegate back into the groove of official business. On May 14, the very day he arrived, he was put on a committee with John Adams and William Livingston to read letters from General Washington and his subordinate generals and, on the basis of them, to make any recommendations that might seem advisable. Thus he scarcely had time to reorient himself to city life when this responsibility brought him once more into contact with the rugged delegate from Massachusetts.

For a short time Jefferson occupied rooms at the Chestnut Street home of a cabinet-maker, Ben Randolph, where he had stayed the preceding summer and fall. But a premature heat wave was then engulfing the city, and he thought it wise to seek a location somewhere "in the skirts of the town," as he put it.[21] The new brick house into which he moved within a few days stood at the corner of Market and Seventh streets, a spot which even at that time was not precisely suburban. On the second floor of this residence, with several windows in his rooms and no other building very near, he found living conditions more to his liking. To be sure, there were no mountain breezes such as he enjoyed at home, but it was preferable to the muggy place he had just left.

At his lodgings down on Second Street, Adams sweated out the hours he spent there as stoically as he could.

The pace of events accelerated as the days grew warmer. Only partially familiar with what was happening, Ben Randolph fashioned in his shop a small writing desk, with no prescience regarding the use to which it would soon be put. By some arrangement between himself and his former tenant this unobtrusive piece of furniture was transferred to the latter's possession.

In Congress, the day after Jefferson rode into the city was a redletter one on the calendar of John Adams and others in that body who shared his spirit. Adams had been chosen to write a preamble for a resolution, already passed, recommending that those colonies which had not already done so form governments of their own, "sufficient to the exigencies of the situation." Now the delegates sat tense with interest, as Adams read his explanatory paragraph. Even Jefferson, we may well believe, showed fewer signs of lassitude than he sometimes did when listening to the proceedings of Congress. "It is necessary"—so it was written and read—"that the exercise of every kind

[21] Jefferson to Thomas Nelson, May 16, 1775, *ibid.*, I, 292.

of authority under the said [British] crown should be totally suppressed, and all the powers of government exerted under the authority of the people of the colonies."[22] No clouding of meaning, no mincing of words, in this pronouncement. Before the day was over and after some heated debate, this explicit preamble was adopted, not overwhelmingly, but definitely.

This action was the high-water mark, up to that date, for the flood of colonial resistance. Some time before midnight Adams wrote to his friend, James Warren: "This day the Congress has passed the most important resolution ever taken in America."[23]

During that same week there was, by proclamation of Congress, another day of fasting and prayer. Not long afterward, a number of Presbyterian ministers in the city for a meeting of their synod decided that the hard-working delegates needed relaxation as certainly as they did the benefits of prayer. They sought and obtained permission to stage a war dance, with the honorable members of Congress as especially invited guests. For this function the services of twenty-one Indians were secured.[24] Perhaps the invited spectators, watching an exhibition of primitive art, forgot the serious business to which they had been giving daily attention. And there is, too, the possibility that a few of them, as they heard the throbbing of the drums, became for the first time really militant in their attitude toward oppressors.

At any rate, the cause vigorously espoused by Paine and Adams and Jefferson and others was winning converts daily in many places. Early in the month of June the trend toward an ultimate crisis appeared to many, for the first time, as irresistible. Prayers recently made for an extension and strengthening of the spirit of liberty were being answered, it was said, as there came from both north and south, not requests, as before, but official instructions issued by several of the colonies stating in substance: "Cut the Gordian knot and set us free."

On the fifth, Adams and Jefferson were chosen, along with Edward Rutledge, James Wilson, and Robert R. Livingston, as a com-

---

[22] *Journals*, IV, 358.

[23] Adams to James Warren, May 15, 1776, Burnett, *Letters*, I, 445.

[24] Caesar Rodney mentions this "war dance" in a letter to Thomas Rodney, May 29, 1776, *ibid.*, I, 467.

mittee to outline procedures for the treatment of spies and persons found guilty of supplying provisions to the enemy. No battles had as yet been fought in the vicinity of Philadelphia, but rumor had it that some of the local citizens were trafficking with officers and others in the King's army. Important business this was, brought officially to the attention of Adams and Jefferson and the others selected to serve with them. Shortly the representative from Braintree and the one from Monticello would be members of another small group entrusted with greater responsibility. More frequently than in the preceding session they were being brought into close encounter.

On the morning of the seventh, delegates filed, according to their custom, into the State House through the high arched gateway on Walnut Street or by the Chestnut Street entrance. In due time each found his place in the familiar white-paneled room which was the nerve center of revolution. Scarcely a member was missing. Word had been passed around that this morning's session would be an extraordinary one. And no one had been misinformed. When the proper moment came, Richard Henry Lee stood up, one of his hands, the crippled one, enclosed as always in a neat silk bandage, the other holding a piece of paper. From it he read: "Resolved, That these United Colonies are, and of right ought to be, free and independent States, that they are absolved from all allegiance to the British Crown, and that all political connection between them and the State of Great Britain is, and ought to be totally dissolved." With this resolution he presented two appropriate concurrent propositions.

He moved the adoption of all three of them. Instantly John Adams was on his feet to second the motion. He had crossed his Rubicon long before. Now he thrilled with the realization that this body of accredited leaders was finally being given the opportunity to do likewise, in behalf of and response to every protesting colonist.

The inevitable debate occupied three days. The vote was then postponed until July 1, the more forward members, who were now in the majority, agreeing that time should be allowed for a few hesitant colonies to step into line and solidify the ranks. Soon the wisdom of this delay was apparent. During the interval New Jersey gave assurance that her delegates would "vote plump" for independence. Toward the end of it, word came that the Maryland Convention had withdrawn an earlier decision and was now ready to support Lee's resolutions. As the fateful day drew near, their adoption became as certain as any future event could be. And there was full realization that dire consequences might ensue for those going on record for independence.

Yet there was no disposition on the part of the so-called radicals either to turn back or to stand still. Time would be saved, it was agreed, if in the days remaining before July 1 the necessary declaration could be formulated, giving, with a "decent respect for the opinions of mankind," the reasons for the separation.

Extreme care was taken in setting up a committee to prepare this document. The choice was by ballot. The tally having been completed, it was announced that Jefferson had received more votes than anyone else. Adams was runner-up. Next in line were Benjamin Franklin, Roger Sherman, and Robert R. Livingston. So to these five men was given a responsibility demanding, among other talents, the utmost skill and force in written argument.

The reception room in Franklin's house on Bristol Road was probably the place where they met for preliminary discussion. Never before had any of the members of this little group shared in a deliberation of such significance. And never before had the two of their number with whom we are most concerned been drawn so closely together in pursuit of a common objective.

Very little is known of what these two said to each other on that occasion, and still less about the general conversation that took place, but four of these committee members were in agreement on one point of procedure—that Jefferson should write the Declaration. Livingston was a capable lawyer and statesman and skillful *entrepreneur*, who had been chosen to serve on the committee on the strength of the supposition that wavering New York, of which he was a representative, might thereby be won over more readily to the majority side. Roger Sherman, while no more pleasant than a chestnut bur to some of his acquaintances, was nevertheless one of the New England stalwarts in this rebellion, highly respected and valued by those who worked with him on committees. He had commended himself to many of his associates as a man who combined sound judgment with his commitment to the cause of the patriots. But neither of these men was thought of as the logical person to write out the first draft of the proposed document. It is not likely that either regarded himself as being well fitted for the task.

The aging Franklin had just returned from a grueling mission to Canada. Had this committee been given a less important task, he might not have been willing to share in its deliberations. He was still suffering from an outbreak of boils, which had added to his misery on the long journey. Moreover, he was being subjected to another attack by his persistent enemy, gout. He was avoiding company as much as possible. And even in his best days he had been reluctant to prepare a paper which would be submitted to any group for approval or rejection. Now, even if pressure had been exerted upon him to write the Declaration, he would have resisted to the utmost.

Long afterward, when advanced age had undoubtedly blurred the edges of his memory, Adams stated in a letter that he and Jefferson were appointed by the other members as a subcommittee to do the actual work. Against this assertion must be placed Jefferson's flat denial that there was such a subcommittee. But if this denial be accepted, there is good *a priori* reason for believing that the two men conferred informally about the matter. Indeed, Adams could not have been completely fanciful when, in the letter referred to, he reported a conversation at this stage of the proceedings between Jefferson and himself. Some such bald statement as the forthright Yankee attributed to himself may well have been made by him at that time. Quoting his own words, he told Jefferson, in blunt, straight-from-the-shoulder fashion: "You ought to write it."

He was ready, too, as it appears, with his reasons, and they were probably phrased very much as he set them down in his summary of the conversation. The first reason: Jefferson was a Virginian, and a Virginian ought to appear at the head of the business before them. The second: Adams was obnoxious, suspected, and unpopular. (Here

Adams was surely using his talent for exaggeration.) On the other hand, Jefferson was in general favor with the delegates. The third reason (and this one, he honestly felt, was reason enough): Jefferson could write ten times better than himself.

We are told that to these arguments Jefferson simply responded that he would do the best he could with the assignment.[25]

Back to his living quarters, where the air was as fresh as it could be in that flat, semi-urban neighborhood and where interruptions would be few, went this man, appointed by his peers, constrained by duty, and no doubt exultant with a sense of privilege. On that same day, or the next, or one that very shortly followed, he sat down at the desk recently acquired from his former landlord, dipped his pen in ink, and in clear, fine script spelled out on the page before him the words: "When in the course of human events . . . ." And for a while he kept on writing.

Indeed, this commission called for many hours of concentration. One pictures him, as the long summer days came and went, returning again and again to his diminutive desk, writing with even more than his customary care, striking out here, adding there. When the promise, certainly made to himself if not to others, that he would do his best was fulfilled, he showed the finished product first to Adams and later to Franklin. Each suggested a few changes in the phrasing. Adams had some mental reservations about certain strictures directed against George III; he believed the English king was a dupe rather than a tyrant. He did not, however, make an issue of that point. His opinion that no better person could have been found in all the colonies to state America's case to mankind was strengthened.

A "fair copy" was made and then submitted to the other members of the committee, who voted approval. In this form it was presented to the entire group of delegates on June 28, well in advance of the day set for the "great debate."

The next move, foreordained by the logic of events, the ultimate one in the political phase of the struggle, was up to Congress.

[25] Adams' report of this conversation appears in his letter to Timothy Pickering, August 6, 1822, Adams, *Works*, II, 514n.

Average weather conditions prevailed in Philadelphia during the first week of July. If there was a slight deviation from normal in the temperature, it was in a direction welcomed by residents and transients who earlier had sweltered in oven-like heat. Frequently cool breezes blowing up from the bay fanned away sultry air masses hanging over the city. While there was an occasional thunderstorm, for the most part Nature was in a placid mood. Usually at night the long rows of dwellings, the public buildings, and the harbor were bathed in clear moonlight.

Early on Monday morning, it being the first day of the month, John Adams found time to write at least one letter. In it he clearly indicated, as he had done several times recently, his realization of the fact that he was participating in awesome events. The hour he had been waiting for, often impatiently, was about to strike. The protestations he had made to Jonathan Sewall and others were soon to be submitted to a crucial test. It was more than a casual news item that he reported, as he wrote to Archibald Bullock, "This morning is assigned for the greatest debate of all."[26]

He was at the State House at the hour appointed for meeting—nine o'clock. So were most of the other delegates, more than fifty of them. Following the call to order, a long list of routine business was started on its way through the parliamentary mill and for much of it the process was completed. Some members fidgeted in their seats and sometimes caucused informally as the hour-hand of the great tower-clock above crept toward the mark of twelve. It was not far from that mark when President Hancock announced that Congress would become a "Committee of the Whole" and take up for consideration the resolutions introduced on June 7.

As soon as he could be recognized, John Dickinson, holding in his hand a bulky sheaf of papers, began to speak. Adams and Jefferson and others in the hall were expecting this oration, and each man maneuvered into as comfortable a position as the seating arrangements permitted. Tall, slender, ashy-pale, presenting at first sight, as Adams later described him, the appearance of one who might not live

---

[26] Adams to Archibald Bullock, July 1, 1776, Burnett, *Letters*, I, 521.

a month and yet, upon closer inspection, looking as if he might last for years, the Pennsylvania farmer proceeded with a lengthy speech. The familiar arguments of the moderates were repeated and amplified, not without eloquence. Adoption of the proposed resolutions would divide rather than unite the colonies. There was no definite assurance of getting help from France or Spain. Establishment of a federal government should precede severance of union with England. Some other day—or year—was the proper time, not now. And so on, and on, to the disgust of those already fed up with demands for postponement.

There was as little doubt on the part of Adams' close associates that he was the man to answer Dickinson as there had been that Jefferson was the best qualified to write the Declaration. The lawyer from Braintree was ready with his rebuttal. Years before he had confided to his diary that only some unforeseen "animating occasion" would enable him to shine with all his forensic powers.[27] He must now have sensed that this was that occasion. The time, the place, the subject under discussion, the entire pattern of circumstances, presented him with an opportunity seldom afforded a public speaker.

What he actually said was not recorded. No one of his hearers bothered to take notes, and Adams himself made no written record of his words. But there is evidence that the effect was tremendous. Nature herself provided an accompaniment as a storm broke outside. Thousands of raindrops beat upon the windowpanes; now and then thunder crashed. Strange, was it not, that for the second time in his life, in a situation very important to him, a violent storm was in progress. He had proposed to Abigail in the kitchen of the Weymouth parsonage, when the old house was being shaken with wind and thunderblasts. His speech on that occasion had been most effective. So, too, was this one of much greater portent.

No one in that august company followed the arguments of this persuasive advocate of independence with greater interest than the man who had written the Declaration. Lacking a precise, close-up description of Jefferson in that setting, one can see, with the exercise

[27] Adams, *Diary and Autobiography*, I, 133.

of a little imagination, his long, lean figure hunched carelessly on a chair, and note him listening intently as Adams gave oral expression to truths which he himself had just set forth in another medium. He could scarcely have questioned the value of eloquence, directed, as it was now, toward approval of the document to which he stood in paternal relationship.

Other remarks were made that afternoon, for or against the proposition under consideration. Adams was obliged to repeat his speech, in substance, for the benefit of tardy delegates from New Jersey. There was some rehash of points Dickinson had made. At the end of a nine-hour session devoted to arguments and to a preliminary and indecisive vote on the question, the delegates emerged from the State House into welcome open spaces. The air now was clear. Only a few scudding clouds remained in the night skies. Gone, too, were any doubts that may have lingered in the minds of a few "patriot" members regarding the rightness of their course. They had been strengthened in willingness to pledge their lives, fortunes, and sacred honor in a hazardous venture. In the case of others, opposition had been weakened, procrastination made to seem less worthy. A few, hitherto irresolute, were ready to step over the line which had divided them from the majority.

Reconvening the next morning with the understanding that a final vote would be taken, the members again shifted parliamentary gears. To make the action that was imminent official, the "Committee of the Whole" resolved itself into the Continental Congress proper. Then Lee's resolution that the "United Colonies are, and of right ought to be, free and independent States" was adopted, not a colony dissenting. Only New York refrained from voting, and her spokesman guaranteed that very soon she would take her stand with the others.

Next in the order of business was discussion of the Declaration. While the prevailing opinion was that this item should be disposed of as expeditiously as possible, nevertheless wisdom dictated that a document of such a nature, to be submitted to the court of public opinion, receive most careful scrutiny. Sentence by sentence it was weighed in the balance of collective judgment, and at a few points, none of them vital, was found wanting. Jefferson squirmed uneasily in his chair as his composition was subjected to what he afterward called "mutilations." He could now understand better Franklin's aversion to writing any paper to be reviewed, perhaps amended, by a deliberative body. But a sense of propriety and his disinclination to take part in public debate kept him quiet.

In reality, it was not necessary for him to say anything. Frequently Adams leaped to his feet and argued against change or omission. If he wished to soften some of the charges made against the British king, he had no desire to be suspected of having friendly feelings toward that monarch. Why, anyhow, pick microscopic flaws in a statement that approximated flawlessness?

A few days after July 4, Richard Stockton, one of the New Jersey delegates, in speaking to some of his neighbors at home, who were eager for a first-hand report of the proceedings, had much to say about John Adams. "I call him," he told them, "the Atlas of American Independence."[28] It is not on record that Jefferson gave any similar testimony in writing at the time, but it would be unrealistic to think that he lacked appreciation of Adams' efforts while they were being made. In later years he wrote gratefully about Adams' advocacy of the "fair copy" reported by the committee. His comment was that his colleague kept "fighting fearlessly for every word of it."[29]

The few changes that were made, in spite of all Adams' arguments, strengthened rather than weakened the Declaration. George III shared in responsibility for many injustices, although he had never, as was alleged, directed that slaves be brought to America or given sanction to that practice. Astute lawyers in the assembly were successful in eliminating an indictment that would not stand up in a court of law. Moreover, the majority decided that the "everlasting Adieu" to the British people as a whole, was neither necessary nor

[28] A letter written by Richard Stockton, Jr., a son of the New Jersey delegate, contains a reference to these remarks of the elder Stockton. This portion of the letter is quoted in Adams, *Works*, III, 56.

[29] Jefferson to James Madison, August 30, 1823, *The Works of Thomas Jefferson*, edited by Paul Leicester Ford, (12 vols., New York, 1904), XII, 308 (cited hereafter as Jefferson, *Works*).

desirable. It was pointed out that many persons living in England were sympathetic toward the aggrieved Americans. Sound wisdom prevailed; there was no positive and inclusive farewell to those still subjects of the British monarch. Several other changes, unimportant in comparison with the main propositions, were made. Jefferson's handiwork was not really mutilated. It emerged from this test retaining its original splendor.

Many hours over a three-day period were devoted to this process of judicious review. Finally, late in the afternoon or early in the evening of July 4, the amended Declaration was adopted. There was no rush to ring bells or light bonfires. Indeed, the celebration that followed was very quiet by comparison with many that have taken place since on anniversaries of that day.

It seems that Jefferson did not make any public display of his feeling. Part of his time on July 4 was spent in prosaic activities. He visited a number of shops and bought a thermometer and seven pairs of women's gloves. Adams was more inclined to outward expression of emotion. His forte was not prophecy, but he did foretell with fair accuracy, and with some ecstasy, the manner in which this event would be recalled by future generations. He believed, however, and with good reason, that the action of Tuesday, July 2, was climactic, and mistakenly predicted that July 2 would be observed as a "great anniversary Festival."

In general, his fellow delegates did not behave as if they had just taken part in one of history's important scenes. When they disposed of the main item on the agenda that day, they did not adjourn immediately. Instead, they proceeded in even fashion with other business claiming their attention.

At noon on the Monday following, the Declaration was read from the Observatory platform in the State House Yard. Adams reported that a "great crowd of people" gathered to hear it. Another observer, who evidently had Tory inclinations, stated that "there were very few respectable people present," using "respectable" in the eighteenth-century sense. He added that a "General," whose name was not mentioned, spoke against the Declaration and that there were many others who opposed it.[30]

Whatever the size of the crowd that gathered near the State House that day or the quality of the people who composed it or the nature of the reaction to what was heard, bells did ring throughout the afternoon and the evening, heralding the good news which Adams and many others had been eagerly anticipating for months. In the evening, a mild starlit one, soldiers paraded and there was a *feu de joie*. Adams and Jefferson surely took some pride in their part in accomplishing the result thus made public for the city dwellers and hailed by some portion of them. No pair of men in Congress, a group in which ability and a sense of mission were of remarkably high order, had done as much to make America free. Mingled with their pride was mutual appreciation of efforts made in that soul-testing time. They were now bound together by a tie which had no parallel in the relationships, one with another, of their companions in this great adventure.

After the adoption of the Declaration, less than two months of concurrent service in the Continental Congress remained for these two leaders. To both of them it probably appeared at times as anticlimactic, but it was not lacking in importance and it continued to make great demands upon them.

On the very day that Congress declared the fact and the right of independence, General Howe's transports, carrying a rejuvenated army, sailed up through the Narrows toward New York—a dagger thrust that was meant to divide the rebellious colonies. News of this offensive and reports of a military situation that seemed to be steadily deteriorating, from the American point of view, kept the delegates on tenterhooks of anxiety and presented them with a new and very disturbing set of problems.

[30] The other observer was Charles Biddle. The account given in his autobiography of this reading of the Declaration and the one written by Adams in a letter to Samuel Chase, July 9, 1776, may be found in the *Diary of Independence Hall*, by Harold D. Eberlein and Cortland VanWyck Hubbard (Philadelphia, 1948), 178, 180.

Before them also was a blueprint for confederation. Forward-looking Franklin had done some preparatory work along this line, and the essential features of his plan were incorporated in the report of a special committee to which the intricate subject had been assigned. The presentation of this report precipitated a more spirited debate than that preceding the adoption of the Declaration. Adams argued, with the support of Franklin and others, that representation in the governing body should be on the basis of population, and that the unit rule of voting by colonies, which had hitherto been followed, should be set aside. Some of the delegates, however, believed that this rule provided necessary safeguards for the smaller states, and their spokesmen insisted that it be incorporated in the proposed Articles. While he was not one of those spokesmen, Jefferson was in the group represented by them, and in private correspondence with Adams stated his opinion on the subject. The latter, looking back after a lapse of many years on some of his experiences in the Continental Congress, and having in mind some intervening developments, rather tartly and not quite accurately wrote, "Jefferson *in those days* never failed to agree with me, in everything of a political nature."[31]

During that eventful summer they had repeated opportunities to converse about their common interests, also those few differences of opinion which existed between them and which, for the time being, escaped Adams' attention. After July 4 they met frequently, as they had done before, for committee work in a little circle of *confrères*. With Dr. Franklin they contrived an intricate design as an official seal for the United States of America. One feature of it was a central inscription, *E pluribus unum*, fittingly expressing the essential unity of the federating states. Many other ideas which they approved were less than appropriate. The Latin motto, rather fortunately, it seems, was the only feature of the proposed design that presented a strong appeal to the majority of those making final decisions. It was incorporated in the seal finally approved and remains to this day a visible symbol of the last joint labors in the Continental Congress of three great leaders.

Within a short time after independence was proclaimed there was a

[31] Adams, *Works*, III, 68–69. Italics mine.

close approximation to unanimity in the purpose, on the part of the delegates in Congress, to maintain it. This purpose, with the moral force back of it, was dramatically, but semi-secretly, attested on August 2.

On that day, before any other business was transacted in what was now Independence Hall, there was a ceremony, simple in its main features, which, had it taken place a few centuries earlier and more openly, might have attracted the interest of Shakespeare. The large silver inkstand, which had been resting for more than twenty years on the Speaker's table, served a purpose which those who purchased it could not have foreseen. In sober succession members of the Congress, including a few who had become delegates since July 4, took the pen provided for them and affixed their respective signatures to a parchment copy of the Declaration.[32]

First among them, Speaker John Hancock spelled out his name in huge letters. As he leaned over to make some marks that have become familiar to later generations of Americans, he is reported to have quipped that John Bull might now double the reward of £500 offered for his head. And when affluent Charles Carroll signed, a fellow delegate allegedly remarked that it meant a few millions for the common cause.[33]

Probably Jefferson did not speak a word when he stood near the inkstand and the pen was handed to him. But surely that moment was for him another one of pardonable pride. Even if he still thought of this document as "mutilated" to a certain extent, it was, after all, his creation.

John Adams waited his turn and, when it came, signed with the firm, clear strokes characteristic of his signature. As the proceedings continued, there was tension that could be felt. This was an act that

[32] There was no general signing of the Declaration on the day it was formally approved. Moreover, the signers, bold as they were, exercised prudence to the extent of withholding for a time any public announcement of the ceremony of August 2. They believed that British authorities would regard the act as prima facie evidence of treason.

[33] John H. Hazelton, *The Declaration of Independence, Its History* (New York, 1906), 209.

might well serve as evidence of treason. If serio-comic comments were actually made, they issued, presumably, from a desire to provide a measurement of relief. Dr. Franklin had warned, "We must all hang together or hang separately." Now, as he signed, he could not be sure that it was a clear alternative. Near him was Dr. Benjamin Rush, one of the new delegates from Pennsylvania, an ardent patriot who belonged to a group of intimates, including both Adams and Jefferson, drawn together by the developing crisis. Not far away was Abraham Clark of New Jersey, ready and resolute, even though he had recently seen by night a disturbing vision, in which the principal object was a high gallows with a long row of halters, one for each of the signers.[34]

If there was any visible trace of flinching on the part of any of these men, there was no such inner fear or weakness as would result in defection. Now, by signature as well as by vote, they had taken deliberately, with open eyes and determined spirits, a calculated risk.

Zealous as he was for the life of the newborn nation, Jefferson by this time was chafing under the necessity which kept him in Philadelphia longer than he had expected. He believed that he had made his maximum contribution to the common cause. In the foreseeable future any one of several Virginians could, in his opinion, represent the state in Congress as well as he.

One of the impelling reasons for his desire to be replaced quickly by another qualified representative proceeded from his keen interest in political affairs in his own state. He was convinced that his services were needed there because of an impending battle between ultra-conservatives and liberals who shared his ideas of government. The lines were being drawn for an extraordinary confrontation of opposing philosophies. At stake were provisions of a new constitution, and the battleground would be a meeting of the Virginia Assembly, scheduled to begin in October. He learned that the voters of Albemarle County had elected him to represent them in this Assembly. He regarded the election as a clear summons to duty. He felt morally obligated to be in the thick of the fight for Virginia's liberation from an archaic administrative system.

[34] Edmund C. Burnett, *The Continental Congress* (New York, 1941), 221.

There were also personal considerations back of his determination to break off, as soon as he could with propriety, his connection with Congress. The mistress of Monticello was not well. While the news of her condition came to him indirectly, it was of such a nature as to make each additional day spent in Philadelphia most anxious. On one of those days he was notified that Richard Henry Lee, who had gone home in June, had been chosen to take his place in the Virginia delegation. It was, apparently, the claims of a sick wife that had kept Lee away from the State House while so much history was being made there. Those claims were not now urgent. Lee certainly understood, so Jefferson reflected, what it meant to a dutiful husband to be hundreds of miles from home under such circumstances. There is something almost pathetic in Jefferson's written plea to him to speed his return, and so relieve himself of the necessity of staying longer. "For God's sake, for your country's sake, and for my sake, come," he urged. To which he added a postscript emphasis: "I pray you to come. I am under a sacred obligation to go home."[35]

In lesser degree a similar conflict of loyalties was in progress during those midsummer weeks within the breast of John Adams. An epidemic of smallpox was raging along the coast south of Boston. While it lacked the virulence of the previous year's dysentery scourge, knowledge of it added another anxiety to those under which this absentee husband and father was weighed down. Abigail and all the children underwent a belated vaccination which, even with two repetitions, did not keep six-year-old Charles from getting the disease. And it was clear now to his mother that Adams had been wise in having himself inoculated some years before. Unlike Jefferson, he continued to hear regularly and directly, during that summer, from his wife. He was kept informed about afflictions and the threat of them in the home circle. And from him there went to his family expressions of solicitude. One of them was in the form of advice to get plenty of fresh air as long as there was any danger.

One of his recurrent anxieties related to his own health. On days when the temperature soared and at times when the round of com-

[35] Jefferson to Richard Henry Lee, July 29, 1776, Jefferson *Papers*, I, 477.

mittee sessions and of State House debates was especially wearying, he felt that his physical resources were practically exhausted. Once, when the midsummer heat was relentless, he wrote to Abigail that he needed desperately the "bracing quality" of his "native air."[36] The urge to get away from the hot city, to go back to Braintree as fast as horses could take him, was almost—but not quite—overpowering. And it continued. Several weeks later, at a time when the weather was again oppressively sultry, he made an honest confession in another letter to Abigail: "If our affairs had not been in so critical a state in New York, [a reference to the landing of Howe's army on Long Island], I should have run away before now."[37]

Probably he felt more than ever like playing truant when Jefferson's release was announced at the beginning of September and that most impatient delegate, his term ended, started for Monticello. It was then three weeks beyond the date which he had originally set for his departure. In the interval he had settled his accounts, purchased a few articles which would be useful at home, and packed personal belongings. His impedimenta now included a writing desk of more than nominal value. As the day to which he looked forward drew near, he bade farewell to his colleagues, many of them comrades in counsel and action over a period of more than a year. High on the list of those for whom he had a warm, fraternal regard was John Adams.

Adams' good friend Elbridge Gerry and his cousin Samuel had recently obtained leaves of absence and, quitting the scene temporarily, had begun the long ride homeward. It is possible that sometimes at night, tossing restlessly on his bed, he wondered if either of them, or even Jefferson, had better reasons than he himself could advance for absence, temporary or otherwise, from the deliberations of the new country's governing body.

But, as his custom was, he hewed to the line of duty. It brought him repeatedly to sessions of the Congress and in mid-September to Staten Island with Benjamin Franklin and Edward Rutledge. There, as representatives of Congress, they held fruitless discussions with

[36] Adams to Mrs. Adams, July 11, 1776, Adams, *Familiar Letters*, 200.
[37] Adams to Mrs. Adams, August 14, 1776, *ibid.*, 211.

General Howe regarding terms of peace. Even after the completion of this mission, Adams did not feel free to make an application immediately for respite from his official labors. When he did so, it was granted; and early on an October Sunday morning he started on horseback along the now familiar route that led to Braintree.

Eight months had elapsed since he used that means of transportation, and he did not find the experience a comfortable one; but he was in a hurry, and did not dismount for any extended rest until evening. His mileage for that day was thirty. A little later in the month, alert with expectancy, breathing the "native air" which he had missed so much, he made his way along the main street of his native village to the modest farmhouse, with lean-to back, which was home.

One morning in the following spring, Adams, who had resumed his duties in Congress, picked up a letter directed to himself and read it with great interest. Neither he nor the writer had any idea of the extent and general scope of the correspondence then beginning.[38] But in this communication, the first written one from Jefferson to Adams, were features that would be repeated, singly or in combination, in many letters to follow. Jefferson, busy as he was at Williamsburg, had taken time to write to his associate in the struggle for independence requesting information, conveying a suggestion, and expressing esteem for the man to whom it was addressed.

News of the proceedings at Philadelphia was trickling so slowly in the direction of Williamsburg and Richmond and Charlottesville that many Virginians had become "lethargick and insensible of the state they are in." Could not the Congress reissue its former directive that the post riders "travel night and day"? It was important that citizens everywhere know, with as little delay as possible, what was going on.

But Jefferson's main reason for writing was concern about the Confederation, which was "again on the carpet"; especially about the difficult problem of assuring fair representation in the law-making

---

[38] As we shall see, the two men exchanged letters during a period of almost half a century, there being, however, some long intervals in which, for one reason or another, there was no written communication between them.

body. He reminded Adams of their private conversation on this subject, making special reference to his suggestion that any proposition introduced in that body could be voted down, not only by a majority of representatives of the population, but also by a "majority of the colonies of America"—that is, by use of the unit rule.

This was, in germinal form, a plan later incorporated in the United States Constitution. But now, in 1777, the need for an efficient federal government was pressing, in Jefferson's opinion. The lack of it, he believed, threatened the existence of the nation that had so recently come to birth. While he was at this time, as always, a loyal Virginian and would have been unalterably opposed to any complete surrender of state sovereignty, he was not—to quote from one of the better biographies of him—"specially local or particularistic; almost all his colleagues were that, to a considerable degree. He was willing to concede much to the cause of union."[39] His interest in that cause, held in balance with his belief in local government, led him to call Adams' attention again to the proposal he had made in the matter of representation in Congress. Would Adams be "so good" as to resurrect it and use his powers of persuasion to have it adopted?[40]

The day on which this letter was received had not ended when a reply to it was made ready. It was a typical Adamsesque mixture of optimism, pessimism, frankness, appreciation, and snap judgment.

The writer did not despair of the "great work of Confederation." But, he complained, it "drags heavily on." Jefferson's "Industry and Abilities" were, he declared, greatly needed there in the city which General Howe was now stigmatizing as the "rebel capital." The new nation was in a bad way financially. Nor was it secure enough from any point of view to excuse Jefferson's "Retreat to the Delights of domestic Life." It can scarcely be doubted that Adams knew the reasons for Jefferson's withdrawal from Congress. This inaccurate reference to a "Retreat" is one of a considerable number of indications that he was sometimes hasty in writing, just as he was in speaking.

[39] Dumas Malone, *Jefferson the Virginian* (Vol. I of *Jefferson and His Time*, Boston, 1948–), 244.
[40] Jefferson to Adams, May 16, 1777, Jefferson *Papers*, II, 18–19.

As for the proposal to make unit voting by states of equal effect with voting of individual members of the legislative body, in the sole capacity of representatives of districts, a polite brush-off was administered. Adams agreed to give attention to it only in the event that a system of representation then being discussed was defeated. He frankly stated that in his opinion this scheme was "perfectly equitable."[41]

This, the first exchange of letters between the two statesmen, could not have been entirely satisfactory to the one who initiated it.

Later that same year Jefferson had some interesting talks with one of his neighbors at Monticello, Philip Mazzei. The latter had brought over a company of *vignerons* from his native Italy and was experimenting extensively with grape growing in Virginia. The two men spent much time chatting about a variety of subjects, including grapes (if not cabbages) and kings and generals and statesmen, and eventually they talked about money. Jefferson learned that ten million crowns were lying idle in the coffers of the Grand Duke of Tuscany. And others as well as Adams had made him aware that, in terms of national welfare, the pound shortage was more serious than the soldier shortage.

He decided to write another letter to the man who he still believed was the most persuasive of the delegates at Philadelphia. To him he broached the idea of securing the authorization by Congress of an effort to tap the source of credit of which he had been informed. This could be done, he wrote, by approach through an intermediary to the Grand Duke. And neighbor Mazzei was an ideal man for the job. He was "conversant in courts, of great understanding, and equal zeal in our cause." Jefferson could do no more than leave the matter to the discretion of his former colleague at the State House. He clearly implied, however, that it was worthy of "further thought."[42]

There is no record of how much thought Adams gave to the idea, but apparently it was never considered seriously by those who were directing the business of revolution. Not long after Adams heard of

[41] Adams to Jefferson, May 26, 1777, *ibid.*, II, 20–22.
[42] Jefferson to Adams, August 21, 1777, *ibid.*, II, 28.

the idle money in Tuscany and of the service Mazzei might render, American forces won a victory at Saratoga, France extended recognition to the infant nation, and for a while at least the problem of financing the war was less difficult.

However, nearly three years after Jefferson first mentioned the Italian husbandman as a possible agent for Congress, Adams, then residing in Paris, received him at his lodgings in that city. It was a visit which seems to have been arranged by Jefferson and took place on the eve of Mazzei's departure for his native land. The latter was looking forward to a meeting with the rich duke for the purpose of securing a substantial loan to the United States, as much in need of that kind of help as it had been in the very early years of the struggle. But it appears that the Tuscan royalist was not interested in making such investments. The rate of interest offered may have been too low and the enterprise in which the American states were engaged may have seemed too dubious.

At any rate, Mazzei's call on Adams was the occasion for the latter's second letter to Jefferson, closing the short chapter of their correspondence during the years of the Revolution.[43] They were far apart geographically, and there was little overlapping of their most pressing concerns. For some time there was no direct contact between them.

But each of them in his first letter to the other, had expressed a willingness to keep open a line of mutual communication. Jefferson coupled with his declaration of such willingness praise of Adams' worth and abilities in these words: "The esteem I have for you privately as well as for your public importance will always render assurance of your health and happiness agreeable."[44] Adams responded in the same spirit: "I shall ever esteam it a Happiness to hear of your Welfare."[45] The years that went by, prior to their next meeting, without such assurances brought no lessening of their mutual esteem and respect. On any day during this long period in which

[43] Adams to Jefferson, June 29, 1780, *ibid.*, III, 469–70.
[44] Jefferson to Adams, May 16, 1777, *ibid.*, II, 19.
[45] Adams to Jefferson, May 26, 1777, *ibid.*, II, 22.

their separate paths of duty kept them far apart, both would have welcomed an opportunity to meet and counsel together.

Two great men, brought together in a historic setting by a combination of momentous circumstances, had become friends.

CHAPTER II

The Transatlantic Phase

꘡꘡꘡

Two American travelers, having completed a rough night trip across the English Channel, were directed by a friendly Irish stranger to the Hotel L'Aigle d'Or in the French port of Le Havre, where they found welcome accommodations. It was early morning on the last day of July, 1784.

These new guests at the hostelry scarcely needed to introduce themselves as father and daughter. Hazel-gray eyes, auburn-reddish hair, angular frame, taller than average stature—all common characteristics—were good evidence of their relationship. The daughter, too young to be called a woman or even an adolescent, but in appearance too mature to be taken for a child, carried a cage containing a yellow-green parrot. Her father gave attention to the disposition of their other baggage and at the same time kept a watchful eye upon herself. Both were mildly excited as they breathed the air and looked about on scenes of a country about which they had read and heard much.

For Thomas Jefferson, in age not yet beyond the early forties, and for twelve-year-old Martha the end of a long land and water journey was in sight.

They were not conventional tourists and this was not primarily a sight-seeing expedition. In Jefferson's portfolio were his official credentials for diplomatic service with John Adams and Benjamin Franklin, both of whom had been in Europe for some time representing American interests. The three were to negotiate treaties of "amity and commerce," in every case where it was possible, with approximately a score of specified governments. The political independence of the

United States had increased dependence upon international trade relations.

Father and daughter had met in Philadelphia, where the latter, motherless and occasionally homesick, was for some time an apt but incongruous pupil in a fashionable boarding school. Then there had been visits to New York, New Haven, Providence, and Boston, followed by a memorable voyage across the Atlantic in a three-masted sailing vessel. They stopped first at West Cowes, England, then went on to Portsmouth, where they stayed long enough for Patsy, as the girl was familiarly called, to recover from the effects of a fever, possibly attributable to *mal de mer*. Now, on their first morning in France, there remained only the final stage of their journey—the 130-mile trip to Paris.

There was no occasion for haste, and two days elapsed before they were on their way. Very little escaped their attention as hour after hour their carriage followed the windings of the Seine, at times through quaint villages but usually past scenes of pastoral beauty. It was harvest time in Normandy, and Farmer Jefferson noted the paradox of poverty in a region where soil fertility was evident. For two nights and a day they lingered in Rouen, where William the Conqueror and other kings, as well as the Maid of Orleans, had long before played important roles in the human drama. Another long day of travel brought them almost to the edge of the city. On the next morning they came to St. Germain with its important chateau, then to Marly, where the waters of the Seine were caught and funneled to the cascades of Versailles—a mechanical arrangement which intrigued Jefferson as much as anything he had seen on this trip. From there it was a short ride to the Hotel d'Orleans, where they were to stay until more suitable quarters could be found. Their interest in people and places around them was high. A dream had come true. They were in Paris.

Meantime, other Americans were getting about Europe in a series of movements directed toward the same destination. Abigail Adams and her daughter Abigail had crossed the ocean two weeks and several hundred miles ahead of Jefferson and his daughter. They had seen as much of London as they could in the brief period before meeting Adams and the oldest son.

It had been a protracted separation. John and John Quincy had been abroad for more than five and one-half years. Since in those times there was no such rapid communication as the telegraph and telephone, some misunderstanding arose about the time and place for this family rendezvous. One day, when July was almost over, John Quincy, looking older than a boy of seventeen should, as his mother thought, suddenly appeared at the hotel where the two Abigails were staying. Through him they learned that the husband and father expected to wait for them at The Hague, where he had been serving as the appointed American representative. Immediately John Quincy and his mother and sister began making arrangements to go to the Dutch capital. While they were so engaged, impetuous John Adams suddenly changed his mind. He crossed the North Sea, it being what he called a "tedious passage," then hitchhiked inland a distance of twenty-four miles, the means of conveyance a farmer's cart. After that ride, he still had more than a few miles to go, but in a matter of hours he put them behind him. Seldom had his wife and daughter been more completely—and pleasantly—surprised than when he arrived, travel-stained but with high-pitched expectations, at their lodgings.

This reunion took place on an evening in early August. Two mornings later, at Calais, young John and his father, seasoned travelers that they were, introduced the ladies of the family to France. For the four of them there had been a choppy ride across the Channel. Now, as Jefferson and his daughter had done upon their arrival in the country, they made themselves as comfortable as possible in a vehicle which was to transport them to the capital. For several days they were to spend the greater part of their time in an English carriage, recently bought.

Abby, as the young lady of this little group was frequently called by members of her family and by friends, dutifully followed the recommendation of her father that she keep a diary. Doing so, he pointed out, was one means of getting full benefit from her travels.

The route which they took was the one followed by Yorick of the *Sentimental Journey*, whose acquaintance Abby had made in her reading. She noted in her record that the villages were wretched in appearance, many of the houses in them scarcely fit for human habitation. And this was a country, she observed, in which nearly everybody worked as if separated from starvation by only a narrow gap. On the other hand, there was the prince's estate which they stopped to visit, with two hundred horses and two hundred dogs and a private theater and palatial gardens.

Father and son had become accustomed to these contrasting scenes, but to the impressionable young woman and her mother those first days in France were most revealing. For all of them there was being established one more point of contact with the other Americans who had just seen a cross-section of life in the French provinces.

On August 13 the two young people and their parents registered at the Hotel de York in Paris.

There was little time to do more than remove the dust of travel and get some needed rest before going to a dinner party at the home of the American consul, Mr. Thomas Barclay. In her account of this experience Abby wrote, "Mr. Jefferson and daughter dined with us."[1]

This was the first meeting of all those members of the two families who were now in a foreign land.[2] It was also the first time that the two statesmen had met in eight busy years. Perhaps they were not as

---

[1] *Journal and Correspondence of Miss Adams*, edited by her Daughter (2 vols., New York, 1841–42), I, 14 (cited hereafter as Miss Adams, *Journal and Correspondence*).

[2] There can be little doubt that Abigail and her daughter met Jefferson and his daughter in the interval between June 18 and June 20, 1784, even though Abigail made no mention of it in the diary in which she related, in some detail, events of those days in her own experience. All four of them were in Boston from some time on the eighteenth until midday of the twentieth, at which time the Adams ladies boarded the ship *Active*. On the nineteenth Jefferson wrote to Adams: "I have hastened myself on my journey hither in hopes of having the pleasure of attending Mrs. Adams to Paris and of lessening some of the difficulties to which she may be exposed. But after some unexpected delays at Philadelphia and New York I arrived here yesterday and find her engaged for her passage to London and to sail tomorrow." (Jefferson *Papers*, VII, 309). The assumption that the two pairs of travelers did meet at that time seems reasonable.

effusive in their greetings as present-day Americans might be under similar circumstances, but there was certainly cordial warmth in their exchange of salutations and in introducing those of the company previously unacquainted.

In her personal narrative Abby reported that it was a friendly party, although not free from the restraints of a foreign custom. Dinner was served in the French style, the host believing that Americans in Paris should do as the Parisians did. This compliance with custom precluded the free table-conversation familiar to and preferred by the honored guests.

But there was opportunity that day or soon afterwards for Abigail to relate to the gentleman from Virginia some of her adventures since leaving home. She would never forget the voyage in a three-hundred-ton trader across the wide ocean. She could still feel, almost, the pitching and rolling of the vessel. And she could still smell, almost, the nauseating odors that came sometimes from various parts of a craft of "horrid dirtiness." Once, while writing her diary account of the voyage, she had remembered what she previously read about the Roman Cato, who, it seems, was a very poor sailor. Of him it was said, as Abigail reported, that "one of the three things which he regreted at the close of Life; was that he had gone once by sea when he might have made his journey by land."[3]

No such choice had been possible for Abigail as she planned this journey to Europe. She probably learned, after having engaged passage for herself and Abby, that Jefferson, knowing of her intention to make the trip and solicitous of her welfare, had made tentative arrangements for extra accommodations with the captain of the more commodious French packet in which he and Patsy were to sail. On that assumption, she must have wished many times before she and Abby saw the cliffs of Dover that they had become fellow passengers with this friend of her husband.

On the day of the consul's dinner party, all these recent travelers were safe, relaxed, and comfortable. On the lower age level there began certain relationships that for a while, at least, were to be most

[3] Adams, *Diary and Autobiography*, III, 163.

interesting and helpful. As the meal and the post-prandial conversation continued, there was, on Patsy's part, more than cursory appraisal of two young Americans of her own generation. The range of her interest was wider than that of the average person of her age, and she knew that back of whatever John Quincy said was a wealth of experience prematurely accumulated. He had gone to school in Amsterdam and Leyden. He had traveled eastward as far as Russia. If there had been time and opportunity, he could have told many stories about distant places and strange peoples.

Nor was it a small privilege for Patsy to be in the company of Miss Adams. The seven years' difference in their ages was partially balanced by the fact that Patsy was mature for her age. But she could not speak or understand French, and one appeal of these new acquaintances was that she could get the meaning of every word that either of them spoke.

In fact, this very young lady, as well as her father, had much in common, on the domestic plane, with the family from Braintree. Neither family circle was complete. Patsy's younger sisters, Mary and Lucy Elizabeth, were with Jefferson's brother-in-law, Francis Eppes, and his family at the home called Eppington in southern Virginia. Mary, six years old, better known as Polly, had told her father in a letter she spelled out shortly before he left for Paris "I can almost read."[4] But she and Lucy Elizabeth, just past babyhood, were much too young to be taken to a distant continent on a trip of indefinite duration.

There were two missing, likewise, in the Adams family, as four of them began life together in the foreign capital. Charles and Thomas, both nearing adolescence, might not have been left behind if father and mother had been less eager to have them properly prepared for college. With that purpose in mind, they, too, were given a temporary home with a hospitably inclined uncle and aunt. This uncle was minister of a church at Haverhill, Massachusetts, a well-educated man and a good tutor. Naturally, there was solicitude on the part of each of the three parents concerning their absent children. Also, Abby, and

[4] Mary Jefferson to Thomas Jefferson, April 1784, Jefferson *Papers*, VII, 58.

to a lesser degree John Quincy, missed their two brothers, even as Patsy missed her two sisters.

If we may judge what these newcomers to Europe talked about in their first meetings by what they wrote to friends and relatives, we know that some of their conversation related to differences they had recently observed in ways of living. France was different from England, and both countries were different from America. Abigail's few days in London were enough to make her believe that city was better than Boston, and when she had spent a like period in Paris, she was sure that it was worse than Boston. Her husband and son reminded her that she had not really seen the French metropolis. To which she retorted, "I have smelt it."[5]

Young Abby frequently contrasted the French with the English, and apparently could think of no particulars in which the former excelled. They seemed industrious after a fashion, but showed no such alertness and verve as the people across the Channel. French food was not nearly as good as English. Even the women's dresses were not as stylish and attractive as those she had seen in London.

Jefferson's daughter had similar opinions about the people who now surrounded her and about their habits. Most of those opinions were based on what she had seen en route from Le Havre. She would not trade her corner of Virginia for all of France. To be sure, many of the churches were beautiful, their architecture magnificent, and the rural regions lovely, but never had she seen so many beggars. Worse still, strangers in the country were in danger of being treated abominably. In every town, it seemed, there was practiced the hook-or-crook method of extracting the foreigner's money.

The elder Adams and John Quincy, too, sophisticated by years of residence abroad, were mildly amused at the reactions of the travelers just arrived from America. It was obvious that they had good powers of observation, and they would learn more as they stayed longer.

With the exception of a few days spent, by necessity rather than

---

[5] Mrs. Adams to Miss Lucy Cranch, September 5, 1784, *Letters of Mrs. Adams, the Wife of John Adams, with An Introductory Memoir by her Grandson, Charles Francis Adams* (Boston, 1840), 251 (cited hereafter as *Letters of Mrs. Adams*).

choice, on the Isle of Wight and at Portsmouth, Jefferson had never been in England. As in former years, he was inclined to discount any favorable opinion of that country which he heard expressed. To him there were many more interesting topics for discussion.

In the consul's drawing room, on the occasion of that first social function in Paris, he may have edged into the conversation a few remarks about elephants and moose and quadrupeds in general. Recently he had been reading and thinking about the habits of various species of the animal world. Also, just before he left America, he had read a learned treatise on balloons, containing information that they could even carry a passenger. Some Parisians were still excited about the first ascension of such an object that they had witnessed—an event of the preceding year. How wonderful it was! Man could at last travel through the upper air.

Adams himself had been intrigued by this new form of navigation. At the Barclays' on that summer Sunday, and later as these two Americans and their ladies got together, there may have been some talk about the wonderful accomplishment. If so, it was in line with many conversations that had taken place, in preceding months, as city dwellers met on street corners, in public cafés, or at fashionable salons.

Certainly there was no lack of topics about which to exchange comments. It would have been strange if there was no talk of business at the very beginning of this resumption of close personal companionship between Adams and Jefferson. As certainly as in their earlier experience at Philadelphia they were brought together here in a foreign land by constraints of patriotic duty. Within a few days they were to meet with Franklin and with him assume directly a responsibility entrusted to them by Congress—to carry on negotiations for treaties of "amity and commerce" with a score of specified governments. Each looked forward with satisfaction to the opportunity of working with the other. Adams was especially pleased that Congress had seen fit to send Jefferson as one of its representatives. Shortly before they first greeted each other in the new surroundings, he wrote James Warren that Jefferson's appointment gave him "great pleasure." "He is an old Friend," he commented, "with whom I have had occasion to work at many a knotty Problem, and in whose Abilities and Steadiness I always found great Cause to confide.''[6]

In the immediate prospect before them were more knotty problems. To the advantage of tackling an important assignment together, however, was added that of having once more the venerable Franklin as a counselor and coworker. Moreover, as the day approached on which their labors were to begin, there was substantial encouragement in the fact that the two families found each other mutually agreeable.

Passy, on the outskirts of Paris, where Franklin had been living and entertaining for several years in semiluxurious style, was the scene of the first and nearly all the subsequent formal meetings of the three commissioners. In the elderly diplomat's home, overlooking pleasant vineyards that sloped down to the Seine, they met on August 30 to begin work.

In the choice of Jefferson for a place on this mission, Congress had taken into account the fact that he came from south of the Potomac. His appointment was assurance that Virginia and states farther south would not be forgotten in the negotiations that were being contemplated. Adams could be depended upon to look out especially for the interests of New England. Similarly, Franklin represented the middle states. But no one of the three was provincial in his outlook. There was no doubt that all would do as much as possible for any group of Americans who might profit by access to foreign markets. In each of them, lumbermen of New Hampshire, shore fishermen and far-cruising whalers in others parts of New England, wheat and flour producers of New York and Pennsylvania, tobacco growers of Virginia, processors of tar and turpentine in the Carolinas and Georgia, and all others in the new country who might have surplus goods to sell, would have a sympathetic spokesman.

They faced serious and, as it turned out, almost insuperable obstacles. Franklin, a little tremulous as he contemplated the directive of Congress to himself and his colleagues looking toward treaties with

[6] Adams to James Warren, August 27, 1784 (Massachusetts Historical Society; Adams Manuscript Trust) quoted in Jefferson *Papers*, VII, 382.

nearly all the principalities and powers of Europe, observed, "We are not likely to eat the bread of idleness."[7] No one of them expected that the task before them would be easy, but neither did any of them anticipate that the results achieved would be so meager.

For a while they met every day, later at less frequent intervals, and in the concluding stages of the proceedings only as the dwindling opportunities of the situation required. It became clear as they proceeded with exploratory moves that the "Most Serene Republic of Genoa" and the "Most Serene Republic of Venice" were as little inclined to enter into a compact with the "Citizens of the United States of America" as was the "High, Glorious, mighty and most Noble Prince, King and Emperor of Fez, Morocco, etc.," sovereign of a state that specialized in piracy. Such replies as were authorized by these "Serene" states and this "Glorious" ruler were less than enthusiastic, and there were few hopeful responses from other governments.

As apparently fruitless months went by, Jefferson's belief that most of the Old World monarchs were individuals of low intellectual and moral caliber was strengthened. Scarcely one of them, he came to think, had either the ability or the virtue that would qualify him to be a good vestryman in a parish church in Virginia. He attributed the rebuffs which he and his fellow commissioniers experienced partly to a widespread decadence in high places, manifesting itself in such common symptoms as ineptness, laxity, and narrow vision. Moreover, and Jefferson was quick to notice this, some members of England's ruling class were diligent in spreading anti-American propaganda through the press and all other available channels.

But it was a lack of political unity at home as much as a dearth of statesmanship and good will in foreign countries that blocked most of the combined efforts of Franklin, Adams, and Jefferson. The more astute of those exercising authority in the royal courts of Europe were hesitant about entering into agreements with a remote nation whose component units were, they believed, loosely federated. As a matter

[7] Franklin to Adams, August 6, 1784, *Complete Works of Benjamin Franklin*, edited by John Bigelow (10 vols., New York and London, 1887–88), IX, 41.

of fact, the United States was not then united enough to warrant the hopes animating members of Congress when they saddled these men with such a responsibility.

Before he sailed for Europe, Jefferson had made some efforts to have the powers of Congress over commerce increased. While he was perpetually haunted by fears of an overly strong central government, he was not oblivious of the dangers inherent in a merely nominal confederation. His argument was strikingly similar to that later set forward by his political opponents. As he put it, "Nothing can preserve our Confederacy unless their band of Union, their common council, be strengthened."[8] Now, as he grappled with the difficulties of this mission, he saw from a new perspective the need for the establishment of a "more perfect union."

Within a few years this result was achieved. Gradually arteries of foreign commerce were opened up; and to these American diplomats, laboring against heavy odds, belongs the credit for initiating formally an enterprise of incalculable value to many other countries in addition to their own.

The overtures sent out from Passy were favorably received at Sans Souci, where Frederick the Great manipulated a power approximately absolute on the basis of principles comparatively enlightened. It was within the compass of such a power that the treaty submitted by the American agents was accepted, with only a few changes. In due course, it was signed and ratified.

The trade advantages accruing to the young nation of the West from this agreement were not great. Nevertheless, there were in it some idealistic provisions, bearing Jefferson's special imprint, overreaching the mere mechanics of commerce and far in advance of most of the accepted stipulations of that kind in that century. "Why should not the Law of Nations go on improving? Ages have intervened between its several steps; but as knowledge of late increases rapidly, why should not those steps be quickened?"[9] So Jefferson and his co-

---

[8] Jefferson to Madison, July 1, 1784, Jefferson *Papers*, VII, 356.

[9] *Ibid.*, VII, 491. The quotation is from a document attributed to Jefferson, entitled "Reasons in Support of the New Proposed Articles in the Treaties of Com-

agents argued at the time these proposals were made. "Old Frederick," in whom military genius was combined with some real regard for human rights, responded in effect, "Why not, indeed?"

The particular point in which improvement in the "Law of Nations" was sought related to more security for civilians, on land and sea, in time of war. Thus it came about that some harsh practices of contemporary warfare were abjured by the two nations, and to that extent there was a foregleam of civilization at its best in the century that followed. This treaty has been characterized by a modern scholar as "symptomatic" of an "idealism that the New World felt might be made practicable," placing the United States "in such a position among the nations as to make possible the preservation of an original liberalism."[10]

There is grim irony in the fact that early in the twentieth century the war lords of Germany virtually mocked agreements authorized by an earlier ruler in that part of Europe, dismissing modern international compacts as "scraps of paper." Nevertheless, the "original liberalism" which Franklin and Adams and Jefferson championed in Paris, as they had done in other ways in Philadelphia, has been preserved. Moreover, in the opinion of many competent observers, its range has been extended. While confirmed pessimists would undoubtedly deny the hypothesis that Jefferson and his associates set forth at Paris, that the "Law of Nations" goes on improving, others, admitting that the rate of progress is slow, insist that there is continuing justification for that point of view.

There must have been frequent periods of relaxation as these three American knights of diplomacy spent time together in the spacious rooms in Franklin's house. At such times, laying aside for a while the business with which they were immediately concerned, they would not fail to recall more exciting experiences which they had shared a few years before. Over wine cups filled from an ample supply of

merce." This document was enclosed in a letter from the American commissioners to Baron de Thulemier of the Prussian government, and was dated November 10, 1784.

[10] William Kirk Woolery, *The Relation of Thomas Jefferson to American Foreign Policy* (Baltimore, 1927), 19.

Bordeaux and Burgundy in the cellar, there was, we may assume, some reminiscing about the long fight for American independence and their respective parts in it. After these "wine breaks" they could go back with fresh vigor to the tasks confronting them.

It was a goodly fellowship, even if marred to some extent by Adams' growing feeling, not entirely free from envy, that Franklin had lived too long in France and had become too popular with her people to be of maximum service to his own country. Within a few years Adams would come to believe that Jefferson himself was enamored of the French to such an extent as to impair seriously his usefulness as a public servant of America. And by a process of reasoning not as clear to others as to himself, the man from Massachusetts, throughout much of his career, regarded any appearance of altruistic motives on the part of France as a misleading, if not deceptive, mask. But now, in meeting the responsibility delegated to them, he was pleased with evidence that Jefferson was free from any taint of foreign influence. He continued to be grateful to Congress for having provided Franklin and himself with such a partner.

In less than four months after the first meeting of the three commissioners at Passy, he wrote to Elbridge Gerry, who was still a member of Congress: "Jefferson is an excellent hand. You could not have sent a better. He appears to me to be infected with no Party Passions or national prejudices, or any Partialities, but for his own country."[11] A few days later he reported in similar vein to Henry Knox: "You can scarcely have heard a Character too high of my Friend and Colleague Mr. Jefferson, either in point of Power or Virtues. My Fellow Labourer in Congress, eight or nine years ago, upon many arduous Tryals, particularly in the draught of our Declaration of Independence and in the formation of our Code of Articles of War, and Laws for the Army. I have found him uniformly the same wise and prudent Man and Steady Patriot."[12]

[11] Adams to Gerry, December 12, 1784 (Massachusetts Historical Society; Adams Manuscript Trust) quoted in Jefferson *Papers*, VII, 382.

[12] Adams to Henry Knox, December 15, 1784 (Massachusetts Historical Society; Adams Manuscript Trust) quoted in Jefferson *Papers*, VII, 383.

In general, albeit in less outspoken fashion, Jefferson reciprocated these sentiments. As they wrestled with problems posed before them, each looked upon the presence of the other, in a land where friends were far outnumbered by strangers, as an inestimable blessing.

As has already been indicated, a new phase in the development of this friendship was introduced when the two men began meeting each other in the presence of one or more of the other members of their respective families. If they had lived in Paris as they had in Philadelphia, separated from everyone of their own flesh and blood, the story now being told would have been very different.

For Adams and the others in his little family circle a home away from home was established in a large house belonging to the Comte de Rouault, in suburban Auteuil. Having located there less than a week after reaching Paris, Adams referred to this new residence as the best he could wish for. Very appealing to him were the "House, the Garden, the Situation near the Bois de Boulogne, elevated above the River Seine and the low Grounds, and distant from the putrid Streets of Paris."[13] Here he enjoyed, in a manner unprecedented in his experience, the emoluments of a foreign diplomat. Frequently he walked for exercise, strolling along the tree-bordered paths near the mansion.

Abigail, accustomed to the narrow confines of an average New England dwelling, found herself mistress of a house where forty beds could be made. Under her supervision were seven servants to help in attendance upon the needs of the household. As for Abby, Alice in Wonderland could not have been more thrilled than she was by this new environment. And for John Quincy, as for his father, such luxury, combined with domestic satisfaction, was a new experience.

To this home, in a setting that appeared rather exotic to recently arrived Americans, Thomas Jefferson came in response to a dinner invitation on the first Sunday following the consul-general's party. In a very short time he was on such friendly terms with all the residents at Auteuil that he felt free to go there without preliminary formalities.

[13] Adams, *Diary and Autobiography*, III, 171.

For a while this association appeared to him as a patch of blue sky in the midst of dark clouds. Patsy had been placed, soon after arrival in Paris, in a convent school, where good educational advantages were offered with the understanding that no attempts were made to convert Protestant pupils to Roman Catholicism. Admittance to this school was restricted, and acceptance of Patsy as a *pensionnaire* was most fortunate for her. But as her father came out through the wooden gate of the convent, a symbol of separation from the child whom he had just left in care of Mother Louise Thérèse and her assistants, and as he went back to his lodgings, he was far from being a happy man. He could visit Patsy regularly, and on occasion she could get permission to join him for a little while outside, but of the joys of family life which had been allotted him for a few short years, only this small remnant now remained.

The death of Martha Wayles Jefferson two years before had plunged him into an abyss of grief from which he had emerged painfully and slowly. But he had no natural inclination for the life of a recluse, and now, as one duly accredited by the United States on a mission of importance, he needed more spacious living quarters. Early in the fall he rented a fairly elaborate suite of rooms in the Hotel de Landron, equipped them with appropriate furniture, decorated them with costly fabrics, and started a collection of paintings and sculptured works. To take care of this establishment he employed a full staff of servants. Partly for the sake of companionship he began sharing these accommodations and accumulations with David Humphreys, secretary of the American Legation, and William Short, a young Virginia lawyer who had become his private secretary. In this elegant house he succeeded, apparently, in insulating himself from the offensive city odors which had disturbed Mrs. Adams. Even in these pleasant and commodious surroundings, however, he experienced frequent moods of dejection.

A very natural contributing cause to his recurring melancholy was a physical affliction, not very clearly diagnosed, but attributed by him to unwholesome water and damp air. Whatever its exact nature, it was severe enough to keep him indoors most of the time for several weeks. His general outlook was further darkened by the same appearance of neglect which frequently disturbed his peace of mind while he was living in Philadelphia. Relatives and friends in Virginia did not keep in touch with him to the extent he desired. News about them and about domestic events in general seldom came. "Nothing can equal the dearth of American intelligence in which we live here," he lamented to one of his irregular correspondents at home. To this he added, "We might as well be in the moon."[14]

But shortly after penning this complaint, he received some letters brought by his good friend Lafayette, returning from America. In one of them was devastating news. Lucy Elizabeth had died at Eppington. Whooping cough, referred to in this message as the "most horrible of all disorders," had cut short the life of his youngest daughter. Of the six children born to Martha and himself only Patsy and Polly were now left—and Polly was half a world away. To his brother-in-law, who had also lost a child at the same time and from the same malady, he wrote, "It is in vain to endeavor to describe the situation of my mind; it would pour balm neither into your wounds nor mine."[15]

He had brought with him to France a violin, for which he had a feeling as near affection as any inanimate object could arouse in him. The hours he spent with it provided a certain satisfaction which compensated in part for his afflictions. Bow in hand and instrument in position, he whiled away parts of many gloomy days that followed one another in late fall and early winter.

Even the recollections of gastronomic delights at Monticello at times induced a nostalgic mood. Once, soon after getting settled in his residence, he wrote this directive to his brother-in-law: "Send me a doz. or two hams from Monticello if any vessel from James river to Havre."[16]

Jefferson's deprivations and anxieties, coupled with indisposition and bereavement, stood out, before his own mind at least, in sharp

---

[14] Jefferson to Francis Hopkinson, January 13, 1785, Jefferson *Papers*, VII, 602.

[15] Jefferson to Francis Eppes, February 5, 1785, *ibid.*, VII, 635.

[16] Jefferson to Francis Eppes, November 11, 1784, *ibid.*, VII, 501.

contrast to the manner of life being followed by occupants of the Auteuil mansion. A pleasing picture is provided by Abigail in one of her descriptions of life that winter with husband and daughter and son. It depicts an experience normal for many people, but one which she and other members of the family had seldom known in the troubled years of the Revolution.

It was eight o'clock on a December evening. A heavy snowstorm had carpeted with white all the landscape about their temporary home. Inside, John Adams sat in an easy chair by a table, reading Plato's *Laws*. Opposite him was Abigail herself who, when not occupied with her writing, was reading Mr. St. John's *Letters*, inferior, very probably, to her own. Next to her, in a low chair and in a "pensive posture," was Abby. She was thinking, one may well assume, of Royall Tyler, a youthful barrister back home from whom she had parted tearfully with mutual pledges of love and devotion. The course of their romance had been blocked by jealousies, intrigues, and, to no small extent, by parental objections.

The reading and the pensive thoughts were interrupted as John Quincy entered the room. He carried a number of letters, brought out from the city that day by himself. As far back as he could remember, he had accepted among his other duties those of a postboy. He handed this bundle of messages to his father, who leisurely distributed them to the little group around him. All were as eager as small children about a Christmas tree. These were letters from dear ones on the other side of the ocean.

Abigail received two. For John there was only one. For John Quincy, bearer of letters to others, there was, unfortunately, none. But for Abby there were six. It seems that Royall Tyler had not forgotten her. She and her parents shared what her mother described as a "rich repast."[17]

One pictures Jefferson on that same night in his widower's establishment, still ailing physically and starving, as it were, for the letters that did not come, missing the touch of vanished hands and the sound of once familiar voices.

[17] Mrs. Adams to Mrs. Cranch, December 12, 1784, *Letters of Mrs. Adams*, 260–61.

By the turn of the year, however, Jefferson was feeling much better, and there are records that tell of his being host at a charming tea party on New Year's Eve. The company was unevenly balanced between men and women, Abigail and her daughter being the only ladies present in a group that included most of Jefferson's male friends in and about the city. Among them, of course, were John and John Quincy. As Abby poured and host and guests talked together, the ties that connected the individuals from Braintree with those from Monticello were knit more closely.

On the horizon which the new year presented to these Americans abroad one of the bright features was the prospect of more informal social gatherings. Abby, rather deliberate for a young girl in making an estimate of an older man, noted in her private record after her first two meetings with Jefferson that she had not seen him enough to form a judgment about him. But she was not impervious to his charm for any great length of time. Early in the fall she was one of his guests at a dinner party. In her diary comments about the affair is this reference to the host: "Mr. J. is an agreeable man."[18]

Her mother seems to have been even more hesitant in allowing first impressions of the tall, affable Virginian to become fixed. But those impressions were all favorable, in contrast to some she had received in early meetings with Dr. Franklin. Franklin was evidently on familiar terms with a rather dubious character known as Madame Helvetius. At a social function Abigail heard this lady "bawl out"— Abigail's own phrase—"Ah, mon Dieu, where is Franklin," and saw her, upon finding him, kiss him on both cheeks and on the forehead.[19] The Puritan lady from New England was disgusted and continued so even after Franklin told her that the madame was a typical French woman and had no evil intentions. Jefferson, it was clear, kept all ladies of this type at a respectful distance. His consistently sedate behavior called forth her admiration.

Moreover, she was impressed, increasingly so as their acquaintance grew, by his familiarity with subjects which from her early girlhood

[18] Miss Adams, *Journal and Correspondence*, I, 38.

[19] Mrs. Adams to Miss Lucy Cranch, September 5, 1784, *Letters of Mrs. Adams*, 252.

had interested her, particularly the classic Greek and Roman writers and their works. Further, the philosophy which underlay his observations of mankind and the totality of human experience seemed to be in harmony with her own convictions. To her he became a much better than average friend. By the time the turn of events made imminent her withdrawal from the Paris scene, she could give him the most unqualified praise. "I shall really regret to leave Mr. Jefferson," she informed one of her sisters; "he is one of the choice ones of the earth."[20]

Likewise, Jefferson's geniality and learning cast a spell of considerable potency over young John Quincy. The latter, on the New Year's Day that followed the tea party at the Hotel de Landron, made the first entry in what developed into a monumental record of his life. Among the very early notations were these: "Mr. Jefferson is a man of universal learning"; "Spent the evening with Mr. Jefferson whom I love to be with."[21] The elder Adams noticed that his son missed no opportunity to be in Jefferson's company and that the latter appeared to reciprocate this interest. Probably no jealous feeling was aroused, but in a later year, when both of them were nearing the end of life, the father wrote to Jefferson that during the period of their common residence in Paris John Quincy seemed to be as much Jefferson's son as his own.[22] The influence which these inter-family connections had upon the personal relations of the two American leaders in foreign service can scarcely be overemphasized.

In addition to their host-guest relationships and their collaboration as diplomatic agents, there were other ways in which their mutual good feeling found expression. For example, Adams was able to help his colleague out of embarassing financial difficulties. Jefferson had rented his hotel apartments and bought furniture on the strength of the assumption, unwarranted by the facts of the situation, that his salary would be paid on time by Congress. Finding himself in a tem-

[20] Mrs. Adams to Mrs. Cranch, May 8, 1785, *ibid.*, 292.

[21] Quoted in *John Quincy Adams and the Foundations of American Foreign Policy*, by Samuel Flagg Bemis (New York, 1949), 14.

[22] See Chapter VI, Note 89 below.

porary economic predicament, as many others have for reasons not so good, he was tided over through arrangements Adams made. So cordial was their attitude toward each other that no service, large or small, which friendship could render in either direction was intentionally omitted.

Late in April, Adams received notice of his appointment as the first American minister to Great Britain. Soon afterwards came the announcement of Jefferson's selection as Franklin's successor at the Versailles court. (The aged diplomat had outlived his usefulness in France, and Congress was agreeable to his eagerness to retire.) Adams reacted with mixed feelings to his new assignment, but Jefferson looked upon his own appointment as a signal honor.

The news that he was to occupy a post long held by Franklin was coincident with other factors which brightened Jefferson's outlook and made him love Paris more without loving Monticello less. The long winter was over; his personal finances were no longer precarious; his health was normal again; and there was nothing to prevent his facing new duties cheerfully and hopefully. He sent out invitations to a larger party than any he had felt like giving since arriving in Paris.

It was on a day in early springtime that his guests assembled in the well-furnished rooms at the Hotel de Landron. Among them were John Adams, his wife, son, and daughter, John Paul Jones, the naval hero with many laurels, and several additional American friends of Jefferson, along with the still youthful Marquis de Lafayette, his sprightly marquise, and a few other represenatives of French nobility. Franklin certainly would have been in the company if physical infirmities had not kept him a virtual prisoner at Passy.

The occasion was a pleasant one, although darkened somewhat for the host and for members of the Adams family by the shadow of separation. On their way home that evening John and Abigail walked through the Tuileries gardens. Pausing frequently at the *parquets* by the intersections, they surveyed such a scene as only Paris at such an hour afforded. Then back to their house and garden, with the surrounding woods now in full vernal bloom. It was not going to be easy to leave this pleasing environment, always to be associated in their memories with domestic happiness and gay parties.

Echoing Abigail's sentiments, John Adams, on one of his last days in France, wrote to a brother-in-law: "I shall part with Mr. Jefferson, with great Regret, but as he no doubt will be placed at Versailles, I shall be happy in a Correspondence of Friendship, Confidence, and Affection."[23]

This pleasant anticipation was to be realized. Very soon there would be an exchange, across the Channel, of letters such as friends placed in those circumstances might be expected to write.

Even before crossing from Calais to Dover, Adams sent two notes to his friend. As they journeyed toward the French port, husband, wife, and daughter, had spent some of their leisure time reading a book which Jefferson had written—his *Notes on Virginia*. This work had been privately printed that month, and one of the two-hundred copies was presented, with the compliments of the author, to the Adams family. "I thank you kindly for your Book," Adams wrote in one of the two short messages introducing this phase of their correspondence. "I think," he added, "it will do its Author and his Country great Honour. The Passages upon Slavery, are worth Diamonds."[24]

The book may have helped John and Abigail, perhaps even Abby, to forget, at times, the combination of unpleasant circumstances attending their transfer from one post of duty to another. John Quincy, a prospective student at Harvard, had left Paris and started homeward a few days before his parents and sister made their departure. Accustomed as they were to such partings, they found bidding farewell to this son and brother an emotional ordeal from which they did not readily recover. For much of the time in recent years the son had shared with his father the life of a roving ambassador. Moreover, to that father the thought of going to England as the first American minister was far from exhilarating. It was not difficult for him to

[23] Adams to Richard Cranch, April 27, 1785 (Massachusetts Historical Society; Adams Manuscript Trust) quoted in Jefferson *Papers*, VII, 652.
[24] Adams to Jefferson, May 22, 1785, Jefferson *Papers*, VIII, 160.

leave most of the French people whom he knew, but as he looked forward to the duties involved in this new undertaking, he felt certain qualms. There were times when he feared that he might be headed, as he put it, toward a "briar patch."

While he was on the way to this destination of doubtful desirability, the aspect of nature herself was disheartening. The farther north the little family traveled, the greater the contrast between the dry and barren fields—result of a local drought—and the seasonal greenery about Auteuil. When they arrived in Calais, they were covered with dust and still inwardly commiserating with French peasants whom they had seen, even with the sheep and cattle that appeared as "walking skeletons." There was much indeed to make their journey, in Adams' own way of describing it, rather *triste*.

The new ambassador to France was acutely conscious of the break in his social circle occasioned by this shift on the diplomatic front. "The departure of your family has left me in the dumps," he wrote in his first letter to Adams from Paris.[25] However, when he made this confession, he had already presented his credentials as Franklin's successor, and on the whole he continued to be pleased with new opportunities opening before him. Several weeks elapsed between the departures of his two colleagues, and during that interval he consulted frequently with the veteran diplomat whom he was about to replace. These contacts, in addition to easing the transition to the status of high-ranking ambassador, compensated partially for the removal of John and Abigail and their daughter. Also, it was still possible for him to spend some time with Patsy, and that privilege, along with his new duties, kept him from being "in the dumps" for any length of time.

Shortly after he admitted being in that dejected state, he received in one day two letters from Adams, written after the latter's arrival in London. They were forerunners of many to come throughout the remaining period of their concurrent stay in Europe. Jefferson's replies were just as numerous. As the two men began keeping contact with each other in this manner, Abigail was more than ever pleased

[25] Jefferson to Adams, May 25, 1785, *ibid.*, VIII, 164.

that her husband had at least one good friend of high standing on that side of the ocean. For her "dearest friend" was representing a nation, "poor America," against which "venom" was constantly being leveled by a number of English writers and speakers. After all, his new situation did bear some resemblance to a "briar patch." When Abigail had lived for a few months in the British capital, she gave one of her sisters another clear indication of her feeling about Jefferson. This time it related to his role as John's ally and confidant: "In Mr. Jefferson," she wrote, "he [Adams] has a firm and faithful friend, with whom he can consult and advise; and as each of them has no object but the good of their country in view, they have an unlimited confidence in each other; and they have only to lament that the Channel divides their more frequent intercourse."[26]

The letters which the two men wrote to each other, usually sent across this separating body of water in care of a trusted messenger, solicited advice, asked favors, and more often reported progress, or the lack of it, in carrying out objectives officially set before them. The personal requests which they made, while not important historically, are significant as additional evidence of the friendly nature of the relationship between them at the time. Would Jefferson see to the cancellation of an order for shipment of a large stock of wine, stored in the cellar of Adams' former residence at Auteuil, among possessions that were scheduled to be "freighted" to London? One case of Madeira and Burgundy might be allowed to go, but for the rest England's import tax was prohibitive. Yes, Jefferson would undertake to save his friend that expense. Would Adams order for Jefferson the two best London newspapers and arrange, if possible, for them to be sent without postage and without liability to government inspection? Yes, Adams was willing to do so, but it would be better if Jefferson made application directly to the French *Premier Commis* or the *Bureau des Interprètes*.

Naturally, the bulk of their correspondence related to their ambassadorial duties. Some of it had to do with the country to which they had once stood in the relation of "rebels." The chance that England

[26] Mrs. Adams to Mrs. Cranch, October 1, 1785, *Letters of Mrs. Adams*, 321.

might eventually agree to a treaty of commerce with the States of America could not be ruled out altogether, and Adams asked his colleague to prepare a document as a basis for discussion. At the time Franklin was still in Paris, making ready for his last long voyage. Complying with Adams' request, Franklin and Jefferson, the latter doing most of the work, shaped a treaty which they were willing to have proposed at London. In it were included most of the stipulations in earlier documents of the same kind proposed to Denmark and Tuscany, also in the one to which Frederick of Prussia had given his assent. This *projet* was sent to Adams, who shortly reported: "The Proposal is made. Let them [the British authorities] ruminate upon it."[27]

The ruminations were definitely negative.

As for problems arising from the attitude of the Barbary potentates, they were as baffling as they had been the previous year. Jefferson, using some notes which Franklin gave him, drafted a tentative treaty with these practitioners in piracy. This, too, was dispatched to Adams, who suggested certain alterations. But they agreed that one or more personal agents should be sent, along with the written proposals, to the offending powers, with instructions to explore the possibility of coming to an amicable understanding with them. In that early stage of their correspondence the two Americans turned repeatedly to each other with comment, inquiry, advice, and counter-advice relating to this thorny dilemma. Although Adams was naturally more irascible than his associate, he eventually advocated a policy of compromise with these highwaymen of the seas while Jefferson inclined to the alternative of force. The time came, while the latter was still in France, when, if he had possessed the power to do so, he would have sent John Paul Jones with a few selected frigates of war to the Mediterranean and confronted the pirates with the arguments of cannon balls.[28]

[27] Adams to Jefferson, August 7, 1785, Jefferson *Papers*, VIII, 354.

[28] Later, during his first term as President, Jefferson actually carried out this policy. He dispatched naval forces to coerce Tripoli and by this display and exercise of force won immunity from piracy for American commercial vessels in the Mediterranean.

The recalcitrance of the British government, and in lesser degree of the French, in respect to the extension of commerce with the United States elicited discouraging, at times bitter, comments on the part of both ambassadors. Adams grimly held to the hope that both nations would come to understand the advantage of buying, among other American commodities, New England "oil and candles and fins"; payment could be made for them with "buttons and ribbons." Jefferson reported from time to time his efforts to loosen a hammer-lock hold which the Farmers' General of France had upon potential importers of American tobacco. These efforts were not entirely un-availing, but the net result could scarcely be considered success as against Adams' failure. Both men continued to encounter, in separate environments, massive resistance. They were tilting, not at windmills, but at giants in the form of eighteenth-century cartels.

Numerous indeed were the topics about which these two guardians of American interests abroad wrote to one another, sometimes half a dozen or more in one letter. Among them was one of considerable concern to Adams as the first minister of his country to the government of her late enemy. It is also important to our theme, because what each of them said about it helps us to understand better their attitude at the time toward each other as individuals. This topic was introduced by Adams not long after performing one of the more delicate duties of his public career.

In accordance with traditional custom more than with his own desire, he had been officially presented to his former sovereign. Approaching the royal presence, he made the prescribed genuflexions and otherwise observed flawlessly the court ritual. Then he read a carefully prepared speech. Later, reviewing the ceremony, he was moderately proud of his remarks and pleased because he had received a more gracious response than he had anticipated. In his reply the British ruler even went so far as to say, in effect, that he thoroughly approved of the choice made by the States of America for their first minister to the mother country.

Full publicity was given, of course, to this exchange, and from some who were still subjects of George III Adams began receiving compliments for his part in it. He was not at all averse to attention of this kind, but in this case the praise was so general that he began to wonder if as an American patriot he had overstepped proper bounds. Having taken the part that he did in the late revolution, had he, in this ritualistic contact with George III, been more congenial than was necessary? He decided to submit to Jefferson the relevant evidence and ask his opinion. Enclosing the speech he had delivered to the King, he sent his friend a letter revealing his own uneasiness and with it that high regard for Jefferson's judgment which he had previously admitted. "Is there anything said by me," he asked, "which I ought not to have said? Is there any expression exceptionable? Have I compromised myself or the public in anything? more than ought to be . . . ."[29]

One of Adams' biographers has stated, "His vanity and supreme self-satisfaction passed away only with his passing breath."[30] This is a fairly typical example of many references that have been made to one trait of his character. Yet this element in his nature was strangely intermixed with a becoming humility. There were times, not exactly rare, when he turned to others for advice. That Jefferson was the one to whom he turned at this time, without trace of vanity, reveals, as much as any fact emerging from the record, how he felt at this point in his career about his Virginia contemporary.

The reply could not have been more reassuring. "I think . . . you by no means compromitted yourself or your country, nor expressed more than it would be our interest to encourage if they [British government officials] were disposed to meet us."[31]

One suspects that the minister accredited to the Court of St. James breathed a little more easily when he read those words.

Paralleling and in a way complementing this correspondence was that between Abigail and the man whom she continued to think of as one of the finest specimens of humanity in existence. Soon after her arrival in London, this lady, who never could have been accused of

---

[29] Adams to Jefferson, September 18, 1785, Jefferson *Papers*, VIII, 525.

[30] John T. Morse, Jr., *John Adams* (Boston and New York, 1899), 320.

[31] Jefferson to Adams, September 24, 1785, Jefferson *Papers*, VIII, 545.

disregarding proprieties, made Jefferson the beneficiary of her epistolary talents, not waiting to be "honourd with a line" from him. She wrote him at some length, admitting that an apology was due for her scribbling so freely, but explaining that she had heard him remark more than once that he liked to hear from absent friends "even the Minutia of their Situation." In this, the first letter that passed between them, she assembled for his information a fair-sized collection of "Minutia."[32]

Jefferson gallantly responded with thanks for her "condescension" in making the first approach to this pen-and-ink phase of their friendship. But his animus against the British led him to comment with unnatural tartness upon the preference which she had indicated for London as compared with Paris. Almost rudely he alluded to her praise, mild as it was, of the city on the Thames. He considered it a "flout." This verbal blow was delivered in connection with a clear statement of his contrasting attitudes toward the French and the British people—an expression pointing forward like an index finger, as one looks at it with knowledge of later historical developments, to political schisms. The people of France, he declared, were "polite, self-denying, feeling, hospitable, goodhumored." He loved them with all his heart. But for those among whom Abigail now lived he had a very different string of adjectives. They were "rich, proud, hectoring, swearing, squibbing, carnivorous." He even had an uncomplimentary noun for them. They were "animals."[33]

At this point Jefferson was guilty of gross exaggeration. Adams himself could not have written less judiciously. But if Abigail took any umbrage from the manner in which he manifested these symptoms of Anglophobia, there is no record of it. As a matter of fact, the longer she lived in London, the less inclined she was to write about its people with enthusiasm. She came to be particularly displeased with the "polite circles," of which she knew more by observation than by direct contact. "Such a set of gamblers the ladies here are," she confided to one of her sisters. "And such a life as they lead! Good

[32] Mrs. Adams to Jefferson, June 6, 1785, *ibid.*, VIII, 180.
[33] Jefferson to Mrs. Adams, June 21, 1785, *ibid.*, VIII, 239.

heavens! Were reasonable beings made for this?"[34] Before completion of her first year of residence in London this minister's daughter
was thinking in terms of getting away from there as soon as possible.
Contemplating European courts in general, and in particular those
with which she was more familiar, and the lives being spent uselessly
in and around them, she wrote in another letter sent back to the homeland, "I wish I was well out of the way of all of them."[35]

In the category of "Minutia" there were, on both sides of the
correspondence, items such as lifelong friends or close relatives might
include. She wrote about her family's lodgings at Grosvenor Square,
procured after a diligent, lengthy search, which she was obliged to
make herself. Jefferson wrote about his new residence, located on the
Champs Elysées, more pleasing to him than the one he had just occupied. Both of them alluded to the high cost of living in a style becoming to their station, a fact of which they were painfully conscious.
She gave him first-hand information about a rendition of Handel's
Messiah in Westminster Abbey, also about Mrs. Siddons' superb
dramatic performances, voicing regret that he could not be present
to see and hear. He told her about the new opera by Marmontel and
Piccini. The problem of disposal of a new cask of wine which had been
belatedly delivered at Auteuil was presented for Abigail's decision:
"It is yours," she replied, it being necessary, anyhow, for her husband
to procure a new supply of that commodity. Jefferson accepted the
gift "chearfully."

One of Abigail's anxieties throughout much of her first summer
in England was of a maternal nature. Many weeks went by without
any word from John Quincy or about him. Jefferson shared this
solicitude with her, and when at last, early in September, she received
news of the young man's safe arrival in America, she, knowing his
concern, quickly relayed the information to him. Through her, re-
membrances were periodically sent from Paris to young Abby, who
reciprocated in the same manner. Nor did Abigail forget the very
young lady in the Parisian convent. More than once she wrote, "Give

---

[34] Mrs. Adams to Mrs. Cranch, April 6, 1786, *Letters of Mrs. Adams*, 333.
[35] Mrs. Adams to Mrs. Cranch, May 21, 1786, *ibid.*, 334.

my love to Miss Jefferson." She even expressed a desire that Patsy might spend a few months with her. And in the same connection she let Jefferson know that she had not given up hope of seeing him in England.

The amenities of this relationship were such that each correspondent was willing to act as a purchasing agent for the other. Here again, it was Abigail rather than Jefferson who took the initiative. She could not find any shoes in London that suited her. She also needed a few articles of dinnerware and some ornamental figures of a certain kind, these being obtainable, she had reason to believe, in Paris shops. If Jefferson would be so good as to buy these articles for her and have them forwarded, it would be a gracious favor.

Very soon he was attending to these errands. He bought shoes of the right size and shape, *plateaux de dessert* of the kind specified, and also for her tables four miniature gods and goddesses, all of them Roman. Abigail had ordered Minerva and Diana and Apollo, but Mars was his own choice. Explaining this purchase, he showed again his deep-seated antipathy to the English people. "This [the figure of Mars] will do, thinks I," he wrote, "for the table of the American Minister in London, where those whom it may concern may look and learn that though Wisdom is our guide, and the Song and Chase our supreme delight, yet we offer adoration to that tutelar god also who rocked the cradle of our birth, who has accepted our infant offerings, and has shown himself the patron of our rights and avenger of our wrongs."[36]

He was not, however, averse to business transactions with these inferior members of the human race nor hesitant about asking Abigail to reciprocate favors. He needed cloths and napkins for his own table and had a preference for a particular damask which was of English manufacture. If she agreed with him in that preference, would she make the deal in his behalf and have a sufficient amount of the material sent over? She did as well as she could with the assignment, going from one shop to another to get what he wanted in the right quantity and dimensions. Then, as if to make up for some possible

[36] Jefferson to Mrs. Adams, September 25, 1785, Jefferson *Papers*, VIII, 548.

dereliction in the performance of this duty, she offered to buy, on his order, some superior Irish linen. To which he responded by asking her to get for him twelve shirts made of that linen. Having done this, she bought for him, as a good-will bonus, two pairs of nut-crackers, of the same kind she had bought for herself and found very convenient.

Her hope that he might come to England for a visit was fulfilled in the late winter and early spring of 1786. Adams had been given some reason to think that commercial treaties with Tripoli and Portugal could be put into a form that would insure ratification. The deputies from those countries now seemed amenable to approaches made earlier. Indeed, the bearded African and the courtly Count de Pinto had intimated that their respective governments desired to enter into formal arrangements with the States of America. Also, the odds were more favorable than they had been for some time that the men shaping British foreign policy might belatedly see the light and be disposed to give serious consideration to American proposals. The presence of Jefferson was the more necessary, Adams believed, because the powers originally delegated to them and Franklin, while still in force, would soon be withdrawn. The time limit placed upon them was not far distant.

He therefore sent a written request across the Channel insisting that Jefferson come to London straightway. Colonel William S. Smith, a young officer who had been serving as secretary of the American legation in London, carried the message and reinforced it orally. He was the bearer also of an invitation from Abby, supplementing the similar one previously extended by her mother: "When you come to London, bring with you amiable and lovely Patsy." While that personable young lady could not leave her studies at the convent, her father was receptive to Adams' appeal, and early in March left Paris, in company with the Colonel, bound for London by way of Calais and Dover. They arrived at their destination on the evening of March 11, and, weary as he was, Jefferson did not sleep before having a conference with Adams.

In due course he was welcomed by the ladies of the family at

Grosvenor Square. It was the beginning of an experience which, although it included some unpleasantness and more frustration, may be accurately described as a pleasant interlude in that extended period in which he was far from home and all but one of his kindred.

Included in the prospect before Jefferson as he rode into London on that March evening was a presentation to Marquis Carmathen, the British minister of foreign affairs, also a more formal one to George III himself. The presumption is that he would have avoided both of these functions if there had been any convenient escape. As it turned out, these concessions to necessity were more distressing to him than he had expected them to be.

Adams had lost no time in arranging an appointment with the Marquis for Jefferson and himself. While both of them clung to some hope that this official might see fit to treat with them on matters of commerce, the interview that followed showed more clearly than ever that the basis for that hope was fragile. The response to the propositions of the two ministers was given with a cold politeness and an obvious evasiveness. Jefferson came to the conclusion that nothing could be gained, except keeping the record straight, by making further advances to the intransigent foreign minister.

A few mornings after being balked in this manner, Jefferson prepared for a face-to-face meeting with the King, an individual whom he still regarded as primarily responsible for most of the troubles experienced by his own Virginia and her sister colonies and then by the United States of America. One can imagine his feelings as the hour appointed for this encounter approached.

He and Adams appeared at the palace and, having been admitted to the reception room, made the ceremonial approach to His Majesty required by protocol. It was a dramatic meeting, never reported to the world as fully as it could have been. But in the records set down by one of the American participants there was no attempt to gloss over the monarch's behavior.

Almost a decade had intervened since the adoption of Jefferson's Declaration, but many of the events leading up to it and following from it were vivid in the memory of each of the three men present.

Two of them, at least, could have repeated some of the language of that Declaration verbatim. And George III, whose mental faculties were still unimpaired, remembered the manner in which he had been indicted before the court of public opinion by the author of the document. Such traces of cordiality as were evident at the time of Adams' presentation were now missing. If, therefore, the royal back was turned on the American ambassadors, as was alleged, it was an affront directed especially to the one who had used his vocabulary so vigorously in castigating his sovereign.[37]

Jefferson, sensitive even to ordinary rebuffs, returned to his temporary residence in London's fashionable West End nursing more than ever a personal bitterness from which, apparently, he never became entirely free. In his old age he commented acidly on the reception given by the King to Adams and himself on that occasion. "The ulcerations in the narrow mind of that mulish being," he wrote, "left nothing to be expected on the subject of my attendance."[38]

On the other hand, if that phase of his diplomatic experience was clouded by disappointments and incivilities, there was much in the round of his activities to lighten his spirits. The necessity of lengthening his stay added to his store of information in many areas. He was intrigued by the displays in the London shops. As assiduously as any bargain hunter he visited many of them, patronized some, and before returning to France was willing to admit that, on the whole, they were better than those of Paris. The opportunity to see and hear the famous Mrs. Siddons was not missed, and in addition to the evening spent at Drury Lane Theater, where she was playing, there were others set aside for theater or opera. One day he went out to Windsor, inspected the ancient castle, and found much worthy of his attention in that handiwork of man. Also, there were frequent dinner engagements, some of them accompanied only by shallow chitchat, but a few, more acceptable to his taste, involving meaty conversation.

Best of all the hours spent in dining and wining were those when he was a guest at the Grosvenor Square house, which recalled similar

[37] See Adams, *Works*, I, 420.
[38] Jefferson, *Works*, I, 97.

occasions in the great mansion at Auteuil. John Quincy was absent, but his place was taken to some extent by the tall, dark, and handsome Colonel Smith, soon to be a member of the Adams family. Long absence had lessened, it seems, Abby's fondness for Royall Tyler; but even more influential in making her decision to break off relations with that young man was her mother's maneuvering in the interest of the Colonel. The latter's persistent wooing was likewise an important factor in the flowering of this new romance. There was rejoicing in the Adams household when Abby's engagement was definitely announced. And the good friend who was frequently a guest during the early springtime following the announcement shared in the general satisfaction. He believed, along with the parents of this capable and amiable young lady, that the man whom she was preparing to marry was most worthy. While for Jefferson these congenial associations in the British capital did not constitute paradise enough, they provided as near an approximation to it as he could hope to find there.

He had read about the famous English gardens, and, with the idea of future landscaping at Monticello very much in mind, devoted some of his free time to sightseeing in the rural provinces. Adams was his sole companion on the most extensive of these outings.

While Jefferson took the initiative in planning the expedition, his friend was by no means averse to the suggestion that he spend a few days in the open country, away from the city and the tiring routine of duty. For the first, and with one exception the only, time in their lives they became, under these circumstances, literal fellow travelers. It seems appropriate, therefore, to trace the course of their journey and in some detail to note incidents of it.

Leaving Colonel Smith to attend to such diplomatic business as might develop in their absence, they left London on the morning of April 4 for approximately a week of direct contact with the charms of the English countryside. Their method of transportation was the familiar post-chaise, and the accommodations which they found at inns and taverns were not unlike those to which they had become accustomed in their earlier journeyings to and from Philadelphia.

Neither in Adams' sketchy diary nor in Jefferson's memoranda is there any reference to the weather during that week. But they were in England, and it was April. As they traveled northwestward into the heart of the Midlands, the pastoral vistas which opened before them were at or near their springtime best. They must have had much to say to each other during the many hours when there was nothing to do but sit as comfortably as possible in their hired coach, watch the scenery, and talk. About their conversations, as about the weather, they evidently had neither time nor inclination to write. They could have talked business or recalled the times that had tried their souls when their country was winning its freedom. They could not have failed to discuss what they were seeing and otherwise experiencing. Certainly two such men, almost as free, for the time being, as the birds that kept singing along their way and with such an opportunity for man-to-man tête-à-têtes, were not embarrassed by any lack of topics.

Jefferson kept jotting down notes about the gardens. Many of his notations were factual, others criticized or commended particular features, and all were of more value to himself, in making long-range plans for his own estate, than to anyone else. Adams' interest in the large manor houses and grounds was not as keen as that of his companion. His Yankee sense of values made him question the wisdom of spending vast sums of money to create and maintain such "Residences of Greatness and Luxury." Penn's Hill, standing sentinel over his native place, might, he thought, be embellished similarly if someone had the money and enterprise and inclination to undertake the project; but he preferred the familiar landmark just as it was. He expressed the hope that the time would be far distant when such "ornamented Farms" would become fashionable in his own America. "Nature has done greater Things and furnished nobler Materials there," he boasted. "The Oceans, Islands, Rivers, Mountains, Valleys are all laid out upon a larger Scale."[39] This was in the spirit—certainly not without some merit—of a proud Texan or Californian of this generation.

If the "Gentlemen's Seats" which they visited on the first two days

[39] Adams, *Diary and Autobiography*, III, 186.

of this trip did not exactly fascinate Adams, he was willing enough to give some attention to other places of the same kind. Writing to Abigail about these earlier experiences on the tour, he admitted, "We have seen Magnificence, Elegance and Taste enough to excite an Inclination to see more."[40] And there was much more to see. Following the course they had mapped out, the two tourists traveled along the Avon and Severn valleys, stopping, among other places, at Stratford, a mecca for the curious and the reverential since the days of Shakespeare. They saw the house in which the poet was born, the slab beneath which he was buried, the souvenirs offered for sale—chips from a chair on which he was accustomed to sit, they were told, and bits of wood advertised as having belonged to a mulberry tree which he planted. Adams was duly impressed by this visit. He took time to write in his account that Shakespeare's "Wit, and Fancy, his Taste and Judgment, His Knowledge of Nature, of Life and Character, are Immortal."[41]

Jefferson did not number the bard of Avon among his literary favorites. It seems that he preferred Ossian, the Gaelic poet, whose writings had recently been popularized by James McPherson. Nor did he manifest an interest equal to that of Adams when, two days later, they stood at the site, near Worcester, where Oliver Cromwell and his "Ironsides" had repelled the invasion of Charles II. He kept a respectful silence as his Puritan friend lectured, in the style of a schoolmaster, a group of peasants who had gathered about them. "This is holy Ground," he told them, "much holier than that on which your Churches stand. All England should come in Pilgrimage to this Hill, once a year."[42]

Posterity is the loser because of not having an audio-visual record of John Adams and Thomas Jefferson meeting with the plain folk of a rural English neighborhood, and of the former, in his role as spokesman, reminding them of an important event in their national history. There is preserved only his brief record of the episode and his terse

[40] *Ibid.*, III, 187.
[41] *Ibid.*, III, 185
[42] *Ibid.*

comment upon the manner in which his informal address was received. "It animated them," he confided to his diary, "and they seemed much pleased with it."[43]

The turning point of the journey was Leasowes, a lovely spot deep in the heart of England. There an "umbrageous" walk through verdant woods, part of an estate on which a minor poet had made some major improvements, provided a welcome relief from the steady joltings of the carriage. As they headed southward, they stopped at Birmingham, pausing long enough for a walk about the "Town," as Adams designated it. Then they came to Blenheim, a "truly princely habitation," with its great castle, its gardens merging into a magnificent park, its large herd of fallow deer, and its monument to Marlborough, the silent, imposing tribute of his duchess. A little later they tarried for a while at Oxford. The man who would found another university looked upon the towers and spires and walked about the halls of that ancient seat of learning—and wrote no description of it that survives. As they neared London, there were more gardens to be seen, and more statistical and other factual descriptions of possible use in the future were written down in the pocket notebook of the gentleman from Monticello.

Abigail heartily welcomed the pair of travelers when they returned to the city. It was the first time in almost two years that she and John had been separated. In London, so different from Braintree where good neighbors were plentiful, she had sorely missed him. In his absence, the "routs," the balls, and the dinners which she attended were even more "stupid" than similar London functions to which she had gone in his company.

Jefferson's stay in London was prolonged beyond his expectations, partly because of this pilgrimage with Adams, but more in consequence of an unforeseen sequence of proposals and counterproposals made while the projected treaty with Portugal was being shaped into final form. He took advantage of the delay and of the leisure time at his disposal to patronize other shops, to make additional visits at Grosvenor Square, and to see more places of interest in and around

43 *Ibid.*

the city. On April 20 he went with John and Abigail and Abby to another magnificent country estate, Osterly Park. They strolled about the battlements and towers and through the ornamented apartments, and at almost every turn Adams was strengthened in the impression that such establishments were "Ostentations of Vanity"; he came to doubt that even their owners enjoyed them. And in his little book Jefferson made a condensed record of facts about the mantels and interior friezes and cornices. It is quite probable that these pencilings, hastily made, along with many of the notes he had taken earlier that month, were useful to him when he was ready to draw up plans for remodeling his own home.

During the latter part of this sojourn in England, his only lengthy visit in that country, Jefferson found time to sit for a portrait, an experience that was probably arranged for him by Adams. The artist was a young American, Mather Brown, who apparently had decided to present his subject as a man of fashion. The powdered hair, some of which was done into a curl which all but covered one ear, the ruffles at the sleeve and neck, the small delicate hand—these suggest the courtier and the gallant rather than the statesman and the philosopher. But Abigail thought enough of the portrait and its original to procure a replica when it was available and to have it hung on one of the walls of the house in which the Adamses lived. It became one of the prized possessions of the Adams family.

The conferences with responsible officials of the British government came to nothing, and attempts to reach an agreement with Tripoli's ambassador, whose extortionate demands had the flavor of bribery, were equally unproductive. Even the long-drawn-out negotiations with Count de Pinto proved to be wasted effort. When it came to the showdown of ratification, the Portuguese government was as obdurate as the majority of other European powers. Beginning his journey back to Paris on April 26, Jefferson did not know how complete was the failure of his mission; he did understand, however, that the visible results fell far short of the hopes which had induced Adams to summon him to London.

On the brighter side of the picture which the memory of seven weeks in England held before him as he returned to France, and long thereafter, were scenes entirely unrelated to official business. It was good to live over again, as well as he could, the hours of friendship with his colleague, the visits with the lady whose talents as hostess, as letter writer, and as shopper he knew so well, and with the young couple who were soon to exchange marriage vows. He repeated congratulations, which he had earlier extended to himself, on his good fortune in having with him, on the same continent at least, such worthy and dependable American friends.

Back in the French capital after a trip which was, in some degree, a vacation, Jefferson eased into the routine with which he had become familiar since qualifying as Franklin's successor at the court of Versailles. Soon he and Adams resumed their contact by correspondence, but in their capacity as government officials they were compelled to write in terms of bafflement rather than accomplishment. Naturally, as men still charged with the promotion of American commerce, they made frequent references to such commodities as whale oil and tobacco. (Jefferson told Abigail in one of his letters that her husband's head was "full of whale oil." She was too polite to retort that his own seemed to be full of tobacco.) But more and more they came to resemble salesmen offering goods for which there was no appreciable market.

As well as they could on paper, they consulted further on how to deal with the Barbary potentates, who continued to get away with wholesale blackmail, if not with murder. On this question their difference of opinion persisted. Adams calculated, to his own satisfaction, that it would be cheaper to buy peace than to wage war with the offenders, and forwarded the figures to his associate. Jefferson countered with figures of his own that war would be the better bargain, and added that justice and honor and consideration for the respect of European nations pointed to that alternative. Moreover, he argued, if the United States would take the initiative in a move to deal forcibly with these maritime highwaymen, she would not lack for allies, and in time there would be a powerful confederacy capable of stamping out an evil too long tolerated. "The same facts impress us differently," he wrote. "This is enough to make me suspect an error in my process of reasoning tho' I am not able to detect it."[44]

Adams was far from being obdurate in the matter. Admitting the force of Jefferson's arguments, he affirmed that he would be for "eternal War" with the Algerians, provided that "our States could be brought to agree in the Measure."[45] That this could be done, however, he was very doubtful.

The continuing friendly feeling between the two American ministers is evidenced in occasional sentences crowded "edgewise" into the dull mass of official business. After Adams returned to London from another rural excursion, this one with Abigail and the young lady who by that time was Mrs. Smith, he wrote to Jefferson that they all missed him on the journey, that his presence would have added to their enjoyment of it. Later in that same year, Jefferson, having learned that Adams and his wife were visiting Holland, found an opportunity to send a letter to his fellow minister by a messenger. In it he brought Adams up to date on parleys centering about the "pirates," and with a tinge of regret added, "I think if I had had a little more warning, my desire to see Holland, as well as to meet again Mrs. Adams and yourself, would have tempted me to make a flying trip there."[46]

Writing to Colonel Smith while the memory of his springtime visit in England was still fresh in his memory, he interjected this directive: "Present me affectionately to Mr. Adams and the ladies, and tell them that I never offer prayers to heaven for myself without including them."[47] It may be presumed that this firm token of friendship was devoutly reciprocated.

Neither Adams nor Jefferson was at this time driven hard by pressure of business, if we may judge their activity by modern American standards. Increasingly each of them felt that as an agent of his country he was "marking time." But no indication appeared that

---

[44] Jefferson to Adams, July 11, 1786, Jefferson *Papers*, X, 124–25.
[45] Adams to Jefferson, July 31, 1786, *ibid.*, X, 176.
[46] Jefferson to Adams, August 27, 1786, *ibid.*, X, 303.
[47] Jefferson to Col. William S. Smith, May 4, 1786, *ibid.*, IX, 447.

Congress was disposed to release them from their assignments. They did not go "out of bounds" entirely, but, as was natural, they departed to some extent, in angular fashion, from the straight line laid down by their commissions.

Jefferson's most interesting deviation was in a form which may be described with fair accuracy as a love affair.

Some time in August, 1786, very probably early in that month, he met Maria Cosway, the golden-haired, Anglo-Italian wife of an English painter. The Cosways, who gave some indications of being mismated, had recently come to Paris from their home in London. Their errand, as first planned, included certain professional services arranged for the artist husband, also some common indulgence in pleasures habitual in the colony of Parisian *intelligentsia*. But it turned out that Cosway spent most of his time at his easel, while his young wife chose a path which had a certain appearance of dalliance. Following it with her, the American ambassador actually broke a wrist, came near, it would seem, to losing a hand, and almost, if one refers to the circumstances figuratively, lost his heart.

The evidence indicates that it was a case of mutual infatuation at first sight. Looking back to the day of their first meeting, marked with a round of pleasures enjoyed together, Jefferson recalled that at heart he wanted it to be "as long as a Lapland summer day." Had she possessed it, Mrs. Cosway herself would have used the power to make the sun stand still. There were other days and also evenings during that late summer and early autumn when they enjoyed each other's company. At such times the widower ignored the vexing problems of his official position, while the lady, married to a man who may have seemed to her a kind of robot specializing in painting, found partial relief from her marital problems. The two of them, sometimes without other company, rode about the hills and valleys and strolled though the chateaux and gardens near Paris. Perhaps there were hours when the harvest moon smiled on them, returning from long, happy excursions. At any rate, it was as if the gallant recently pictured by Mather Brown had come to life and stepped out of the frame.

If this interesting situation were to be depicted mathematically, it would not be in the shape of the eternal triangle. There was no divorce; nor was there any scandal, although the sequel of many such episodes has been one or the other, or both. The injury to Jefferson's right wrist marred the otherwise happy course, restricted as it was, of this affair of the heart. He and Mrs. Cosway had just returned from a long walk when, evidently in a playful movement, he lost his balance and fell on his wrist in such a manner as to snap and dislocate the bone. One of the physical effects was permanent, but an immediate consequence was that his rendezvous with the lady of the golden curls could not take place as frequently as before.

Nor were there many days left in which he could spend his time in that way. Cosway completed the assignment which had brought him to Paris, and one morning Jefferson, in true courtly fashion, helped the lady into the carriage which was to take her away from him. His throbbing wrist had kept him awake the night before, and this farewell attention could not have been physically painless. Moreover, according to his own testimony, the act of separation was the source of another kind of anguish for which there was no quick relief.

It appears that in the week following he used some of his time in writing laboriously, with his left hand, a letter to Mrs. Cosway. In it is included a very interesting dialogue between the Head and the Heart. It took the form of an extended argument in which, while the Heart had the last word, the Head won out, the final arbiter being the Will. On the whole, the Cosway affair constituted another interlude in the ambassador's European experience, this one spiced with romance. Out of it emerged, in contrast to the usual issue of excursions along a primrose-bedecked path, a long-continued friendship. One who has qualified as an authority on Jefferson's career wrote, with some restraint, that it was an "ascetic love affair" which passed "like a whirlwind through his life, and leaving him more than ever devoted to an ideal love from which he was never to swerve."[48]

Of all this John and Abigail heard only indirectly and incompletely. In fact, Jefferson maintained a discreet silence about his romantic

[48] Marie G. Kimball, "Jefferson's Farewell to Romance," *Virginia Quarterly Review*, Vol. IV, (July, 1928), 403.

adventure in all his correspondence except that directed to Mrs. Cosway herself. He informed Colonel Smith that if he were to explain how he had injured his right hand, it would require a long story—too long for his left one to write. This statement was probably cover for an understandable reluctance to admit the infatuation which was associated, however indirectly, with his accident. When Abigail finally heard of the injury, she showed her sympathy by directing Jefferson's attention to a home remedy, describing it as "British oil." She had personally known it to produce "very salutary effects" when used "upon a spraind joint."[49]

But by the time Jefferson received this well-meant recommendation, nature had wrought some improvement in his wrist, and he was not in the market for "British oil." Meantime, Adams was occupied with an undertaking which, although lacking a romantic flavor, was quite as interesting to him as Jefferson's emotional "Whirlwind" had been to that ordinarily sedate philosopher.

Having returned from his summer visit in Holland, the American minister in London began a major literary project—his third venture of that kind.[50] It would take a scholar seven years, he declared, to do justice to his chosen theme. Apart from the time involved, he stated, he lacked the necessary scholarly qualifications. But like many other writers he could not escape an inner compulsion to give his ideas to the public.

The imposing title of this opus, *Defence of the Constitutions of Government of the United States of America against the Attack of M. Turgot in his Letter to Dr. Price, Dated the 22nd of March, 1778*, points to the fact that it was essentially a lawyer's brief. The French writer had criticized the framers of constitutions in American

[49] Mrs. Adams to Jefferson, January 29, 1787, Jefferson *Papers*, XI, 86.

[50] Hitherto, Adams' principal literary efforts had been in the form of newspaper articles. A series of such articles, questioning the legality of the Stamp Act, was published under the title, "A Dissertation on the Canon and Feudal Law." In 1774, some essays which he had contributed to the *Boston Gazette*, using the signature "Novanglus," were published as a pamphlet. In 1782 a publishing firm in Amsterdam brought them out in regular book form, the title being *History of the Dispute with America from its Origin in 1754 to the Present Time*.

states for their tendency to copy the English system, particularly in the division of governmental powers, including the bicameral arrangement for legislative functions. His theories, based on the political philosophy of Rousseau and Montesquieu, were poisonous in the view of Adams, who had been one of the principal architects of his own state's fundamental law.

On those early autumn days which Jefferson and his feminine friend were enjoying together, Adams was digging laboriously in ancient tomes, doing the spade work for the *Defence*. Elaborately, even if hurriedly, he collected evidence from centuries of experience in civil government to make his case for the Anglo-Saxon principle, which had governed most of the men who helped to write the constitutions then in force in America. For many weeks he kept as busy with this project as he ever had in preparing a case for a jury. If he did not adequately telescope a seven-year undertaking into a few months, nevertheless he accomplished *multum in parvo*. The book was printed in January, 1787, and Jefferson was one of several friends in Europe and America to whom he sent copies.[51]

Acknowledging receipt of the volume Jefferson expressed his thanks, noted that its subject was "interesting," and stated that he had no doubt of its being well received. A little later he gave the author his personal opinion of its merits. "I have read your book with infinite satisfaction and improvement," he wrote. "It will do real good in America. It's learning and it's good sense will I hope make it an institute for our politicians, old as well as young." He added that in order to give it a wider circulation, he had secured the services of a competent French translator.[52]

Straightway Adams replied that this approbation was a "vast consolation" to him. It helped to balance his uneasy anticipation that for a long time the work would be unpopular at home.

Throughout much of the time in which Adams was occupied with the preparation of this ponderous brief, his friend was contemplating

[51] This was the first part of a three-volume project which was completed and published before the end of 1788.
[52] Jefferson to Adams, February 23, 1787, Jefferson *Papers*, XI, 177.

an extensive tour through central and southern France. It was another *divertissement* made possible because his duties as American ambassador were relatively light. But there were several postponements, beginning with the one made necessary by his wrist injury. When he finally got away, spring was advancing northward from the Mediterranean. He rode forth to meet it with the eagerness of one long snowbound and with his native curiosity whetted to a keen edge.

This time he traveled alone, except for a servant and now and then a *valet de place* employed for a short time. He explained to one correspondent that he could reflect better without the distractions of a companion. Had Adams been too garrulous to suit him on their journey the preceding spring? In the explanation of his preference on this journey for comparative solitude, there is a vague hint that his fellow traveler in England had sometimes been overly communicative.

He went unhurriedly, and almost unrecognized, by way of Dijon and Lyons toward the destination upon which he had tentatively decided. Not until he reached the Rhone valley did he meet the balmy season, but having made that contact, he was moved to near ecstasy. In this mood he reported to his secretary: "I am now in the land of corn, wine, oil and sunshine. What more can one ask of heaven?"[53] For his physical ailments he had more faith in the healing properties of the spring zephyrs and the Provençal sunshine than in the medicinal waters of Aix, to which his doctors had directed him.

Actually, the warm springs of the resort town did his aching wrist little good, whereas the splendid weather and the zest of travel affected him, body and soul, as a tonic. He extended his itinerary to include the Italian Riviera, the northern Apennines, and the plains of Lombardy. After turning northward, he cruised for several days along the Canal de Languedoc. From Toulouse he crossed to Bordeaux and then, completing his own "grand circle," returned to the capital by way of Brittany and the valley of the Loire. In the afterglow of this experience he wrote to a friend, "I . . . never passed three months and a half more delightfully."[54]

[53] Jefferson to William Short, March 27, 1787, *ibid.*, XI, 247.
[54] Jefferson to John Banister, Jr., June 19, 1787, *ibid.*, XI, 477.

While he was roaming from place to place, the existence of the Barbary pirates, if not dismissed from his mind entirely, was not permitted to interfere with his enjoyment. And, for the time being at least, he was not disturbed by most of the other problems with which he and Adams, and at an earlier stage Franklin, had struggled, for the most part ineffectively. The lady with the violet-blue eyes and the golden ringlets must have been in his thoughts often, but not a line passed between them that spring. And if John and Abigail had been on another planet, they would not have heard less than they did, in a direct way, from their wandering friend.

The reflections of the solitary traveler were evidently related, in large degree, to his day-by-day observations. It is not likely that by any marvels of telepathy he shared directly in the thinking of the Founding Fathers who assembled in Philadelphia that springtime to formulate and adopt a federal constitution. The days on which they began their labors Jefferson spent in traversing, under usually cloud-less skies, the course of the Canal de Languedoc, the nightingales often in full chorus on both sides of the slow-moving barge.

If in that delightful setting he was moved to meditate for a time about an organic law for the new government, he must have reviewed the arguments of Adams' "interesting" book. Already it had appeared in New York and Philadelphia. James Madison and Alexander Hamilton and John Jay were familiar with it. The author's fear that it would be unpopular in America was not entirely groundless, but it was influential to a degree which he did not anticipate. The astute Madison realized that there was political dynamite in it. This was his comment to Jefferson about it: "Mr. Adams' Book, which has been in your hands of course, has excited a good deal of attention. . . . It will probably be much read, particularly in the Eastern States, and contribute with other circumstances to revive the predilections of this Country for the British Constitution. . . . It will be read and praised and become a powerful engine in forming the public opinion. The name and character of the Author, with the critical situation of our affairs, naturally account for such an effect."[55]

[55] Madison to Jefferson, June 6, 1787, *ibid.*, XI, 401–402.

But neither Jefferson's younger friend nor his older one, the lawyer who had prepared and submitted the *Defence*, could foresee just how powerful an "engine" it would become within a few years and the effect it would have, directly or otherwise, upon their own political fortunes and that of Jefferson himself.

A few weeks after returning from his journeying in southern France and Italy, Jefferson, having surveyed again the scene to which he was closest, commented in a letter to Jay, "The face of things in Europe is a little turbid at present; but probably all will subside."[56] He did not realize that France was sitting on the edge of a volcano. Moreover, as was true of Adams and Madison and lesser statesmen, he was only partially aware of the subtle logistics by which antagonistic philosophies were being brought within clashing distance in his own country. These movements were being initiated and carried forward as if by operation of some force outside the range of human history.

The courtship in which the wooer and the wooed were Colonel William Smith and the younger Abigail Adams, respectively, led, as has been told, to the marriage altar. All omens associated with the ceremony, performed on a day in June by the good Bishop of St. Asaph, seemed auspicious. The bride's mother, born a Smith, shared in the general happiness as her only daughter took that surname as her own. But, as in the case of the average mother on such occasions, there was sorrow mingled with her joy. John Quincy and the younger boys were far away. The prospect before her, in terms of human companionship, was further dimmed by this event. As the summer advanced, there came times when, even more than in the period preceding the wedding, she thought of herself as living in a kind of exile. At such times the big house on Grosvenor Square seemed strangely, almost intolerably still.

One day that summer she wrote to Jefferson that the "contrivance" arranged between Colonel Smith and the Bishop had left her, in one sense, without a daughter. She took no pains to conceal from him the natural yearnings of a mother so situated. More in jest than in earnest

[56] Jefferson to Jay, June 21, 1787, *ibid.*, XI, 490.

and yet thinking of a possibility that might not be too remote, she asked Jefferson if he could let her have Patsy and, in return, at some future date, take one of her sons as his own. To lessen the chance of his missing the point, she added, "I am for Strengthening [the] federal union."[57]

The reply to this semiplayful overture combined delicacy with firmness. The widower father would be delighted to have Abigail's son (he was thinking of the only one he knew), but he could not give up his daughter.

No one ever called Jefferson a humorist, but in his correspondence with Abigail there are little strokes of whimsey, bits of facetious comment which no dull pedant would have written. A facet of his personality which usually remained lusterless when he was dealing with Adams and with most of his other associates lit up more often when he was talking or writing to lady friends. After a few months in which no communication passed between Abigail and himself, he began a letter to her with the observation that if his most recent communication was written in the reign of King Amri, she had not deigned to make a reply since the time of one of Amri's successors, Ochasias or Joachar or Manahem.

Later, introducing to Abigail as well as he could on paper another one of his friends, Madame de Corny, who was about to visit in London, he treated himself to one of his rare chuckles, writing, "I asked her to carry me in her pocket, that I might have the pleasure of bringing you together in person but on examining the treaty of commerce she found that I should be contraband, that there might be a search-and-seizure—and that the case would admit very specially of embarras."[58]

It was with Abby, however, that he became most playful, by way of correspondence, at this time. At times in her first year of married life he was in direct communication with her. Remembering her mother's business dealings with him, she had asked him, modestly

---

[57] Mrs. Adams to Jefferson, July 23, 1786, *ibid.*, X, 162.
[58] Jefferson to Mrs. Adams, November, 1786, *ibid.*, X, 557.

using her Colonel as intermediary, to purchase two corsets for her, stipulating the price to be paid. A few months later, not having received them, she made bold to write to him about the matter. Evidently the Parisian *corsetière* was lacking in punctuality. When finally the garments could be forwarded, he wrote to her, pointing out that if the articles ordered were not large enough, they could be stored away and used later. Well on the way to her first experience of motherhood, she could read the meaning in his cryptic words: "There are ebbs as well as flows in this world."[59]

At that time Abby's mother was making use, as she had formerly, of Jefferson's talents as a shopper. When she needed shoes again, she ordered through him some custom-made ones, specifying that they should have straps and that one pair of the lot should be "blew sattin." Moreover, her need of black lace and of white and colored gloves could not be satisfactorily supplied in the London stores. And so, at her direction, the good friend in what was even then, apparently, the world's fashion capital for ladies, saw to it that all these articles, as well as some others that she wanted from the same source, were bought as economically and sent to her as expeditiously as possible.

From time to time Abigail had opportunity to return these favors, as she had done in the earlier months of their correspondence. Jefferson was still willing to patronize some English merchants, not from love of the English, as he made clear, but from "love of himself." However, he thought it inappropriate to ask Abigail to go marketing for certain objects he wanted, such as a chariot and cabriolet harness and a harpsichord. He therefore entrusted her son-in-law with this responsibility.

For all concerned these arrangements were most convenient, and the commissions were carried out faithfully and satisfactorily. The American minister to France and his friends in England evidently considered it a privilege to go from store to store and carefully compare prices and quality, after the manner of average shoppers,

[59] Jefferson to Mrs. Abigail Adams Smith, January 15, 1787, *ibid.*, XI, 45–46.

with due consideration for needs and desires expressed by correspondence. Of course, they kept a record of purchases and periodically settled accounts.

Meanwhile, the bond of friendship between the two families was being strengthened further by a sequence of events that centered about Jefferson's younger daughter.

From the time that he heard of the death of infant Lucy, the lonely father was determined that the family circle should not continue to be incomplete because of any circumstance he could control. The existence of the broad Atlantic had no effect upon his purpose. After a time Polly was informed of her father's wishes, but she had different wishes, which she did not hesitate to express, either to the uncle and aunt who were providing a home for her or to her parent. When that parent read a letter which came from her, he knew that he had to deal with a child who had a mind of her own.

"I am sorry you sent for me," she scrawled. "I don't want to go to France, I had rather stay with Aunt Eppes." Then she added the names of other relatives from whom she did not wish to be separated. "I hope," she continued, "you and she [Patsy] will come and see us." If they could not do so immediately, there was another way in which her father could make her happy, if he really wanted to. "I hope," she wrote, "you will send me a doll."[60]

Probably the indulgent father provided the doll. But the obstacles which stood in the way of getting her to Paris, including her own feelings, the perils of ocean travel, involving at the worst the horror of capture by pirates, and the difficulty of finding a suitable companion for the child while en route—these were to him just so many difficulties that must somehow be surmounted. The thought of being separated from her during all the remaining time, uncertain as it was, that he would be in Europe was intolerable. Not until several months of the third year of his stay abroad had gone by was it possible for him to make preliminary plans for her coming. He then informed Abigail of an arrangement he had effected, one justifiable only on the basis of close friendship.

[60] Mary Jefferson to Jefferson, May 22, 1786, *ibid.*, IX, 560.

Just before Christmas of that year, spelling out the message slowly with his left hand, he told her the good news: "My friends write me that they will send my little daughter to me by a Vessel which sails in May for England." Thinking it unnecessary to secure Abigail's consent, he had informed those friends that she would receive Polly as a guest in London and care for her long enough for news of her arrival to get to him, and then for himself, or a trusted proxy, to go across the Channel to fetch her to Paris. With a frankness that was understandable in the circumstances, he admitted, "I have taken the liberty to tell them [presumably the relatives with whom she had been staying] that you will take her under your wing.... I knew your goodness too well," he explained, "to scruple the giving this direction before I had asked your permission."[61]

Abigail looked forward with eagerness to the coming of this young visitor. It was something on the credit side of an existence which, on the other side, was stacked with demands upon her patience and forbearance. She would, of course, remain with John to the bitter end of his tour of duty; but her residence in the British capital, lengthened beyond the point of her expectation, was becoming less and less tolerable. In one of her letters sent that winter to Sister Cranch, she wrote, "I shall quit Europe with more pleasure than I came to it, uncontaminated, I hope, with its manners and vices."[62] Frequently her feelings reflected the dreary fogs along the Thames, but for the former there were compensating rays in the expectation of having this child with her for a time. She assured Jefferson that nothing would be lacking in her attention to his daughter for however long she might remain in London.

Back in Virginia, the problem of getting Polly started on the way to her father was perplexing. No amount of coaxing availed to get her consent to make the trip. Finally, rather than carrying her forcibly aboard the vessel on which she was to sail, her uncle and aunt resorted to stratagem. With the connivance of the captain, she was lured into attendance, in company with a few small cousins, at what was repre-

[61] Jefferson to Mrs. Adams, December 21, 1786, *ibid.*, X, 621.
[62] Mrs. Adams to Mrs. Cranch, February 25, 1787, *Letters of Mrs. Adams*, 370.

sented to her as a picnic on the decks and in the cabins. After a period of play so arranged, she went to sleep, which was the cue for her cousins to leave the ship. When she awoke, she learned that the sea voyage had actually begun. With her, as her only caretaker other than the captain, was a fourteen-year-old maid.

About six weeks later she was safe and sound, but tearful and confused and no doubt a bit rebellious, in the big house in London, the pre-arranged way-station on her long journey. In a matter of minutes after her arrival, Abigail was writing to Jefferson, giving him the assurances he had been awaiting. She reported that she had shown Polly his picture, that it meant nothing to her, that she had talked to her about Patsy, stressing the point that Patsy never cried. She had promised to be good and not to cry any more. Then, having sent her "duty" to her father, she "wiped her eyes and laid down to sleep."[63]

Jefferson, prevented from making the trip to London himself, straightway dispatched his servant to accompany the young traveler from there to her destination. The servant found her unwilling to leave her new friends. While she was not as adamant about remaining in London as she had been about staying in Virginia, she was much disturbed by the new arrangements made for her. Her first hours of distress in an unfamiliar environment had been followed by days of unexpected happiness. More such days were preferable, in her view, to any hasty reunion with a father and sister who were comparative strangers. In fact, she had fallen in love with the good lady who had taken her "under her wing." That lady, in turn, was captivated by her young guest. Obstinate though she was in some ways, she had many charms that could be accounted for, as Abigail may have reasoned, by heredity.

"Her temper, her disposition, her sensibility," Abigail commented to the father, "are all formed to delight." Thinking of her own experiences as Polly's temporary guardian, she continued, "Perhaps at your first meeting you may find a little roughness but it all subsides in a very little time, and she is soon attached by kindness."[64]

---

[63] Mrs. Adams to Jefferson, June 26, 1787, Jefferson *Papers*, XI, 502.
[64] Mrs. Adams to Jefferson, July 10, 1787, *ibid.*, XI, 575.

It was on July 15 that Jefferson and his older daughter spent together their final moments of waiting for this reunion, their long-cherished anticipation about to be realized. When the coach which had brought Polly from a French port halted in front of his house at the corner of the Champs Elysées and the rue de Berrie, she stepped out, a figure tall for her age, an utterly charming child, but bewildered, as if she were about to be greeted by total strangers. But Abigail's prediction that in short order the child's best self would be in evidence proved accurate. Within a few days she was, her father reported, "perfectly happy" and a "universal favorite" with the "young ladies and mistresses" of the convent, where she had joined her sister as a *pensionnaire*.

For years afterwards it was told how, soon after the first greeting from her father, she flung her arms about him, exclaiming that while she loved a number of people, she loved him and Patsy best of all. Among the others whom she named as belonging in the circle of her affections was "Aunty Abigail."

The benefactor who had earned the title of "Aunty" continued for some time under the spell of fascination which Polly had brought into her life, nor could the passing of the years and the pressure of an unfortunate antipathy entirely suppress it. While the memories of the motherless child's stay with her and of the displays of affection associated with it were still fresh in her mind, she wrote to Mrs. Cranch: "A fairer child of her age I never saw. So mature and understanding, so womanly a behavior, and so much sensibility, united, are rarely to be met with. I grew so fond of her, and she was so much attached to me, that when Mr. Jefferson sent for her, they were obliged to force the little creature away."[65]

Nor was Adams unimpressed by this visitor in his home. Of course, his head was not "full of whale oil," nor even of constitutions, good and bad, for states and nations. Like most other men, he responded to the appeal of childhood. On the eve of Polly's leaving Grosvenor Square, he expressed his feeling in this fashion to her father: "I am extremely sorry that you could not come for your daughter in

[65] Mrs. Adams to Mrs. Cranch, July 16, 1787, *Letters of Mrs. Adams*, 377.

person, and that we are obliged to part with her so soon." In endorsement of Abigail's praise he added, "In my Life I never saw a more charming child."[66]

Against these amenities in domestic relationships, strengthening as well as expressing friendship, must be placed factors of another kind in the Old World environment of the two American ambassadors. As the period of their service abroad lengthened, both Jefferson's dislike of monarchy and Adams' innate distrust of democracy became more pronounced and divisive.

That ill-fated pair, Louis XVI and Marie Antoinette, together provided living corroboration of the Virginian's conviction that the rule of kings and queens, perpetuated by heredity, was fraught with danger to human liberty. Although neither one of this royal couple was as offensive to him personally as was George III, yet the stupidity of both of them, drifting toward the cataract of revolution, added to the contempt with which he regarded their system of government. They belonged to an order of society whose members could best be likened to predatory beasts. To "besiege the throne of heaven" to "extirpate from creation this class of human lions, tygers and mammouts called kings" was to him a devout exercise in which every lover of mankind could worthily engage.[67]

On the other hand, the better acquaintance with the French people made possible by his long residence among them increased his admiration for them. On his trip through southern France he had deliberately made contact with some of the poorer peasants in their hovel homes, broken with them such bread as they had, and commiserated with them. Out of such experiences arose a purpose which he openly avowed—to do something which, in at least an indirect way, would put a "morsel of meat" in their thin vegetable stew. He estimated that twenty-four out of twenty-five of the people in the lower economic brackets were to such an extent victims of a "scourge" that their existence was a prolonged misery. That "scourge," he contended, was the hereditary autocracy incarnated in a pitiful king and queen.

[66] Adams to Jefferson, July 10, 1787, Jefferson *Papers*, XI, 575.
[67] Jefferson to David Humphreys, August 14, 1787, *ibid.*, XII, 33.

As the first scenes, comparatively peaceful, of a great tragedy unfolded, he watched with more interest than that of a casual spectator. He noted carefully the proceedings of the Assembly of "Notables" on February 22, 1787, at Versailles. Later he saw, not once but many times, long lines of the hungry waiting for such meager handouts as were offered. Now and then he stood near as thousands of the poverty-stricken milled about the streets, masses of humanity only a few steps from the mob state and destined to take those few steps eventually and with defiance. He wrote to Adams, "The king, long in the habit of drowning his cares in wine, plunges deeper and deeper; the queen cries but sins on."[68]

Throughout all the period in which the plot was thickening, his sympathy for the downtrodden was accompanied more by hope that their condition would be ameliorated than by apprehension of wholesale bloodshed. It was not a hope shared generally by the French people. The period immediately preceding the outbreak of the revolution bore little resemblance to the France of 1784, its citizens living, as Thomas Carlyle described it, in a "Golden or Paper Age of Hope, with its horseracings, balloon flyings, and finer sensibilities of the heart; ah, gone is that, its golden effulgence paled, bedarkened."[69]

Jefferson himself was no longer afflicted with the nostalgia which helped to make his first winter abroad a season of discontent. Both of his daughters were now with him, he was near the stage where a real-life drama that riveted his attention was being enacted. He had no desire, such as that expressed by Adams, to get back to his "turnip yard" as soon as possible. As the forces of revolution began to coalesce, he felt an obligation to conform, in keeping with the usages of diplomacy, to a code of neutrality in respect to the groups moving toward collision; but the importunities of his friends of the "Patriot Party," particularly Lafayette, coincided with his own desire to make his talents in statecraft available. He was eventually constrained to share inconspicuously his insights and wisdom with kindred spirits. The time came when a group of leaders, looking toward the overthrow of

[68] Jefferson to Adams, August 30, 1787, *ibid.*, XII, 680.
[69] *The French Revolution* (3 vols., Boston, 1884), I, 104.

tyranny without excesses of passion, met for mutual counsel at Jefferson's house.

The Archbishop of Bordeaux, chairman of a committee laying the groundwork for a new order in the country, wrote to him, directly soliciting more active participation. "There are no foreigners any more in our opinion," Jefferson was told, "when the happiness of man is at stake."[70] While the American minister did not feel that he could take part as openly as he desired in the labors of such a committee, he persisted unofficially in giving as much aid as he could to those who were seeking redress of wrongs. The man who played a major part in one revolution did not maintain an attitude of aloofness as the course of events led on to another more violent one.

Although Adams was giving some of his attention to the social ferment in France, he continued to spend many hours at his desk compiling additional evidence for the case he had already presented to Western civilization in general and to his own country in particular. His investigations preparatory to the writing of the second and third volumes of the *Defence* strengthened certain predilections which he had when he began the project. As between a government operated according to principles of pure democracy and one in which a preponderance of power would be lodged in hereditary executives and senators, his preference was decidedly for the latter. He argued that democracy was outside the bounds of possibility in this world, that Montesquieu's outlines of it were "figments of the brain," "delusive imaginations." Conditions in Europe were never more critical, he declared, than they were at that time; and while he could not logically attribute them to popular rule, he believed they would be much worse if such a rule were to be generally established. "What dependence can be placed," he inquired in one of his letters of this period, "upon the common people in any part of Europe?"[71]

Whether by conjugal association or by her own independent reasoning, Abigail came to share her husband's feelings about the vaga-

[70] The Archbishop of Bordeaux to Jefferson, July 20, 1789, *The Letters of Lafayette and of Jefferson*, edited by Gilbert Chinard (Baltimore, 1929), 144.
[71] Adams to Jay, September 22, 1787, Adams, *Works*, VIII, 451.

ries of ordinary human beings. The greater part of one of her letters to Jefferson in 1787 was devoted to comments on Shays's Rebellion in Massachusetts, an important event of the time. It was an organized defiance of state authority having a few points of resemblance to the movement which was acquiring momentum in France. She was greatly agitated by this Massachusetts uprising, and in her letter referred to its leaders as "ignorant, wrestless desperadoes, without conscience or principals," to their followers as "mobish insurgents," and to their voicing of grievances as the "mad cry of the mob."[72]

Jefferson did not condone lawlessness in Massachusetts or elsewhere, but the usurpation of human rights which he had witnessed inclined him to be tolerant of Shays and his fellow adventurers. His expressed reaction to her somewhat caustic observations had a rather peppery flavor. He wrote: "I hope they pardon them [the leaders of the rebellion]. The spirit of resistance to government on certain occasions is so valuable that I wish it always to be kept alive." With this statement he linked another which must have brought a mild shock to the one who first read it: "I like a little rebellion now and then. It is like a storm in the Atmosphere."[73]

A few months later, when Abigail wished to bring her correspondent up to date on Shays's uprising, she indicated an unwillingness to write to him on "so disagreeable a subject." Instead of doing so, she would send him a parcel of Boston newspapers.[74]

Still later that year another difference of opinion appeared between Jefferson and Adams himself. This one became quite obvious as they engaged in a candid discussion of the new United States Constitution.

Adams was one of several persons who forwarded to his colleague in Paris a copy of this important document, approved by the Philadelphia Convention on September 17, 1787. His opinion of it was set forth in terse, optimistic, and, with one exception, appreciative terms. He thought that a mistake had been made in allowing "Senates and Assemblies" to have veto power over the actions of the Executive.

[72] Mrs. Adams to Jefferson, January 29, 1787, Jefferson *Papers*, XI, 86–87.
[73] Jefferson to Mrs. Adams, February 22, 1787, *ibid.*, XI, 174.
[74] Mrs. Adams to Jefferson, July 10, 1787, *ibid.*, XI, 573.

"I think," he declared, "that Senates and Assemblies should have nothing to do with Executive Power."[75] This flaw could be remedied, however, by amendment; and as soon as the new system was put into operation, the chances were good—a rather naïve guess—for a spirit of unity on the part of all Americans.

The letter in which these ideas were expressed was on the way to its destination when Jefferson wrote to Adams inquiring about his views of the new basic law and imparting information about his own reaction to it. During the preceding summer he referred to the American constitution-makers as a group of demigods, but by this time he had no doubt that there was a sizable portion of mortal clay in their makeup. Certain features in this product of their creative labors staggered, he declared, all his dispositions to subscribe to it. He was particularly displeased with the failure to place any limit upon the length of time the Chief Executive might serve.

To other correspondents, Jefferson pointed out, as Adams had done, that the provision for amendments made its improvement possible. As it stood, however, it would never, in his opinion usher in a millenial dawn. On the contrary, as he pictured the possibility for Adams' benefit, some "Galloman" or "Angloman"—an early use of semipolitical labels which would become common later—might be re-elected several times, get absolute control of military forces, found a dynasty, and eventually undo the good accomplished by the Revolution.[76]

From our twentieth-century perspective it appears that he was unduly fearful. But the rather dim view that he took of the Constitution in its original form was natural for one whose congenital dislike for monarchy was accentuated by proximity to Louis XVI, his queen, and vassals.

Responding to Jefferson's adverse remarks about the work of the founding fathers, Adams stated as honestly as he could the antithesis

[75] Adams to Jefferson, November 10, 1787, *ibid.*, XII, 335.

[76] Jefferson to Adams, November 13, 1787, *ibid.*, XII, 351. After more than a century and a half of the government's functioning under the Constitution, this mistake, as Jefferson regarded it, was rectified by adoption of the Twenty-second Amendment, limiting the President to two terms, or to a maximum of ten years, in office.

in their evaluations. "I am so unfortunate as to differ somewhat from you," he wrote. Against Jefferson's fear that the United States might, in the absence of safeguards, become a monarchy was his own apprehension that in the new government the Senate might unduly curb executive power, causing "Faction and Distraction." And what if a president should be re-elected as long as he might live? "So much the better, as it seems to me." He thought that free elections, involving the danger of foreign influence, would be a greater menace to the country than an executive with unlimited tenure of office. He looked with "terror" upon any political system wherein choices for "offices which are great objects of Ambition" would be made directly by the people. According to his view, matured by his researches and to some extent also by close observation of the British monarchy, admittedly perverted by George III, the device of an electoral college might prove to be insufficient protection against mass hysteria or ignorance.[77]

By comparison with this difference in their basic conceptions of government, their earlier differences relating to problems posed by the piratical states were of minor importance. Within a few years the arguments which they set forth in this exchange of letters were taken up, amplified, at times twisted out of their original shape, but in general made the ideological basis for a political conflict that rocked the foundations of the new republic.

Largely because of his prolix *Defence* and letters such as those he wrote to Jefferson about the Constitution, Adams emerged as a leading advocate of "Federalism." *Vis-à-vis* this system of ideas was "Anti-Federalism." These designating titles, a little later assumed in derivative form by party organizations, were first used during the time when debates over ratification of the Constitution were in progress, and their repetition prompted Jefferson to disavow connection with any groups so specified. Not too seriously, and rather ironically in view of his later involvements, he expressed a willingness to remain out of heaven if he could enter it only after being tagged by any such distinctive label.

But, willy-nilly, he, and Adams, too, were beginning to be forced

[77] Adams to Jefferson, December 6, 1787, *ibid.*, XII, 396.

into a situation where anonymity of this kind was impossible. At the same time, being the kind of men they were, they could not escape the suction of a current of circumstances which eventually would work havoc to a friendship built up during years of collaboration.

As, in the latter part of their residence abroad, they attended to their respective duties in London and Paris, they continued to keep abreast, or as nearly so as possible on their side of the ocean, with happenings in the homeland. Even so, and fortunately, neither of them could discern any indication that in the comparatively near future they would be pitted conspicuously against each other, after the fashion of Roman gladiators, in an epic encounter.

There were long months of waiting between Adams' official notification of his desire to be relieved of his duties in London and the response that Congress had acceded to his request. The period of his stay abroad was further extended by an unexpected delay. During the course of it he and Jefferson once more broke bread together in a foreign land and joined with other men of influence in conferences affecting their country's welfare.

More than a year before that time Jefferson was informed that John and Abigail had definitely resolved to go home as soon as they could do so with propriety. Writing to his fellow-ambassador about that decision, Jefferson declared that the news had brought him "real pain." He had come to value Adams' judgment in matters of diplomatic policy, and the thought of being deprived of it, to the extent that this move would necessitate, was disturbing. He even ventured to suggest to his friend an alternative course, with possibilities of value to their country and certainly more appealing to himself. Adams' commission as minister to Holland had never been terminated. Might it not be appropriate for him and Abigail, whose stay in England had become so very irksome, to go to The Hague? There he might do a "great deal of good." But Jefferson was not very hopeful that his friends across the Channel would be amenable to this suggestion. Permaturely, but with genuine feeling, he wrote, "I shall now feel bewidowed."[78]

[78] Jefferson to Adams, February 20, 1787, *ibid.*, XI, 170.

The truth was that John and Abigail no longer saw any indications of possible usefulness in Europe that could counterbalance their desire to re-establish themselves in their native surroundings. And as month after month went by, there was mounting eagerness on their part to get out of England as speedily as possible. For Adams it was an anomalous situation to be representing in a foreign land a country to which, by deliberate intention, no reciprocating ambassador was sent. His earlier anticipation that this irregularity would be remedied had not been realized. Now his intention was firm to refuse outright, even if his credentials were renewed, further involvement in such a set of circumstances. There is a suggestion of pathos in what he wrote to Jefferson long before Congress sanctioned his release: "I am not at home in this country."[79]

The idea broached by Jefferson that he might transfer to Holland met with the response which was probably expected. "No Consideration" would tempt him to settle again in that country. One important reason for his outright dismissal of such a possibility was the nature of the climate there. It had already been very harmful to his health; he dared not risk it further. Even more effective as a deterrent to any protracted residence there was his feeling that Abigail could not live long in such a low-lying country. And she was indispensable to him. As he put it, upon her depended all the satisfaction that life brought to him.

As he looked forward to withdrawal from the European scene, Adams informed Jefferson that his general satisfaction with the move would be accompanied by two regrets. One was that in Braintree it would be impossible to get many books that he might want or need. He seemed to think that even in Boston he could not find all the volumes necessary to supply his possible demands. The other regret arose, as he phrased it, out of the impending "Interruption of that intimate Correspondence with you, which is one of the most agreable Events in my life."[80]

He knew, of course, that return to America was not equivalent to

[79] Adams to Jefferson, March 1, 1787, *ibid.*, XI, 190.
[80] *Ibid.*,

putting himself entirely outside the limits of communication with his friend, but for a long time he had been near enough to Jefferson to make it possible for a letter between them to go, in either direction, within a few days. By contrast, the Atlantic Ocean presented an insurmountable barrier to satisfactory correspondence.

It was in early December, 1787, that Adams finally received word of the adoption by Congress of a resolution approving his petition for release, commending the manner in which he had performed his duties and fixing February 24, 1788, as the effective date for the expiration of his commission. Straightway he and Abigail began arranging their affairs with the intention of hazarding an early spring voyage. Their expectation was that by the end of March a westward-sailing vessel would have carried them far on the way to the dearest spot on earth for them.

In February, as boxes were being packed and civilities of leave-taking were being attended to, letters came from Jefferson repeating his personal good wishes and regrets that the two families would be so widely separated geographically. Mindful of the uncertainties of travel between the Old World and the New, he assured Adams, "Nobody will pray more sincerely than myself for your passage, that it may be short, safe, and agreeable." He would follow that petition with one that Adams might have a happy reunion with relatives and acquaintances in America, and might there be placed in a station of high honor and influence.[81] In a separate letter to Abigail he reiterated a sentiment he had expressed twelve months before. He told her that the homegoing to which she and John looked forward would leave him "insulated and friendless" and asked that she write to him when settled again in her native place. Thereby he implied that Adams had overestimated the effectiveness of the ocean barrier to communication. The long months ahead would be more tolerable if she would continue to honor him with her correspondence.

She did not postpone her reply to a possible time of leisure in the Braintree home. Amidst the bustle of preparations for departure she

[81] Jefferson to Adams, February 20, 1788, *ibid.*, XII, 611.

snatched some moments to write a few lines of farewell to her "Esteemed Friend." The request which he had made concerning unbroken correspondence was, she affirmed, "much too flattering, not to be gratefully accepted."[82]

But it turned out that these adieus were not the final ones. Because of a shuffle of circumstances, which brought surprise along with other feelings to at least one of these ministers, their parting in Europe was not by letter but face to face. It came at the conclusion of that delaying errand which, as has been related, brought them together in conversations dealing with the interests of their country. This meeting was the result of another letter which Abigail felt impelled to write to Jefferson a few days after she sent her "farewell" message to him.

She wrote this time with the foreknowledge that her husband would very shortly leave London to pay parting respects to the "Most Serene Highness" and the princes who were "High Mightinesses" of Holland. Congress had omitted to provide him with a formal letter of recall from his mission to that country, and the fear of giving offense by neglecting the proprieties was the inner lever that moved him in that direction, although the necessity of crossing the North Sea twice at that time of year was, he declared, a punishment for sins which he must have committed unknowingly.

As he started on this errand, he had no inkling of the fact that he would have, on the Continent, a few more days of close companionship with his friend Jefferson.

For months the credit of the United States in the money markets of Europe had been shaky. Ways and means of making it more secure comprised one of the subjects in the current correspondence of the two American representatives. In midwinter Jefferson, knowing that the onus of negotiations would soon fall on his own shoulders, had appealed to Adams for all the help that his "friendly dispositions" could give. He added to earlier hints another one that a meeting with Adams in Holland, hitherto a fountainhead of credit, might be of great advantage to himself in the months just ahead. Also, the

[82] Mrs. Adams to Jefferson, February 21, 1788, *ibid.*, XII, 613.

two of them might succeed in effecting immediate arrangements for a new loan. At least they would be making a joint, on-the-spot effort to stabilize a situation which was daily becoming more serious.

Adams' response to this suggestion, made before he yielded to importunities based on protocol, was that he would have to be excused. He was afflicted with an "uncommon" cold, the weather was "formidable," and, in addition, he had many other obligations that were most pressing. However, he advised Jefferson to go to Holland in the spring. Later, after he reversed his decision and while he was making ready to go himself, without informing Jefferson, there was feminine intervention. Abigail played a card which only a woman surprisingly conversant, for one of her time, with matters of international diplomacy could have dealt. While John was busy with preparations for the journey, she wrote thus (without his knowledge) to Jefferson: "He [Adams] would be delighted to meet you there in Holland. . . . As this Letter may reach you about the day he will leave London you will consider whether there is a possibility of seeing each other at the Hague."[83]

One detects here a certain amount of coyness coupled with patriotic considerations. Jefferson was quick in responding to the suggestion. On March 4 he left Paris and six days later, travel-weary, greeted Adams in the Dutch capital. To the latter the appearance of Abigail herself in that city would scarcely have been more surprising. But along with other feelings surging in his breast was pleasure in meeting his valued colleague. On the next day they traveled together to Amsterdam. There over a period of several days they talked persuasively with some influential bankers and brokers.

Still ruffled by the change in plans that were, to a certain extent, forced upon him, Adams wrote to Abigail from Amsterdam that "he should have been in London at this hour if you had not . . . laid a Plott, which has brought me to this Town."[84] But his irritation over the contrivance of the "Plott" was certainly softened when, two days

[83] Mrs. Adams to Jefferson, February 26, 1788, *ibid.*, XII, 624.
[84] Adams to Mrs. Adams, March 11, 1788, (Adams Papers, Library of Congress), quoted in Adams, Diary and Autobiography, III, 211.

after writing the mild rebuke, a contract with Dutch financiers was signed, providing for a million-guilder loan to the United States. This action, he knew, would ease the anxiety of certain other creditors and create a new confidence in the future of his country.

Thus Adams and Jefferson's joint services abroad, not nearly as productive of results as they had anticipated, were rounded out with a significant achievement.

Somewhere in the old seaport city the two men spoke their farewells. Then Adams returned as quickly as possible to London and proceeded with Abigail to make the very last round of calls. Within a few days they went down to Cowes to await the sailing of the *Lucretia*, the vessel on which their passage had been engaged. At the same time Abby and Colonel Smith, now proud parents of a bouncing son, were getting ready for their own return to America.

The main objective of Jefferson's trip to Holland having been accomplished, he started on another extensive journey, one that took him through western Germany along the course of the Rhine and on to Strasburg. On April 20, a day which he spent traveling through Lorraine, noting beggars along the road and blooming apple and cherry trees in adjoining orchards, John and Abigail began their long voyage. The *Lucretia*, powered by westward-blowing winds, sailed out of Cowes harbor.

Some months before, Adams, envisioning in advance the land from which he had been absent for the greater part of a decade, exulted in this fashion: "Huzza to the New World and farewell to the Old One." Now his "huzza" was more directly in order. Abigail shared fully in the spirit of it. Her long-deferred hope was on the verge of realization. While the *Lucretia* was somewhere in mid-Atlantic, she wrote this unequivocal statement of her patriotic feeling in the diary whch she kept for at least a part of the way between London and Braintree: "I do not regreet that I made this excursion since it has only more attached me to America."[85]

On board were boxes and trunks and chests filled with purchases which the couple had made in foreign lands. Among them were

[85] Adams, *Diary and Autobiography*, III, 215.

twelve pairs of silk stockings which not long before had been woven for Abigail by skilled hermit-workmen in a Paris monastery. She was indebted to Jefferson as the intermediary agent in this transaction. Also in their collection of baggage were other articles associated in some way with this good friend. And soon Jefferson would have among his prized possessions a portrait of Adams, painted by the same artist who had performed a similar service for himself during his visit in England.

But neither in Paris nor on the ship carrying John and Abigail homeward was there need of visible mementoes for keeping alive happy recollections. In connection with them, there was, on the part of the trio who had been sharing a hitherto congenial relationship, hope that by the dispensations of the same Providence that had brought them together—man to man in Philadelphia and family to family in Paris and London—their respective paths of life would cross again in the country where they really belonged.

CHAPTER III

Divisive Years

NEW YORK, PHILADELPHIA, 1790–93

❧❧❧

H AVING TRAVELED several dusty miles north from the city of New York, which at the time was the federal capital, a party made up of government officers and their wives, plus a few of their relatives and friends, arrived at the Roger Morris mansion. In due time all found their places at the table in the spacious first-floor dining room, and with appetites whetted by their ride and the clear country air began partaking of a sumptuous meal that had been prepared by the skillful caterer at the neighboring Ferry House Tavern. It was Saturday, July 10, 1790.

At the head of the table sat the austere but benevolent host, President George Washington. Near him were the Vice-President and his lady, Abigail, and farther down the board one of their sons and a companion, referred to as "Miss Smith."[1] Seated at the table were Alexander Hamilton, secretary of the treasury, and his wife, Attorney-General Randolph and Mrs. Randolph, and an obese couple, General and Mrs. Henry Knox, the former being secretary of war; also a comparative newcomer in the cabinet circle, the unpaired widower, Thomas Jefferson, secretary of state. In the company were a few others whom the chronicler of the event designated as the "Gentlemen of my Family," as well as the two Custis children who had been adopted into the family.[2] All together it was a heterogene-

---

[1] *The Diaries of George Washington*, edited by John G. Fitzpatrick, (39 vols., Boston and New York, 1931–44), IV, 141. If Washington's brief narrative of this event were not supplemented by information from other sources, there would be some doubt about which one of Adams' sons he was referring to. Abigail's letters and other records show that both John Quincy and Thomas were in New England at the time. It is certain, therefore that the son present was Charles. The "Miss Smith" mentioned was probably one of Abigail's nieces.

[2] *Ibid.*, IV, 142.

ous mixture of the great, the near-great, and those who had no claim, except by association, to distinction.

For the Vice-President and the Secretary of State the circumstances were quite different from those within which their interlocked careers had advanced on the other side of the Atlantic. They had met a number of times since Jefferson had arrived at New York in the preceding March, and certainly had not neglected opportunities to recall experiences which they shared while in France, England, and Holland. Now, in the homeland, they held high office, in one case by election, in the other by appointment. Most unfortunately, however, along with the change in location and status had come, like a drop in air temperature, a chilling modification in their attitude toward each other. The cordial warmth which was characteristic of their contacts while they were abroad had been affected adversely.

Shortly after Jefferson appeared at the temporary capital, Abigail took brief epistolary notice of his coming: "Mr. Jefferson is here, and adds much to the social circle," she informed her sister.[3] Commenting later, and frequently, to the same correspondent on a great variety of subjects within the framework of social life in the city and of matters pertaining to the Washington administration, she made no further reference to the man who a few years before was the object of her tribute—"one of the choice ones of earth." If now and then he came, as is likely, to the Richmond Hill residence of the Vice-President, he was received hospitably, but at the same time as one who had strayed from the straight and narrow path of political rectitude.

More than a year before the swank affair at the Morris mansion, Jefferson, still in Paris, heard from private sources that Adams had been chosen to serve as the first Vice-President in the new American government. He was neither tardy nor formal in sending direct felicitations. "Accept, I pray you, my sincere congratulations," he wrote to his friend. "No man on earth," he said, "pays more cordial homage to your worth, nor wishes more fervently your happiness. Tho' I detest the appearance even of flattery, I cannot always suppress the

---

[3] Mrs. Adams to Mrs. Cranch, April 3, 1790, *New Letters of Abigail Adams*, edited by Stewart Mitchell (Boston, 1947), 44.

JOHN ADAMS
From the portrait by Mather Brown, 1788

effusions of my heart."[4] But within a few months the "effusions" were coupled with serious misgivings regarding Adams' fitness to occupy the place to which he had been elevated.

The Braintree lawyer had come far since the pre-Revolutionary years in which he was making a modest living in comparative obscurity. His departure from home to take the place next to Washington in the new structure of government was made the occasion for a rousing send-off by his fellow townsmen. Moreover, the route along which he traveled to the temporary capital became the course of a triumphal procession. New England farmers and artisans and shopkeepers and clerks acclaimed him with honors which before that time they had rarely, if ever, bestowed upon a human being. Arriving at the New York state line, he was met by an escort which accompanied him to his new residence. The welcome given him resembled to some extent that given a few days later to Washington as he was ferried across the Hudson and hailed by the New Yorkers in the manner of loyal subjects greeting a conquering king. Never since has an American chosen to be Vice-President been showered with so many congratulatory addresses and personal gifts on his way to inauguration.

The experience was more than Adams could take judiciously. There are good reasons for thinking that the heady wine of adulation had, for a while, a toxic effect upon his powers of judgment.

A few days after his induction into office, he insisted in the Senate, over which, by Constitutional provision, he was presiding, that Washington be given the title, "His Highness the President of the United States and the Protector of the Rights of the Same." If he were designated simply "President of the United States," said Adams, people of foreign countries would "despise him to all eternity." A plain Scot from the hills of Pennsylvania, who was a member of the Senate, William Maclay, made the following note about Adams' speech in his diary: "For forty minutes did he harangue us from the chair."[5] For at least a part of that time Maclay gave some attention to

---

[4] Jefferson to Adams, May 10, 1789, *The Adams-Jefferson Letters*, edited by Lester J. Cappon (2 vols., Chapel Hill, 1959), I, 238.

[5] *The Journal of William Maclay*, edited by Edgar S. Maclay (New York, 1927), 26.

paring his fingernails, probably intending that action to be interpreted as a gesture of mild protest. Later, when his chance came, he registered effective opposition to Adams' idea by his own speeches and votes, being among the majority who thwarted a curious attempt to introduce the nomenclature of royalty.

Before the summer was over, Jefferson, making preparations to leave France, heard of his friend's efforts to put a royal aura about the chief magistrate. To his fellow Virginian Madison, source of much of his information about events in New York, he made this interesting comment in code: "The president's title as proposed by the Senate is the most superlatively ridiculous thing I ever heard of. It is a proof the more of the justice of the character given by Dr. Franklin of my friend, 'always an honest man, often a great one, but sometimes absolutely mad.' "[6]

In the four months' interval between his arrival in Virginia and his assumption of new duties in Washington's cabinet, Jefferson heard much more about certain trends in the higher levels of officialdom. Many of those reports were not conducive to his peace of mind. In New York he found verification for some of them.

He had reason to suspect what was really true, that some of Adams' predilections were rubbing off on Abigail, that indeed this process of abrasion had been going on for some time. That lady, soon after establishing herself as mistress at Richmond Hill, made a social call on Mrs. Washington. Reporting the experience in one of her letters, she referred to the President as matter-of-factly as if no question of appropriateness were involved in her choice of a titular phrase. "*His Majesty*," she wrote, "was ill and confined to his room."[7]

Less seriously and more openly, Abigail's husband was being alluded to in certain circles as "His Rotundity." But Jefferson knew that in other and wider circles Adams was spoken of in more dignified

[6] Jefferson to Madison, July 29, 1789, Jefferson *Papers*, XV, 315–16. In this letter Jefferson misquoted Franklin. He had in mind the latter's statement about Adams, made in a letter to R. R. Livingston, July 22, 1783, that he was "always an honest Man, often a wise one, but sometimes and in some things, absolutely out of his senses." See note in Jefferson *Papers*, XV, 316.

[7] Mrs. Adams to Mrs. Cranch, June 28, 1789, *New Letters of Abigail Adams*, 13.

terms; that while in a broad reckoning his popularity had dipped somewhat since he became Vice-President, his influence was still powerful. Moreover, Jefferson was aware that Hamilton, who had recently declared publicly that the country needed a monarchical form of government, was steadily winning followers. They were being added to the number of those previously drawn toward him by his outstanding abilities. Abigail's semisecret use of a phrase usually applied only to the occupant of a throne was indicative of a current in the stream of events which, Jefferson feared, was gaining momentum.

Into his already ample vocabulary there crept and established itself a new appellative word, "monocrat." It was one which had for him a sinister meaning. And he had come to believe that if this label did not fit Adams exactly, he was at least giving aid and comfort to those whom it did fit.

Meanwhile, Adams was attending to his duties with accustomed fidelity. Abigail complained of his inability to get necessary exercise, of the "tight service" which kept him in his presiding chair five hours daily, hearing debates, putting questions, and so on. However, except for his early tirades on the matter of titles, he avoided, as he was supposed to do, participation in debate. But he allowed no doubt to remain in the minds of members of his family and of friends and correspondents in his confidence concerning his opinions on issues that were beginning to divide his countrymen.

He emphatically denied that he was a "monocrat" and insisted that his basic ideas about government were the same as they had been in seventy-six. Nevertheless, he was openly approving some of the features of a constitutional monarchy; and, as the author of his most comprehensive biography states, he was "convinced that there was nothing about such a form of government that was inherently hostile to the democratic principle." "It was his countrymen," this writer remarks, "who were the dogmatists; for them a king was inseparable from a despot and thus the natural enemy of democracy."[8] In his opinion, strengthened by recent events in Europe, the potential excesses of enraged mobs were scarcely less menacing than the high-

[8] Charles Page Smith, *John Adams* (2 vols., Garden City, N.Y., 1962), II, 725.

handed maneuvers of George III and his ministers had been in the years preceding the Revolution.

More than that, an ignorant majority, not normally inclined to violence but unrestrained by ties of property or of obligation to a Supreme Being, could, he believed, constitute a greater threat to liberty than a king who might happen to go mad. France, well advanced now in the throes of revolution, was, he argued, a large-scale example of the social havoc that could be wrought by illiterate and irreligious human beings, if by mere force of numbers they came to exercise power. He declared that he did not know what to make of a country that contained "thirty million atheists." But he was sure that people bound by no sanctions of heaven and free from all restraints inherent in earthly possessions could, if discontented and if sufficient appeals were made to their baser passions, erupt like a volcano and cast a blight over civilization.

Jefferson deplored as much as anyone the social upheaval in France with the withering consequences already in evidence. But, as has been pointed out, he had observed at close range and with revulsion the heartless oppression of the masses by a little band of tyrants that clustered around the court at Versailles. It seemed very strange to him that Adams, not many years before his fellow champion of liberty and other inalienable rights of man, had veered around, apparently, to another way of thinking. Conversely, the Vice-President, while not saying much about it, viewed with some alarm Jefferson's first steps along a path deceptively alluring, as Adams himself thought of it, with misguided and dangerous companions.

They met at the dining table on that summer day outwardly amiable, as they had done several times in the months just preceding. Indeed, we may well assume that all the members of the little company of which they formed a part enjoyed themselves, in the manner of an ordinary *en famille* gathering. One may picture Washington toying with his fork, as he had a way of doing at such functions, a movement accompanying his efforts to dispense hospitality. Abigail and the others present, basking in the favor of the great man, could not have failed to make the best possible use of their conversational abilities.

One suspects, however, that there were some traces of reserve in the demeanor of the Vice-President and the Secretary of State as they met on this occasion. Something belonging to the essence of good companionship, an intangible quality felt when they had gathered about other tables in Philadelphia, Paris, and London, was lacking. Likely they were not at perfect ease in each other's company, however much they may have desired such rapport and sought to rekindle the inner glow associated with it.

In all the region contained within Manhattan Island there was no finer view in those days than that from the Morris mansion. Near the house was a good barn, and sloping toward the river a meadow, bordered by three orchards and a vegetable garden.[9] The day of this gathering was near the peak of the growing season, and nature's lush bounty was in evidence. What could have been more natural than for Washington's guests, having feasted at the table, to stroll about the grounds and admire the scenery? On such a walk there would, of course, be talk, just as at the meal. Given a quiet nook by themselves and more than a few minutes for a three-way conversation, John and Abigail could have exchanged with Thomas bits of personal news unrelated to politics.

Even if such a visit, assuming that it took place, was not as free and unrestrained as similar ones had been in the past, there must have been keen interest on both sides in hearing whatever could be told about the younger members of the two families. John Quincy, the promising young man in whom Jefferson took such great interest when they were living in Paris, was now a graduate of Harvard and a fledgeling lawyer. Behind him were three years of legal training in the law office of Theophilus Parsons at Newburyport, and just ahead the prospect of a law practice of his own in Boston. Within him the

[9] This house is now within the limits of New York City. In it are kept on display certain relics of the American Revolution. A complete description of it, along with its history, is given in *The Jumel Mansion,* by William Henry Shelton (Boston and New York, 1916).

fires of ambition were being refueled steadily. He had not yet married, an omission due neither to his own inclination nor the lack of opportunity, but to apprehensions about his ability to meet the financial difficulties involved. (John Quincy's parents had helped to keep these apprehensions alive and effective).

His sister, while maintaining an establishment of her own not far from Richmond Hill, was actually spending much of her time with her father and mother, while her Colonel, lured by dreams of wealth, was absorbed in various and sundry business ventures. Their son William was, in Grandmother Adams' opinion, "a lovely child with a temper as mild & sweet as one could wish." Now this splendid child had a brother, John, who, if not as angelic in disposition, lacked nothing in health and vigor. In orthodox grandmotherly fashion Abigail included this bit of information with others she sent to her sister: "The children amuse & divert me much."[10] A third child was due in the near future, and all immediately concerned hoped it would be a girl.

Abby's brother Charles had not always observed carefully the Puritan code of ethics which was an important part of his early training. At times his parents feared that he might turn out to be a black sheep in the family. But he was now living under the same roof as his parents, daily the object of their careful if not strict surveillance, and for the time being his conduct seemed exemplary. Most of his working time was spent in a lawyer's office; he was getting ready to follow, professionally, in his father's footsteps.

Thomas Boylston, youngest of this Adams generation, who might have been christened Thomas Jefferson if he had been born a few years later, was at this time a recent graduate of Harvard College. He had not delivered an oration at the commencement exercises, an honor given to an older brother on a similar occasion, nor had he won any distinction except his diploma; but he, too, was looking forward to a place in the legal profession. The expectation was that he would be reunited with his parents before the summer was over.

[10] Mrs. Adams to Mrs. Cranch, April 21, 1790, *New Letters of Abigail Adams*, 46.

In any exchange of news about their respective families, Jefferson's contribution could not have been slight. These friends of his knew that Patsy, whom they remembered as a gracious twelve-year-old, had become a bride shortly before her father started from Monticello to take up his duties as secretary of state. They had heard glowing reports of Thomas Mann Randolph, the young heir to certain Virginia estates who wooed and won the still youthful daughter of their friend. Probably they heard more about him and his bride on that July day.

As for Polly, the child whom Abigail had taken to her heart a few summers before, the word was that she was living again at Eppington with her uncle and aunt, Mr. and Mrs. Eppes. It seemed that she was happier there than anywhere else. Although she had seen Paris, apparently no difficulty was experienced in keeping her on a Virginia farm. To help during the summer season in raising chickens, in the growing and gathering of peas and strawberries and other garden products, within that rural environment to be generally useful in every season, indoors and outdoors—it was all better than living in a big foreign city.

On the day of this outing, if these three parents, displaced in a sense by the demands of duty, conversed at any length together, they might have had something to say about another change of residence soon to become necessary for each of them.

Most of those sharing Washington's hospitality on that occasion knew that they would be obliged to pack their belongings and move to Philadelphia in the near future. Only the day before, the Senate had given final legislative approval, by a small majority, to a bill stipulating that Philadelphia would be the capital for a ten-year period, to begin within a few weeks, and that thereafter the seat of government would be a new city, to be built on the banks of the Potomac. It is generally believed that by a "gentlemen's agreement" Hamilton helped to win votes for this double move, the compensation being Jefferson's support of one of Hamilton's pet schemes—the assumption of the various state debts by the federal government.

Naturally, the New York City burghers did not accept this decision without complaint. For other reasons a few members of the families of high-ranking officials looked with disfavor upon it. The Vice-President was reluctant to move away from the beautifully situated residence which came as near being a home away from home as he could expect to find anywhere. He declared that he had never lived in "so delightful a spot." Abigail's feeling about the enforced move was almost bitter. She could see no "publick utility to be derived from it."[11] It would mean "going amongst another set of company." She would have to make and receive a "hundred ceremonious visits."[12] She did not expect to get any satisfaction from them. Worst of all, it would involve parting from her daughter and grandchildren and getting farther away from Braintree. All together, it was for her a "sad buisness."[13] It is unlikely that she was aware, as she wrote these words, of Jefferson's part in the "buisness."

Actually, no earthly records give any inkling of what Washington's guests at the Morris mansion talked about, but we cannot believe that they were interested only in the weather and the scenery. It is a reasonable conjecture that those with whom we are here most concerned took some advantage of the opportunity to chat about such matters of common interest as those which have been mentioned.

At any rate, the long day which this select company enjoyed together advanced to the point where everyone had to think about getting home. Reluctantly, we must suppose, host and visitors started back toward the city. One pictures the little cavalcade, headed by the gilded chaise in which the Chief Magistrate rode, proceeding in reverse direction over the route traveled that morning. The shadows would be deepening along the Palisades across the Hudson, and the distant contour of low-lying hills on Long Island would be fading and blurring in the early evening twilight. Probably no one in the group reached home before the squad of hired lamplighters started up and down the city streets on their early evening mission.

A few weeks later, the desks of the government officials were

---

[11] Mrs. Adams to Mrs. Cranch, May 30, 1790, *ibid.*, 49.

[12] Mrs. Adams to Mrs. Cranch, October 3, 1790, *ibid.*, 59.

[13] Mrs. Adams to Mrs. Cranch, May 30, 1790, *ibid.*, 49.

cleared, and the gestures, a few of them suggestive of royalty, signalizing the President's leave-taking, were made. The local citizens bade farewell, some of them unhappily, to the departing statesmen and pseudo-statesmen. For a short time, while the scene of operations was being shifted to another city, echoes of controversy that had begun to emanate from top echelons of the new government died down.

In mid-November the couple from Braintree, bowing to necessity, took up their residence at Bush Hill, two and one-half miles out from the center of Philadelphia. Just as they had anticipated, both of them looked back on Richmond Hill as a kind of paradise, approximating Eden as nearly as any place on earth except Braintree. Some of the natural beauty of this new location had been destroyed by a British army of occupation during the Revolution. The brick house, long unoccupied, became habitable only after log fires were kept roaring upstairs and downstairs for hours. Even the marble statues which cluttered up a grove back of the house, resembling in some ways those which were in the garden of their Auteuil residence, were coldly repellent.

A few days after the informal housewarming at Bush Hill, the Secretary of State arrived at the new seat of government with no one of his own flesh and blood to keep him company. For this lack there was some compensation in the nearness of Madison, who had been his traveling companion on the journey from Virginia. As he had in Paris, he made arrangements to establish himself in a residence that was far from modest. For several weeks, however, he was obliged to defer occupancy of the pretentious mansion, near the center of the city, which he had leased. Extensive repairs were being made on it. Meantime, eighty-six packing cases consigned to him, containing French furniture, scores of books, and numerous odds and ends which he had bought in Paris, were unloaded from a vessel moored at one of the city wharves.[14] Moreover, he had sent for Petit, the

[14] Abigail had been as helpful as possible in giving Jefferson the benefit of her experience in preparing goods for shipment over the ocean. In particular, she had instructed him in the matter of packing chairs. He relayed this information, along with other details of a similar nature, to William Short in Paris. Short superintended

French steward who was for some time his *maître d'hôtel* in Paris, to come to Philadelphia and preside over another retinue of hired servants. Perhaps he thought that he might have to spend much of his time during the next ten years in that city, and democrat though he was, he had no intention of living in a manner unbecoming to his status or of giving up the comparative affluence to which he was accustomed.

Washington's entry into Philadelphia followed shortly that of Jefferson. He and his wife moved into one of the finest residences of the city, a brick mansion belonging to Robert Morris. Soon the machinery of government was reassembled and in running order, and the City of Brotherly Love assumed new dignity as the official center of the nation that had been cradled there. Almost daily Washington, Adams, and Jefferson—a remarkable triumvirate—looked upon scenes which must have renewed soul-stirring memories.

The social season that followed surpassed in outer splendor anything of the kind that had hitherto been witnessed on this side of the Atlantic. Mrs. Washington's first levee, the Christmas Eve reception at the Robert Morris house, the party given in recognition of the President's birthday, the functions at which the dazzling Mrs. Bingham was the hostess—these were events without parallel except in the most aristocratic circles of Europe. If Jefferson attended any of them, he probably did so only as a concession to what was expected of him as a member of the cabinet. However great his love of luxury in private life, he did not breathe easily in the atmosphere of extravagant parties.

Nor did the couple at Bush Hill look with favor upon such displays of wealth and fashion. Abigail was swamped with invitations, some of them to "teas" and "cards" scheduled for Saturday nights—a time which back in Braintree was hallowed scarcely less than the first day of the week. There were ample excuses for turning down nearly all such solicitations. The weather was inclement, the roads were bad,

---

the work of getting Jefferson's possessions in that city packed and started on the way to Philadelphia. See Jefferson *Papers*, XVI, 323.

and for part of the season she and younger members of the household were ill.

Adams himself, whose earlier insistence upon flamboyant titles for his superior seemed out of character, had turned his attention to more appropriate objectives. On the domestic level he was not now, probably never had been, a stickler for false dignity. Through one of his spouse's letters, as if by means of a telescopic instrument, we get a glimpse of the country's first Vice-President which would have interested Maclay and some of his other contemporaries, had it come within their purview. We see him being driven, in the guise of a horse, through the rooms of Bush Hill by his grandson John, wielding a willow stick.[15] While this unconventional antic was in progress, Jefferson at his High Street residence may have been writing to one or the other of his daughters, shutting out as well as he could the sights and sounds of Philadelphia's Vanity Fair. Or he could have been brooding silently over plans for the furtherance of democracy, as he conceived it, in the new nation.

The battle of the pamphleteers and gazetteers began in the early months of Philadelphia's period as the national capital. Preceding it, and providing the immediate occasion for it, was the appearance of another formidable addition to Adams' literary achievements. While in New York he had found time, however demanding his official duties may have been, to write a series of essays which he entitled "Discourses on Davila." These were published in Fenno's *Gazette*, a journal that reflected and propagated Hamilton's ideas of government.

Adams' later description of this effort as a "dull, heavy volume" is accurate, but in spite of its dullness, it was widely circulated and read. His main thesis, a favorite with him, was that there should be a better balance between the executive and legislative branches of government than that provided by the federal Constitution, and that in the interest of national stability, limitations placed upon the power of the President should be removed. The alternative to securing such balance and removing such limitations might well be anarchy. Jefferson

[15] Mrs. Adams to Mrs. Abigail Adams Smith, January 8, 1791, *Letters of Mrs. Adams*, 412.

and some other readers were given excuse for wondering if Adams might not, after all, be envisaging a limited monarchy for the United States.

More widespread in its influence than Adams' stolid essay was Thomas Paine's *Rights of Man*, copies of which began to be circulated in Philadelphia about the time that the social whirl was in full swing. To the printer who was to publish the American edition of Paine's book, a most indiscreet individual, Jefferson wrote a note, praising it highly, expressing satisfaction that "something would at length be publicly said against the political heresies which have lately sprung up among us." To his amazement and without his foreknowledge and consent, this note was incorporated in the book as a preface.

In certain quarters his unintended contribution attracted more attention than what Paine had written. The printer, in his innocence and failure to exercise good judgment, had really given the signal for a contest that would eventually rock the very foundations of the Republic.

Jefferson felt obliged to write an explanatory letter to Washington, who earlier in the spring had started on a tour of parts of "his dominions," as Abigail phrased it, which he had not previously visited. "I am afraid," Jefferson admitted, "the indiscretion of a printer has committed me with my friend, Mr. Adams, for whom, as one of the most honest and disinterested men alive, I have a cordial esteem, increased by long habits of concurrence in the days of his republicanism; and ever since his apostasy to hereditary monarchy & nobility, tho' we differ, we differ as friends should do." In the same context he referred to the author of the "Discourses on Davila" as the "bell-wether" of "Anglo-men" (another word that had recently found a place in Jefferson's vocabulary). In his judgment danger lay in the direction in which this "bell-wether" was leading the flock to which he belonged. But the thought that he might have helped, inadvertently, in injuring Adams "in the public eye" was most disturbing.[16]

Fresh in the Secretary's recollection as he composed this explanatory letter were certain remarks made by Adams and Hamilton in a

[16] Jefferson to Washington, May 8, 1791, Jefferson, *Works*, VI, 255.

meeting which took place on April 11. In that meeting the Vice-President discussed with Jefferson and Hamilton and Knox some matters of public policy, complying with a request of the President that such a conference be held, whenever deemed necessary, in his absence. After the business for which the little group had been called together was disposed of, Adams, so Jefferson reported, began discoursing on the merits of the British system of government. The only change he would make in that system, in concession to the spirit of democracy, would be to provide for a more equitable representation in the House of Commons. As for the king and members of the House of Lords, they were appropriate checks on the whims and passions of the ignorant masses.

Moreover, according to Jefferson's memorabilia, Hamilton added his bit, which seems to have been more than a penny's worth, to the discussion. His remarks were of the same tenor as those he had previously made regarding his preference for the structure of the federal government.[17]

Jefferson went back to his mansion that day confirmed in the belief that his fellow Secretary would accept for his adopted country, if given the chance, the form of British monarchy without any major modifications. And there was no doubt left in his mind that Adams, if not actually a "monocrat," was an "Anglo-man." In what he had just heard directly from the lips of the Secretary of the Treasury and the Vice-President was the essence of the "heresies" which he mentioned in the paragraph intended for only one pair of eyes.

In June of that year the first of a series of articles, written by way of rebuttal to the *Rights of Man*, appeared in the columns of the Boston *Columbian Centinel*. These pieces were at first attributed by many to the Vice-President, and it is not unlikely that he assisted in their production to the extent of discussing their subject matter with the author. That author was John Quincy Adams, whose legal practice was not extensive enough to occupy all his time and whose primary purpose in taking up the verbal cudgels was to defend his father against the charge of "political heresy." He chose the pseudonym of

---

[17] *Ibid.*, I, 179–80.

"Publicola," and shortly from the opposite side came a spirited argument for Jefferson's basic doctrine by one who called himself "Brutus." Also, from the same direction, "Agricola" and "Philodemus" came leaping into the fray.

During that same year Philip Freneau, a poet and journalist who had been one of Madison's college friends, responded to the latter's insistence that he publish and edit a paper which, in addition to printing news of a general nature, would provide a counterbalance to Fenno's *Gazette*. In the words of Jefferson, who was in effect a co-sponsor, it was intended to be a "right vehicle of intelligence." Christened the *National Gazette*, it was, almost from the first issue, a means of propaganda more than of news reporting. Its editor pulled very few punches. There was no precedent in the young republic's history for the skirmish now engaging the forensic talents of Freneau and others, the first phase of a long conflict in which printed words were the means of attack and defense.

Jefferson was not at all averse to having the issues drawn in such a public fashion, but, as he informed Washington, he was genuinely concerned about the effect which these belligerent exchanges and his own unfortunate connection with them might have upon his relationship with John Adams. The truth dawned upon him that the man to whom, more than to any others, he owed a direct explanation was Adams himself.

The Vice-President was spending the summer, as usual, at Braintree. Only by correspondence could the Secretary give his version of what had happened. There were considerations which made him hesitate. This was a delicate matter. He could find the words. The writer of the Declaration of Independence would have no difficulty of that kind. But would they be the right words to send to a man who, although he was "one of the most honest and disinterested men alive," now and then manifested other traits that were less admirable?

A dozen times that summer he picked up his pen with the thought of writing for Adams' benefit a message that would be conciliatory without falsifying his own matured convictions. As many times he put it down without making a stroke. He could have wiped the problem off the list of his immediate concerns and tried to forget it. But finally—and by this time it was midsummer—he chose, to his credit, the alternative of straight approach and appeal.

Starting with the proposition that "truth between candid minds can never do harm," he proceeded to explain how a brief composition of his became, without his advance knowledge and against his will, the preface for the book which had drawn the fire of *Publicola*. "In the presence of the Almighty" he disclaimed any intention of pitting himself against Adams in a public controversy. To be sure, they had different ideas of what was the best form of government, but that had not kept them from being good friends. Adams had known him long enough not to misjudge his ruling motives. Their mutual regard had continued for so long that the explanation being given was no more than what was due.[18]

On the whole, Jefferson could not have stated his case any better; which is to affirm that no man of his time, facing the problem, could have improved upon the presentation. The more impulsive Adams did not pick up his pen hesitantly a dozen times before replying. On the day after he received Jefferson's letter the response was ready to be sent to Philadelphia. The general tone of it was mild; to Jefferson the irenic spirit of nearly all of it was perhaps surprising. It was high time, Adams declared, for the two of them to try to understand each other. Over a period of fifteen years they had been linked together in a friendship which had always been, and still was, dear to his heart. But did Jefferson realize what effect this literary production of Paine's, with "so striking a recommendation" of it made in the preface, had upon his [Adams] peace of mind and his standing as a public official? Thereby the hounds of persecution had been unleashed, and they were still trying to run him down as if he were a rabbit.

This complaint was followed by some especially candid Yankee speech: "If You suppose that I have, or ever had, a design or desire of introducing a Government of kings, Lords and Commons, or in other words an hereditary Executive, or an hereditary Senate, either into the Government of the United States or that of any individual

[18] Jefferson to Adams, July 17, 1791, *Adams-Jefferson Letters*, I, 246.

state in this country, you are wholly mistaken." But the conciliatory note was uppermost in this communication, written without much advance thought and probably without any correction afterwards. "There is no office," he stoutly maintained, "which I would not resign, rather than give just occasion to one friend to forsake me. Your motives for writing to me, I have not a doubt were the most pure and the most friendly."[19]

These assurances might have satisfied anyone normally careful about keeping his friendships in repair. But Jefferson felt that he must clear away in Adams' mind, if at all possible, the notion that the verbal assaults on that statesman were provoked by the printing of the note used as an introduction to the *Rights of Man*. Instead, Jefferson maintained in a second letter, it was the writings of "Publicola" that had released those hounds of persecution of which Adams complained, likening himself to a chased rabbit. This "Publicola," whoever he was, and Jefferson was evidently still ignorant of his identity, had presumed to attack the "principles of the citizens of the United States." In retaliation, personal attacks were made, "very criminally," as Jefferson admitted, upon Adams.

The effect produced by this second explanatory letter must have resembled that which results from rubbing salt in wounds only partially healed. Furthermore, Jefferson appears to have been less than ingenuous in declaring, as he did in this same letter, that he did not have in mind any writing which he supposed to be Adams' when he used the term "political heresies." In other letters he had stated that he was thinking of the "Discourses on Davila" in composing the little piece which pricked the sensitivity of several so-called "Anglomen."[20] If he had any real doubt about the authorship of those "Discourses," it had arisen in very recent weeks, and he could not have been as well informed on that point as most of his contemporaries in public life.

Nevertheless, it is to Jefferson's credit that he had a strong desire

---

[19] Adams to Jefferson, July 29, 1791, *ibid.*, I, 247–250.
[20] See Jefferson to Madison, May 9, 1791, Jefferson, *Works*, VI, 258–59; also Jefferson to Washington, May 8, 1791, *ibid.*, 255.

THOMAS JEFFERSON
From the portrait by Mather Brown, 1786

(matched, it seems, by a similar one on Adams' part) to keep this friendship on the same agreeable plane as it had been for years. And about it he was very hopeful. With an optimism which future events did not justify and which the current situation scarcely warranted, he wrote in the second of these amiable approaches: "The business is now over, and I hope it's effects are over, and that our friendship will never suffer to be committed, whatever use others may think proper to make of our names."[21]

But even in this statement of hopeful outlook, he revealed his awareness of an ironical grouping of circumstances which, reappearing later in other forms, would cause a wider rift in their friendship and eventually bring about a complete, though temporary, estrangement. Both men were being drawn more and more, by forces apparently irresistible, toward an impasse which would have been the dead-end for almost any normal friendship. The Secretary was already the acknowledged leader of a movement whose objective was to sweep all "monocrats" from positions of power and influence. On the other hand, Adams was in the front line of those putting up a sturdy defense against crusaders for democracy.

It was inevitable that this clash of political philosophies would soon be followed by an internecine party struggle. The movement which Jefferson led evolved into an organization to which he stood in paternal relationship as certainly as Washington did to the country as a whole. He and Adams would have been either less or more than human if they could have kept up their friendly association during those years.

In the second year of his cabinet service, while the furor over "political heresies" was at its height, Jefferson and Madison went together on a trip of several weeks' duration. It was only secondarily a vacation. Their main purpose was to combine pleasure, as a minor ingredient, with some business of a noncommercial nature in which they were greatly interested.

Washington was visiting the southern states, but these two travelers turned northward, and covered several hundred miles all to-

---

[21] Jefferson to Adams, August 30, 1791, *Adams-Jefferson Letters*, 251.

gether. As Adams and Jefferson had done in England five spring-times before, they observed the phenomena of nature and visited scenes of historical interest. One day they were at the Saratoga battle-field; on another and for part of the day following they sailed the waters of beautiful Lake George. Then, reversing their direction, they journeyed leisurely through Vermont, Massachusetts, and Con-necticut, and continued on to New York and finally to Philadelphia.

Of course, they admired the scenery and recalled the clash of armies and navies. But more important to them were conferences with Clinton and Burr and other leaders in the rapidly enlarging ranks of the still chaotic opposition. Scarcely less significant were the long, quiet talks they had with each other. It is not difficult to picture them at this or that point in their travels, as, for instance, their arrival on a Saturday evening in the little city of Bennington, where they were obliged to remain until Monday since the law of the state prohibited travel on Sunday. The physical environment of the New England community was delightful, but they may have resented mildly this legal restriction of their movements. However, in those semi-rural surroundings, with very little but the twittering of birds and the humming of insects to break the stillness, they would have opportun-ity to talk without interruption on such worldly matters as the recent enactment of Hamilton's bank bill, the clash of the *Rights of Man* with the "Discourses on Davila," and other more or less related events of the preceding winter and spring.

Perhaps Adams, on that same first day of the week, strolled about his peaceful acres, far from the center of pamphleteer warfare, and meditated on the strange ways of some of his fellow citizens.

It has been suggested that the political party which, after a few years of struggle, wrested power from the Federalists, was born as Jefferson and Madison on this trip reviewed, surveyed, counseled, and planned with each other and with a few other statesmen of kin-dred minds. It is not possible to fix the birthday at any particular moment, but that late spring of 1791 was the time, and the course which the two traveling Virginians followed was the place, or series of places, for a strong forward thrust of this new arrival on the political scene, to which several names would be given in succession. But, continuing the analogy, we may note that it was christened "Anti-Federalist."

At the end of the summer Jefferson left Philadelphia again, this time in the direction of Monticello, the destination which always lured him more than any other. He felt, in some degree, like a returning exile, knowing well, however, that no permanent release had been given to him. And at this stage of his cabinet career he had not become obsessed with the idea of going back to his native place to stay.

But he welcomed the respite. Some months before, as he mentally pictured greening lawns and meadows about his distant mansion, he wrote to his married daughter: "There is not a sprig of grass that shoots uninteresting to me."[22] Now, much more interesting and important than any sprig of grass, there was in that home environment another growing object. His first grandchild, blue-eyed Anne, was well advanced in her first year. Her young aunt, living at Monticello again, had proudly written that she was growing sweeter every day. The responsibilities of leadership, the problems with which he dealt as one of Washington's official family, even the hassle over "heresies," were all forgotten, as this tall man, his homeward journey ended, leaned over and picked up the little one whom he had not seen before. We may be certain that the first representative of a new generation in the Jefferson family was appropriately welcomed.

For a short time Jefferson shared in the domestic and other delights of his home on the little mountain, while Adams continued to oversee autumn harvesting on the farm at the edge of his native village. Each watched, with some feelings that clashed, the steady advance of the days toward time for resumption of his post of duty at Philadelphia.

It is not likely that Jefferson and Madison saw anything portentous in the northeast storm through which they rode while on their way back to the capital. They were not men of the type who look for omens in the vagaries of the weather. But they were well aware of the prob-

---

[22] Jefferson to Martha Jefferson Randolph, December 23, 1790, *The Domestic Life of Thomas Jefferson*, by Sarah Randolph (New York, 1871), 192 (cited hereafter as Randolph, *Domestic Life*).

ability that they would be involved in violent controversy. Happily, the extent and the effects of the repercussions that would follow were outside the range of their anticipation.

Whatever the months just ahead had in store for Jefferson, he was better able to meet it because Maria, now in her fourteenth year, would be near him. (By this time she had discarded, along with her juvenile dresses, the name of Polly.) He had brought her with him as far as Mt. Vernon, where the President's wife, kind-hearted Martha, took charge of her, rendering a service similar to that of Abigail Adams when the reluctant Polly was on her way to France. Maria went on to Philadelphia with the Washington equipage and there rejoined her father. Within a short time she made a number of new acquaintances and renewed an old one.

Loyal Abigail, risking the dangers which the climate of the capital seemed to have for her, had come to spend another winter and spring with her husband. Bush Hill had been relinquished as their place of residence, and they were now living in what she described as a "Thousand Dollars House." When the myriad details of moving had been taken care of, she resumed the social duties associated with her station as the Vice-President's wife. Of a more personal nature was the obligation which she felt to call upon the girl she had befriended and become attached to a few short years before.

One day she appeared at the home where Maria was staying. The visit which ensued must have been unusually interesting to both of them. Memories of the summer days they had spent together came rushing back to both the matron and the adolescent. There was much that had happened in the intervening time that they could talk about. Regarding Abigail's lively grandsons and Maria's lovely niece there were, no doubt, many questions asked and answered. Also, in the recent experience of both of them was a long season spent in rural surroundings; and among the subjects of common interest would be gardens and field crops and poultry and farm animals, perhaps even features of landscapes that were not cluttered with houses and shops.

Presumably Maria, reciprocating Abigail's friendly visit, dutifully called on that lady, but in general the personal connection between the two families became tenuous. The winter was not far advanced when Abigail came down with "intermitting fever," which was followed by inflammatory rheumatism. For weeks she was confined to her room, while at the same time her young friend, under Martha Washington's protecting wing, found diversion in the society of Nelly Custis and others near her own age. Within a few months Maria and Abigail went their separate ways, and the lines of communication between them were again closed.

During that winter, Maria's father and Abigail's husband seldom saw one another, meeting only at state functions or through the necessities of government business. Indeed, they could not have met frequently as friends, except under cover of darkness or by surreptitious maneuvers in daylight, without taking a greater risk as party leaders than either of them was willing to assume. If they had been too openly friendly, one of them would have been courting the disapproval of right-wing extremists, while the other would have been putting in jeopardy his influence over many of his more distant followers. The "upper crust" hostesses of the city understood that it was scarcely proper, and rather useless, to invite both men to the same party.

Meanwhile, Freneau's paper was appearing regularly, with some results that Jefferson had not foreseen. As has been noted, the "vehicle of intelligence," driven by a passionate man with Huguenot blood in his veins, had become, by a quick metamorphosis, a war chariot. At times it was steered in the direction of Washington himself. A report was circulated throughout the city that the chief of state, more than mildly annoyed, had discontinued his subscription. Thereupon, according to rumors readily believed by persons who knew Freneau, that spokesman for the anti-Federalists arranged to have two copies delivered gratuitously at the President's house.

Adams must have lifted his eyebrows or made some gesture of dissent on those occasions, probably infrequent, when he read this journal. In one of the few entries made in his diary during that period, he noted that a copy had been sent to him, and not very lucidly, but, it seems, unappreciatively, commented: "Mr. Freneau, I am told is made Interpreter."[23]

Jefferson did not sanction Freneau's occasional aspersions upon Washington, but he held to the opinion that it was the best periodical that had yet appeared in America. It was effective, as he well knew, in spreading by innuendo the suspicion already fairly common among those having little or no property holdings that Adams was a "monarchist." The tag did not fit, but it was one which the author of the "Discourses on Davila" found difficult to disown. And that so-called "monarchist," who naturally had no sympathy for Freneau's crusade and knew that Jefferson was its most prominent backer, was strengthened in his belief that the latter was, at best, a starry-eyed idealist, a dreamer out of touch with reality.

In her room at the "Thousand Dollors House," Abigail, scarcely able at times to get from her bed to a chair, followed with extraordinary conjugal interest the successive events in this drama; the outcome of it no one could know. She read the papers and sometimes in the privacy of her home listened to her husband's talk about current happenings. In the company of his "dearest friend" he could speak freely about proceedings in Congress, and the charges and counter-charges being made by rival journals in the city and repeated throughout the country. As he usually did, he shared with her the verbal jolts, some light and some heavy, which he was obliged to take. Toward spring, tucking the crisp understatement between comments about domestic affairs, she informed her sister, "As for Politicks, they begin to grow pretty warm."[24]

They grew still warmer, as the weather did, with the approach of summer. When Congress adjourned, the Vice-President and his lady, the latter having recovered sufficiently to be able to travel, started for home. There the climate would be more congenial and the political atmosphere less torrid. The prospect of getting back to their haven

[23] Adams, *Diary and Autobiography*, III, 225.
[24] Mrs. Adams to Mrs. Cranch, March 29, 1792, *New Letters of Abigail Adams*, 80.

near the ocean was as welcome to them as a parallel one would have been to Jefferson.

As a matter of fact, the Secretary was now expecting to relinquish at the earliest possible date his position as one of Washington's official advisers. "Politicks," he told himself, were becoming entirely too warm for him. Wishfully thinking of his own mountainside acres, as he often did, he wrote to Martha on a day when many residents in the city environs were busy with early gardening: "The ensuing year will be the longest of my life, and the last of such hateful labors; the next we will sow our cabbages together."[25]

But there were two considerations that constrained him to postpone for a while a life devoted entirely to country activities such as sowing cabbages. President Washington, in that last year of the term for which he was elected, expressed a desire to go back, at the end of that period, to the quiet of his Mt. Vernon estate. Jefferson argued in a direct appeal, as did others, that the new government might be split asunder if its executive head were to permit himself the luxury of retirement. He was certain that his superior would make a similar appeal if the suggestion of his own immediate withdrawal from public life were to be offered seriously. He could not very convincingly couple a plea for the President's acceptance of a second term with a request that he be relieved forthwith of his own duties as a secretary.

In addition, Hamilton was going to great lengths in the effort to drive him out of the cabinet. Under a thin cloak of anonymity through which most readers, including Jefferson, could penetrate, he wrote articles denouncing the Virginian so thoroughly that only the exercise of great restraint prevented direct reply. In private conversation and in unguarded correspondence with a few of his associates Jefferson let the state of his feelings be known. While at Monticello in the early autumn, a time when the fires of a rare indignation were still burning within him, he made this declaration in a letter to Washington: "I will not suffer my retirement to be clouded by the slanders of a man whose history, from the moment at which history can stoop

[25] Jefferson to Martha Jefferson Randolph, March 22, 1792, Randolph, *Domestic Life*, 209.

to notice him is a tissue of machinations against the liberty of the country which had not only received and given him bread, but heaped its honors on his head."[26]

Meanwhile Hamilton was working diligently for the re-election of Washington and Adams. His attitude toward the latter was not one of unqualified admiration, but he understood that if the dangerous Jeffersonians were to be thwarted, there was no one to take his place. Nominating conventions were unknown in those days; there were, however, less spectacular means of submitting party choices to the electoral college. In a more or less representative caucus of Federalist leaders agreement was reached to submit a Washington-Adams ticket, if such it could be called. Similarly, a number of chiefs and chieftains of the "Anti" group, just emerging into official status, huddled together and then announced that their candidates would be Washington and Clinton.

Hamilton, as much opposed to Clinton, who had recently been elected governor of New York, as he was to Jefferson, nevertheless looked upon him as a formidable contender. Fearful of the outcome, the more so because Adams gave the appearance of being unwilling to lift a finger in the interest of his own re-election, "Mr. Federalist," as Hamilton might have been called, wrote a blunt letter to the Vice-President. The tone of it was that of a general summoning a leading member of his staff. The man chosen, along with Washington, to carry the party standard, was told that his stay at home had already been unduly prolonged. "I learned with pain," Hamilton wrote, "that you may not probably [*sic*] be here until late in the session." "Permit me to say," he continued, as one having authority, "that it best suits the firmness and elevation of your character to meet all events, whether auspicious or otherwise, on the ground where station and duty call you."[27]

Adams did not respond with alacrity to this pointed directive. He

---

[26] Jefferson to Washington, September 9, 1792, Jefferson, *Works*, VII, 148.

[27] Hamilton to Adams, October 1792, *The Works of Alexander Hamilton*, edited by Henry Cabot Lodge (12 vols., New York, 1904), X, 28–29 (cited hereafter as Hamilton, *Works*).

was not convinced that his presence in Philadelphia would bring him any additional support; in addition, both he and Abigail were below par physically. It was not until the end of November that he started, with manifest disinclination, on another trip to the capital city. The journey was exceptionally difficult. Winter storms delayed him, a cold brought physical misery, and, despite his mask of indifference, he was haunted with the fear that, after all, the New York governor might be chosen to replace him.

He would have been surprised—and heartened—to learn that Jefferson was one of his supporters, albeit a rather secretive one. If the truth had become generally known, it would have seemed anomalous to members of Jefferson's party and an occasion for misunderstanding on the part of many Federalists. But by this time there was a line of cleavage between those who were merely opposed to Federalism and the advocates of genuine democracy. Clinton, in Jefferson's opinion, was on the wrong side of that line.

It is all the more worth noting because of the light it throws on the Adams-Jefferson relationship that the latter, one of the greatest of America's political leaders, at least once crossed party lines to favor the election of a man with whom he differed radically at some points, but for whom, nevertheless, he had a preference based on broad considerations of public welfare.

As the returns came in, Washington's reputation as the nonpareil among vote-getters was enhanced. It became evident that every electoral vote would go into his column. But for a while all interested persons shared Adams' doubt about who would get second place. Nevertheless, the incumbent's margin of victory was substantial. The complete tally showed that seventy-seven of the electors were pledged to Adams, only fifty to Clinton. One state, Kentucky, asserted its independence and gave ten complimentary votes to Jefferson.

Naturally, Jefferson was not displeased with the outcome. In advance of the formal certification of results he wrote to one of his correspondents that Adams' triumph was due to the "strength of his personal worth and his services," not to the "demerits of his political creed."[28] In his assessment of the results of the election as a whole, more important than Adams' victory over Clinton and even the implications of the surprising action of the Kentucky electors was a marked increase in the number of Republicans chosen to serve in the House of Representatives. In this evidence of an increasing popular approval of democratic principles there were clear implications, both for Jefferson and those holding the line against the "Anti-Federalist" threat. For the latter, and especially for Hamilton and his associates in strategy, they formed the basis for additional apprehensions. It was recognized, by both those who welcomed and those who deplored the change, that the government was now actually operating under a two-party system.

For the second time, Washington and Adams took their respective oaths of office, on March 4, 1793. There was nothing lacking in the dignity befitting the event. The twice-chosen Chief Executive, dressed in a suit of black velvet, ornamented with powder on his hair and with gleaming knee and shoe buckles, and carrying a light dress-sword, made a striking appearance. His means of conveyance to the State House, a spotless white coach drawn by six equally white horses, was the cynosure of many duly impressed residents and visitors.[29] But there was no suggestion of a coronation. All the rituals appertaining to royalty were taboo. A new spirit and temper abroad in the land made advisable a function that followed a pattern appropriate to a republic.

After nightfall there were fireworks, and in drawing rooms and coffee houses around the city, also by humble firesides, hopes were re-expressed, soberly or convivially. In a few places fears were voiced, and on the part of some there were attempts to drown them in good-sized potions.

As soon as he could get away, Adams, eager to return to his farm, took passage inconspicuously on a stage which was to carry him over a part of the lengthy route. His mood was quite different from that

[28] Jefferson to Thomas Pinckney, December 3, 1792, Jefferson, *Works*, VII, 192.

[29] J. Thomas Scharf and Thompson Westcott, *History of Philadelphia*, (3 vols., Philadelphia, 1884), I, 473.

four years earlier as he rode from Braintree to New York to take the place next to Washington in the government. As if in enforced response to a voice heard through election results, he had just declared that he would have nothing to do with "monarchical trumpery."

Jefferson, more or less resigned to the exigencies of his situation, faced as cheerfully as he could the prospect of a long spring and summer in a rather repellent environment. Its only appeal to him was the opportunity it provided for leadership in the cause to which he was thoroughly committed.

At the beginning of this administrative period the battle for supremacy, in which Hamilton and Jefferson were generally recognized as the opposing generals, entered a new and more rancorous stage. Reverberations from the French Revolution were louder and, to many, more ominous. The most conspicuous, if not the guiltiest, victim of the orgy of bloodshed in Paris was the King—an addition recently made to the long roll of those already done to death. As news arrived, with the inevitable time lag, from the scene of violence, a familiar issue was brought into clearer focus. Hamilton and his satellites seized upon reports from the French capital and wrung out of them every vestige of possible value in the maintenance of their control. On the other hand, Jefferson, while continuing to deplore the excesses of mobs, did so with some reservations, remembering vividly the misery he had seen in France and his observations of its causes. In his heart there was no lessening of sympathy for Frenchmen who were cherishing and struggling toward the ideals of "liberty, equality, and fraternity"; and outwardly he availed himself of every opportunity to champion their rights.

In the same vein in which he had commented earlier about a comparatively minor uprising in New England, he now wrote to his former secretary and long-time friend: "Was there ever such a prize won with so little innocent blood? My own affections have been deeply wounded by some of the martyrs to this cause, but rather than it should have failed I would have seen half the earth desolated."[30] It was his judgment, carefully considered, that the triumph of the

[30] Jefferson to William Short, January 3, 1793, Jefferson, *Works*, VII, 203.

French revolutionists—he was assuming, apparently, that their goal was already achieved—would go far toward insuring the continuance of the republic of the United States, while a victory of the kings who formed a coalition to stamp out the movement would have jeopardized the success of the great American experiment.

To Adams, as to Hamilton, such ideas were too raw. And there were others, among them a number of well-fed and fastidious "conservatives," who could not stomach these notions about the tragic events abroad.

In that spring and summer of 1793, the appearance of Edmond Genêt on the American scene, along with his subsequent behavior, was the immediate occasion for a fresh outburst of hostility between the "Federalists" and the "Republicans," as the latter by this time were frequently designated. Genêt was an erratic representative of the Girondists, then in power in France. In April he arrived at a southern port, and then, as he traveled north to Philadelphia, was entertained in the grand style at a number of civic fetes. In the capital city itself his reception, in which members of the so-called Jacobin clubs took the dominant part, was even more enthusiastic. We do not know to what extent these excessive attentions were influential in shaping his conduct in the weeks that followed. But that conduct was of such a nature as to threaten temporarily to wreck the vessel, designed as the Ship of State, built and launched by mastercraftsmen in the Constitutional Convention.

Genêt made some demands of a near-insulting nature upon the government to which he had come on a diplomatic mission. In other ways he gave evidence of a purpose to force that government to become a military ally of the Girondists. Added up, his actions amounted to a superior exhibition of undiplomatic clumsiness.

Adams remembered Genêt as a small lad whom he had taken one day to see the animals in a zoo located in Paris. Now, because of the nature of his office, he was not directly involved in the affair precipitated by that same individual, who in some ways had not grown up. And he was many miles distant that summer from the epicenter of turbulence. He observed as well as he could from his New England perspective, and with some consternation, the crude emissary's blundering from one act of folly to another. Jefferson, despite his sympathies with the French people, was aroused even more than Adams, and helped to formulate a cabinet decision to request the recall of this extraordinary envoy. In the line of duty he drafted a letter conveying such a request. He well understood that Genêt was doing as much as one individual could to crush the hopes, hitherto lively, of those on the Republican side of the party conflict in his own country.

It should be noted that with Jefferson, as with Adams, patriotic considerations were paramount. In respect to the central issue at stake the two men were of one mind. And while partisan strife became more acrimonious than ever, like other men with lofty motives, Federalists and Anti-Federalist, they were primarily concerned with the safety of the ship of state.

If Adams was not happy as a lark that summer, he was enjoying life about as much as mortals ordinarily do. In Quincy—as the town in which his home was located had been named the previous year, upon its separation from South Braintree—he read his books, fraternized with his neighbors, and spent hours with John Quincy, who came out frequently from Boston for week-end visits. And it was good to feel, occasionally, pine-scented breezes from the hills to the southwest and tonic winds blowing in from the sea.

Quite different in several ways was Jefferson's Philadelphia summer. Anticipating that the severance of his official connection with the government would not be delayed beyond the beginning of the fall season, he vacated his residence in the heart of the city, packed most of his furniture, and made arrangements for its shipment to Virginia. Then he began living quite simply in a three-room cottage, with open spaces about it, near the Schuylkill River. More than one sultry day he spent in the shade of plane trees near the cottage, reading, writing, and at times conferring with one or more trusted lieutenants about the struggle in behalf of the democratic ideal. Once again his younger daughter had accompanied him, and her presence, along with the pleasant rural surroundings, helped to relieve a situation which was daily becoming more vexatious to him. But not even the combination of an idyllic environment and the companionship of "dear Maria" could remove entirely the mental strain which circumstances had forced upon him.

He was paying now the high price of leadership in a cause which was anathema to many of his fellow Americans. One part of that price was the virtual ostracism to which he was subjected by some of the élite of the city. But his patience and good will were being taxed with even more onerous impositions. The President's wife never called him a "filthy democrat," but a rumor was going the rounds that she had used a similar phrase in speaking of plain people whose interests he had at heart. And in every means of communication available to his more rabid political enemies, direct attacks upon him multiplied in number and intensified, as time went on, in bitterness. The charge that he was a "french-fried zealot" or similar charges fell on him like the pellets of a hailstorm.

Moreover, a calumny earlier whispered, to the effect that he was an enemy of his country, was now revived and publicized as much as conditions affecting the traffic in malignity would permit. A few of his irresponsible detractors even stated that he was guilty of offenses involving the nation's welfare, at the same time being shrewd enough not to make himself liable to legal prosecution. It was difficult for a man of his sensitive spirit to withstand the verbal barrage directed against him as a political leader; it was all but impossible to take philosophically repeated allegations that he was, or had been, deliberately imperiling the peace and security of his country.

But all this had no damaging effect on his overmastering purpose. His earlier preference for Adams rather than Clinton as vice-president had been as exceptional as it was private. While he remained in the cabinet and for much of the time in the seven years that immediately followed, he kept directing, as a master strategist, forces propelled by determination to drive "monocrats" and their sympathizers out of positions of responsibility in the federal, state and local governments.

During this portion of his public service, while he was being subjected as never before to the open fulminations of his more hostile adversaries and to defamatory subtleties that were being circulated, articles dealing with the current crisis in foreign relations and domestic affairs were appearing in the *Columbian Centinel*. Once more John Quincy Adams was attempting to influence public opinion in this fashion, and doing so with a logic, trenchant power, and fairness uncommon in such productions of the period. Using successively the signatures, "Marcellus," "Columbus," and "Barnevelt" and writing as an exponent of the more moderate Federalist position, he showed again a prowess with the pen that was almost a match for that frequently shown by Jefferson. And again, as we may suppose, a part of the background for the articles was conversation with John Quincy's father.

The *Centinel* pieces stressed the necessity of "impartial and unequivocal neutrality" in respect to the conflict which was continuing, with awesome consequences, in France. In them were indications that the young lawyer's opposition to democracy of the Jeffersonian type had hardened. Genêt and those who openly encouraged his conduct were singled out for criticism; but there were undertones, frequently repeated, of rebuke for all leaders of what had become a bona fide opposition party.

President Washington, still averse to leading articles in Freneau's paper, was pleased with the offerings of "Marcellus," "Columbus," and "Barneveld." He was certain that they were the products of one creative mind and took pains to learn the identity of the author. If the Vice-President was not the one who gave this information to his superior, he would have leaped at the chance to do so. He was not lacking in fatherly pride as he thought of John Quincy's contribution to the great debate.

Actually, there came a time when the elder Adams believed that it was his son rather than Washington who saved the country from the perils which then threatened it. But being John Adams, he derived some satisfaction from his own part in the maintenance of peace with honor, according to his version of the history then being made. After the worst of the crisis precipitated by the French Revolution was over but while he was still Vice-President, in a letter to daughter Abby, he gave with one co-ordinated movement a left-handed compliment to himself and a fairly heavy slap in the direction of Jefferson. She must not say a word about it to anyone, he wrote, but the truth was that if Jefferson had been presiding over the Senate in that period, with the power of breaking a tie vote, the country, even in the very hour in which he was composing this letter, would be "involved in all the evils of a foreign, if not a civil war."[31]

There is some significance in the fact that Adams imposed strict secrecy on this expression of opinion. It is probable, however, that in that time, when passion rather than reason was ruling the conduct of many citizens, he frequently made similar remarks; it is most improbable that he did so outside the family circle and among a few close friends. He had no inclination to join the pack which was hounding his great contemporary more vigorously than an earlier one, responding to a different hue and cry, had pursued himself. He dissociated himself from all efforts being made, during Jefferson's last year as a cabinet officer, to tear him to pieces politically. With a sense of propriety which he did not always display, he refrained from public criticism of the man who at one time had been his trusted colleague.

Late in August of 1793, Philadelphia's own "reign of terror" began. Its instrument of destruction was not the guillotine, but the scarcely less dreaded yellow fever. With horrifying virulence it swept up from the water front and in certain sections decimated the population. Each breeze wafted outward from the Delaware brought putrid odors; with them were mingled, after a time, scents from tar, vinegar, nitre, and garlic, of supposedly antisepetic value. Not far from where Jefferson and his daughter were living a tent city sprang into existence, as men, women, and children fled from the stricken areas.

There were tumbrils in this terror, too; but instead of carrying those about to die, they were filled with the remains of those already dead. Sometimes the rumbling of these vehicles could be heard at night, as the corpses of hapless victims were hastily and unceremoniously hauled to their graves. Most of the casualties belonged to the

---

[31] Adams to Mrs. Abigail Adams Smith, December 17, 1795, quoted in *Colonel William Smith and Lady*, by Katherine Metcalfe Roof (Boston, 1929), 229.

poorer class, but people who lived in fine houses were not spared. Hamilton himself was attacked by the destroyer, but not mortally.

Jefferson was one of those who lived through the plague unscathed. Almost daily he made the trip to and from his office, seemingly immune to the lethal germs. At the earliest opportunity, however, he and Maria closed up the cottage near the Schuylkill and traveling by way of Washington's Mt. Vernon and Madison's Montpelier returned to Monticello. In mid-autumn Jefferson came north again, this time assuring himself and members of his family that he was beginning the very last round of duty as an officer of the federal government.

By the time he reached Philadelphia, the epidemic was in its final stage and the date set for convening of another session of Congress was near. In November, Adams emerged, rather gingerly, from his long seclusion. Abigail, who for a year and a half had stayed away from the capital as if it were the scene of a constant plague, was quite anxious when the time came to say good-bye to her "dearest friend," more so than usual on such occasions. Probably he promised her, in the moments of parting, as he did a little later in writing, that he would not "run about upon visits, without caution."[32]

On the evening of December 4 he had two visitors at his lodgings. One of them was his son Thomas, the other Thomas Jefferson. That may well have been the last time that the two statesmen met during this portion of their careers in a setting where extended conversation was possible. In a very little while, if the firm resolution of one of them should be carried out, their contemporary service as public officials would be ended. It seems most unlikely that either of them would omit, at such a time and in such a place, telling the other about his family. At any rate, it will serve our purpose to survey again the domestic background of each of them, this time as it was on that evening of early winter.

As has been seen, the oldest and most promising of Adams' sons was making his influence felt to an extent unusual for such a young

[32] Adams to Mrs. Adams, December 5, 1793. *Letters of John Adams Addressed to his Wife*, edited by Charles Francis Adams, (2 vols., Boston, 1841), II, 130.

man. As a lawyer he was as yet scarcely able to support himself adequately, but in other ways, including, of course, his writing for periodicals, he had demonstrated capacities for leadership. Applauded by many Boston residents, he had delivered the patriotic address on the occasion of that city's most recent Fourth of July celebration. International law was his specialty. Those who knew him best believed that, young as he was, he would probably be appointed in the near future to some important post in the diplomatic service.

As for Abby and her peripatetic Colonel, they were, for the time being, on the upgrade financially. All the members of this family of Smiths, having just spent a year abroad, were living in near-regal style in New York. But Abby's parents were still much concerned about her and her children, as they heard more reports of their son-in-law's hazarding his family's future in dubious speculative ventures. The couple's third child, who had mildly disappointed them by not being a girl, had not survived infancy, but the other two were normally healthy and active, and the chances were good that they would have at least one more brother or, perhaps, a sister.

But if all of them, born and unborn, were to be brought up according to the best traditions of the Adams family, the heavier share of the responsibility, it seemed, would rest on their mother. The love-lorn maiden Jefferson had known in Paris was now mistress of a household whose future was more than normally uncertain. Sometimes her father and mother, while talking with less intimate friends about the Colonel, would say "He is very active." But that was a polite and minimum expression, intended to mask the uneasiness in their minds.

The second of the Vice-President's sons, Charles, whom Jefferson scarcely knew, was as charming as ever, more so than some of his near relatives. But less praiseworthy traits, manifestations of which had appeared earlier, were now more in evidence. His father had recently visited him in New York, and optimistically reported to Abigail, "He will do very well." Nevertheless, there was continuing anxiety about him on the part of both parents. Perhaps they thought that what he needed most was a good, steady wife. And yet they frowned on any suggestion of that kind in connection with him. He could scarcely support himself.

Charles's younger brother, who shared with Thomas Jefferson his father's attention on that December night, had completed his apprenticeship in a Philadelphia lawyer's office and was about to take his examination for the bar. If all went well, he would soon be in a position to hang out a shingle announcing his availability to potential clients. But if his character was more stable than that of Charles, he was not as free from peccadilloes as his father desired. He spent entirely too much time in homes where there were young ladies. If he was serious about finding a good wife, using some evenings in search of one would be in order, but to dart like a butterfly from one feminine flower to another, with no purpose beyond temporary pleasure, was, the elder Adams thought, a waste of good time and energy.

Did Jefferson ask the man upon whom he called that evening what the latest news was from Abigail, back in the Quincy home? If so, he could have been told that she was free from "Intermitting fevers" and other physical ills which for many weeks had tormented her in Philadelphia. It was well that her vigor had been restored. No invalid could have coped with the duties which now demanded her attention and energy. Adams' aged mother was failing. There were times when those about her thought that the thread of life would snap very soon. Abigail was doing all she could to compensate for the absence of the son.

In addition, there were many supervisory details relating to the farm. Among other details, it was her duty to see that fresh country butter and other home-produced viands were sent off periodically to her husband, for whose dining table nothing could equal what came from his own cows and orchards and gardens. Indoors, there was a household to be looked after, servants to be hired and instructed, sometimes to be dismissed. And as if these demands were not enough, the intervals between letters to John, who kept complaining about tedious days and lonesome nights, could not be too long.

If Jefferson did inquire about the lady whose conversation and correspondence had delighted him in years past, he could have received information in abundance.

Perhaps, as he and Adams talked, his own impatience to return to Monticello was evident. On his plantation the two daughters were doing their part, but there was no one like Abigail to plan and direct activities. It seemed to him that every one of his ten thousand acres was calling him to remedy the neglect of hired overseers. There was a leanness in the soil, for the cure of which no absentee treatment on the part of the owner was sufficient. Also, there were 154 slaves and more than a few cattle and horses and hogs requiring attention. He may have thought that even the three sheep listed in the assets of his estate were in need of a real shepherd.

Of greater constraining force, naturally, were the yearnings of members of his family for his presence, coupled with his own eagerness to be with them. Although he was only fifty, he was now referring to himself, rather whimsically, as a patriarch; and nothing could shake his belief that he was needed in the exercise of that distinction at home more than Washington needed him. Maria had not come with him on this final trip as a cabinet officer. For that young lady, as for Abigail, there seemed to be something pernicious about the Philadelphia climate. But now, at Monticello, the bloom was coming to her cheeks again. Her father felt that he must help to keep it there. Her sister Martha, while less dependent upon him than she had been in most previous years, still needed more fatherly counsel than could be obtained by correspondence. Then, too, Jefferson could see, in imagination, four tiny hands summoning him in the direction of home. Blue-eyed Anne had a brother, Thomas Jefferson Randolph, by this time old enough to carry on a limited conversation.

Adams and Jefferson were, of course, human beings before they were statesmen, and it is not likely that they passed up the opportunity that evening to exchange remarks appropriate for men with many domestic concerns and responsibilities.

Perhaps very little was said by either of them about Jefferson's forthcoming withdrawal to his Virginia hilltop, but he could not now be accused, by Adams or anyone else, of beating a retreat while under the fire of his arch-antagonist, Hamilton. The latter's efforts to drive him out of the circle of Washington's appointed advisers had met with official resistance, as well as his own firm determination not to appear as the routed leader of a faction diminishing in numbers and influence. He believed that the time had come when he could with honor be "liberated," as he put it, "from the hated occupations of politics."[33]

Washington, who probably knew the worth of his services as secretary better than anyone else, shortly added another plea to those he had already made, that this valued adviser remain where he was. But his repeated solicitation turned out to be resistible; Jefferson was immovable in his purpose. On the last day of the year he submitted in writing a definite confirmation of that fact. As the year terminated, he closed for the last time the desk at which so many important duties had been performed. Mistakenly, he thought that this action symbolized the end of his service as an official in the United States government.

His resignation was regretfully accepted, with sincere protestations that the administration was sustaining a severe loss. "Since it has been impossible," Washington wrote, "to prevail upon you to forego any longer the indulgence of your desire for private life, the event, however anxious I am to avert it, must be submitted to."[34]

One day in the first week of the new year Jefferson rode out of the city, feeling that an intolerable burden had rolled off his shoulders. As he began this journey, he would have scoffed at any suggestion of other meetings with Adams under such conditions as the parting curtain of the future would reveal. But if a look behind that curtain had been possible, he could have seen himself and his old friend, at a time not too far distant, standing against one another in a relationship more openly antagonistic.

[33] Jefferson to Mrs. Angelica Church, November 27, 1793, Randolph, *Domestic Life*, 224.

[34] Washington to Jefferson, January 1, 1794, *The Writings of George Washington*, edited by Worthington C. Ford (14 vols., New York and London, 1889–93), XII, 401.

We are not left in any doubt about the feeling of the Vice-President in connection with Jefferson's departure. Writing to John Quincy in the same week in which the Secretary resigned, he affirmed, "Though his desertion may be a loss to us of some talent, I am not sorry for it on the whole, because . . . his temper is embittered against the constitution and the administration as I think."[35] A few days later he was rather caustic as he expressed this opinion to his closest confidant: "His mind is now poisoned with passion, prejudice, and faction."[36] Certainly he did not regret Jefferson's resignation as much as the President did or with the same sense of loss which he felt when his friend withdrew permanently from the Continental Congress a few weeks after the 1776 Declaration was adopted.

At their best, Adams' judgments of his contemporaries were likely to be faulty; at their worst, they were warped far out of line with reality. His evaluation of Jefferson, at the time the Secretary divested himself of responsibilities connected with the administration, was scarcely rational. The leader who distrusted, when he did not fear, the processes of democracy was not then qualified to judge accurately his Revolutionary comrade, either as a man or as a public servant.

The time came when Adams was more objective in his estimate of this phase of the public service of his Virginia friend. Now, after the passing of many years, most scholars rate Jefferson's accomplishments as secretary of state highly. One modern historian has stated that if Jefferson's career in office had been confined to the years which he spent as a member of the first President's cabinet, he would still deserve notable recognition and a place among the great servants of America.[37] It is pleasant to assume, even though speculation in such matters is rather fanciful, that if Adams were still living among us mortals, he would concur in that judgment.

[35] Adams to John Quincy Adams, January 3, 1794 (Massachusetts Historical Society, Adams Papers), quoted in Smith, *John Adams*, II, 846.

[36] Adams to Mrs. Adams, January 6, 1794, *ibid.*

[37] Samuel Flagg Bemis, in *The American Secretaries of State and Their Diplomacy* (10 vols., New York 1927–29), II, 4.

CHAPTER IV

Parting of the Ways

❧

T HE SCENE in the hall of the national House of Representatives
on March 4, 1797, was a notable one. For the first time in our
history there was at a presidential inauguration an outgoing as well
as an incoming occupant of the country's most exalted position. For
the last time three men, each of whom had taken a leading part in the
pre-Revolutionary movement, were at the center of attention and
interest in the event. The "Father of his Country" was, in a sense,
handing over his child to another for safekeeping. That other was
connected with the man assuming the rank next to him by ties of
varied strength, the strongest being their years of labor together on
two continents for the life and welfare of the new nation.

When the time came for the ceremonies to begin, the name Washington was announced. The retiring President, who had looked forward to this day as a restless child sometimes looks forward to the
last day of school, appeared and was received with an ovation which,
as one spectator reported, "made the hall tremble." Next was heard
the name Jefferson, and immediately the new Vice-President, wearing a long blue frockcoat, came in, and straight as an arrow walked to
the place reserved for him. Again there were loud cheers, but apparently the hall did not tremble as much as it had a few moments before.
Then the announcer called out, "President Adams," whereupon the
man from Quincy, a bit more rotund, nattily attired in a suit of black
broadcloth, came through the entrance and made his way to the
leather chair, occupied by the Speaker when the House was in session.
Once more cheers resounded, but, according to our informer, they
were unequal in volume to those which had preceded. When they
had stopped, Adams arose and impressively delivered his inaugural

address. This duty performed, the oath of office was administered, and then the new President made a final bow and left the hall.[1]

Most of the surface indications on this first day of the new administration were clearly favorable. Jefferson, knowing that it was expected of him, made a short speech in the Senate in connection with his taking the official oath. In a veiled rebuke to injudicious partisans who had been spreading the fiction that he and Adams were enemies, he spoke in appreciative terms about his predecessor. He was an "eminent character"; between them there had been "cordial and uninterrupted friendship"; to him had been "justly confided" the office held by Washington for eight years.[2]

In the presidential address, there was an attempt to remove misconceptions of another kind. Adams tried to make it clear that he was not a monarchist. He vowed that he would uphold the Constitution in its existing form until that document should be "altered by the judgment and wishes of the people." He disowned any antipathy to France. He personally esteemed the French people, and had a sincere desire to maintain friendly relations between France and America and to help perpetuate the honor and advance the best interests of both nations.[3]

These utterances were not the vapid effusions of a narrow-minded politician, directed condescendingly to members of the party that had missed victory in the recent election by a close margin. All available evidence indicates that the man succeeding Washington intended to keep himself above the level of warring factionalism.

We do not know what Jefferson thought as he listened to the rolling periods of this address. He may have remembered how Adams, on a summer day more than two decades before, had made an impassioned plea for the Declaration of Independence. Perhaps he was entertaining some hopes that were not to be realized.

There was no inaugural ball that night. Adams was now as averse

[1] An account of this inauguration by an eyewitness, William McKay, appeared first in Poulson's *Daily Advertiser*, and was reprinted in Scharf and Westcott, *History of Philadelphia*, I, 488.

[2] *Annals of Congress*, Fourth Congress (Washington, 1849), 488.

[3] *Ibid.*, 1582–86.

as Jefferson would have been to any function which could give foundation for fears that the incoming administration might lead the country in the direction of monarchy. However, Philadelphia merchants had insisted on giving Washington a farewell dinner. At the dinner the customary toasts ended with a wish that the country's gratitude to the first President might be "coeval with her existence." As a climax to the proceedings, Washington was crowned with laurel in a tableau.

The news of this mock coronation was not received enthusiastically in some quarters. The new President had long since abandoned the idea of an adulatory title for the position, but he had no doubt about having become, by reason of his position, the most important man in America. Any gesture exalting his predecessor as "first in the hearts of his countrymen" was annoying.

On the day following the inauguration, after a restless night, he wrote to the lady who had just become "first," but unfortunately had been detained at home by her mother-in-law's mortal illness. Briefly, but with justifiable pride, he described the ceremonies. He soberly reported that the only dry eyes in the watching multitude were those of Washington. Without qualification or exception he declared, "All agree that, taken altogether, it was the sublimest thing ever exhibited in America."[4]

And yet, the man leaving the highest office in the land had received more plaudits than the one entering upon it, and this, too, irked that new incumbent more than a little. Even after Washington departed for his solitudes along the Potomac, more space, Adams noted, was given in the journals, and more attention seemingly in the thinking of most people, to the former chief of state than to his successor. Only with difficulty did Adams curb his tendency to jealousy. He had scarcely adjusted himself to the mantle of authority when he wrote to his absent wife, under the seal of secrecy, "All the federalists seem to be afraid to approve anybody but Washington."[5]

[4] Adams to Mrs. Adams, March 5, 1797, Adams, *Letters Addressed to His Wife*, II, 245.
[5] Adams to Mrs. Adams, March 13, 1797, *ibid.*, II, 252.

More disturbing to him, as he looked out over the scene from the summit he had just attained, was the unsettled condition of the young republic. The threat of war from the outside and the reality of internal dissensions posed serious problems—and for many of them there was no solution in sight. Lacking in astuteness as he was, he nevertheless understood that ahead of him was a tight-rope performance calling for exceptional balance. He must have wondered now and then if his own administration could possibly evoke as much enthusiastic praise as Washington's had.

His friendship with the new Vice-President was already more severely battered than he had been willing to admit publicly. New momentum was being given to the forces which were sweeping the two of them, against their will, to an almost complete wreckage of their earlier relationship. Within a few days after his induction into office, Jefferson left to direct springtime activities on his plantation. This was another item of news which Adams sent during his first month as President to his "dearest friend," and to it he added the cryptic comment, " He is as he was."[6]

We have given attention to some links in that chain of destiny which brought Adams and Jefferson to the presidency and vice-presidency, respectively, of the nation which they had helped to bring into existence. It will now be our purpose to note others that were forged in the fires of political controversy during the second half of Washington's administration.

Outwardly, the status quo of their relationship was maintained throughout that period. In the three years immediately following Jefferson's resignation as secretary of state, there were only a few letter contacts between himself and Adams. These few were not communications of the kind which men who had collaborated closely for years might be expected to send to each other; however, they were not unfriendly.

In the spring of 1794, on a day when Jefferson could have been "sowing cabbages" with his daughters, he received a letter from Adams. It accompanied a book sent from some undisclosed motive as

[6] *Ibid.*, II, 250.

a gift. This work, published a short time before in Paris, dealt with political oppressions in Lausanne.[7] In the letter congratulations were extended to one who had escaped from the purgatory of life as a federal official and was now enjoying the paradise of his peaceful home.

In his acknowledgment, the farmer statesman made only a brief reference to the misfortunes of the Swiss city. He wrote at some length about his own good fortune. He seemed to be, if not in paradise, as near to it as an inhabitant of earth could be. Life in the open air, close to growing things, the privilege of being invested with some responsibility for them, the thrill of creativity in partnership with nature—how much better it was than being confined to a desk under the necessity of writing ten or a dozen letters a day. In fact, Jefferson was now pretending to himself that he was just a "dirt farmer." He informed Adams that, like most tillers of the soil, he scarcely ever wrote a letter, except on a rainy day.[8]

At times Adams found it difficult to resist the urge to give up his office and go back to his own farm. Probably that urge was very strong as he read Jefferson's letter. In writing to Abigail, he certainly made no secret of his impatience with the urban environment in which he was placed. Great as her conjugal loyalty was, Abigail had chosen not to gamble with her health, for the time being at least, by living in Philadelphia; and her husband sometimes feared that the climate of the city would ruin him physically. In his letters to her the expressions of dissatisfaction with the role he had to play, and especially the scenery for it, became repetitious. If he could spend only one day at home, it would give him more enjoyment than he could get in an entire winter, cooped up in a city where noise and smoke, along with some displays of luxury by pseudo-aristocrats, induced in him a kind of nausea. Once during this period he wrote, "I wish I had a farm here."[9] Such a possession would to some extent alleviate his mental distress.

[7] This book contained letters of one Jean Jacques Cart to Bernard Demuralt, and was recommended by Adams as "well worth reading."

[8] Jefferson to Adams, April 25, 1795, *Adams-Jefferson Letters*, I, 254.

[9] Adams to Mrs. Adams, December 5, 1794, Adams, *Letters Addressed to His Wife*, II, 170.

Certainly Jefferson's near ecstatic account of experiences on his Monticello estate did not make his own situation any more tolerable. But both men, the "dirt farmer" and the discontented Vice-President, continued to watch, sometimes with the appearance of Olympian aloofness, certain disturbing developments in public affairs. Notable among them was the frenzy caused by the drafting and ratification of Jay's Treaty.

In the summer of 1794, Chief Justice Jay was sent to England to negotiate, if possible, an agreement with the government of that country, then guilty of some of the offenses that had led to the Revolution. His appointment aroused fears in many quarters that his political leanings would make him subservient to designs of the English leaders who still looked upon the American experiment with distrust and a certain measure of contempt. And when he returned the next spring with a treaty which Republicans generally regarded as the "death warrant of American liberty," there was panic, culminating in riots, in several centers of population. Mobs milled in the streets, and the stone that struck Hamilton in a public meeting was a symbol of widespread violence which at times pointed threateningly in the direction of civil war. But the treaty was pushed through the Senate, the President approved ratification of it, the House of Representatives and the Senate enacted the necessary supporting legislation, and passions gradually subsided.

The net result on the political scene, however, was enhancement of the prospects of the Republicans. Their need of an active leader became more urgent than ever. Jefferson was still absorbed in farm management, but he could not disregard claims now being pressed upon him by many party members. Their earlier allegiance had been won under the spell of his influence, and their loyalty was still given to him as the man best qualified to be their standard bearer. Nor was Jefferson himself so constituted that he could continue to maintain an objective attitude. He could not be true to himself and to the cause in which he believed so thoroughly if he were to prolong indefinitely his pose as an uninvolved spectator.

He looked upon Jay's Treaty as an "execrable thing,"[10] and upon Washington's approval of it as the "incomprehensible acquiescence of the only honest man who has assented to it."[11] Under pressure from without and from within he revived his former strategy, and in choosing a time to write letters began paying less attention to the weather than he had in the months just following his retirement. Thus, from his mountaintop he began stimulating and directing the grass-roots activity of a sizable company of interested workers.

With Washington's retirement in the near future a certainty, the country was faced, for the first time seriously, with the question of presidential succession. Jay was out of the picture because of the extensive unpopularity of the treaty which bore his name; Hamilton was disqualified by Constitutional provision since he had been born in the West Indies. Any close observer could have foretold that Adams and Jefferson would be rival contenders for the highest office. Neither had any desire to be placed in opposition to the other in such a contest, but probably did not suspect that their friendship might be a part of the price exacted of them if they were to follow the paths that others seemed to be marking out for them.

As yet, there was no apparent weakening of Jefferson's determination to stay out of public office. Some months after his withdrawal from the cabinet, Washington had tried to recall him and had been rebuffed by Jefferson's declaration that no circumstances would ever tempt him to be an officeholder again. A little later Madison had ventured to take him by the horns, if one may so phrase it, and in consequence had been verbally gored. To this younger friend's suggestion that the state of the nation and the welfare of his party demanded that this resolve be broken down, Jefferson replied that the matter was not even open for discussion, that for all time to come he was to be left out of consideration in the selection of officers in the national government. In the light of what followed, no one can accuse him of having the narrow consistency of small minds.

[10] Jefferson to Edward Rutledge, November 30, 1795, Jefferson, *Works*, VIII, 200.
[11] Jefferson to Madison, March 27, 1796, ibid., VIII, 231.

Even in the early part of 1796 he seemed adamant in his purpose to stay clear of involvement as an officeholder in the federal structure. In February he received another book from Adams, one dealing with the French Revolution. Because of the nature of its thesis, the donor probably reasoned that it might serve as a corrective of his friend's vagaries. Jefferson sent a letter of acknowledgment and thanks, but in it he indicated that he had no intention of reading the book thoroughly. Tersely and rather inaccurately, he observed, "It is on politics, a subject I never loved, and now hate."[12]

We deal here with something too subtle for glib explanation. Men do change their minds, but never in our history has a man of such prominence changed his within such a short time. This much is true: that at that time in his career his emotions were so conflicting, his personality so often at war with itself, as to present occasionally the semblance of abnormality. At times he was Jefferson the husbandman, the plantation owner, and the family man; at other times, the adroit leader of a movement, a man certain that he was mysteriously charged with a mandate to lead a great cause to victory. Actually, while he could not be described as having a split personality in the medical sense, he was often both men at the same time. While his left hand always knew what the right one was doing and vice versa, nevertheless the hands were frequently working at cross purposes. One prominent biographer, referring to this duality of nature, writes: "There were two Jeffersons, and they alternated with some degree of regularity. Whichever situation he happened to be in, he yearned for the other. An understanding of both is essential for a true understanding of the man."[13] Under such circumstances it was not difficult or uncommon for his enemies to bring against him a charge of dissimulation.

No other person then living could have retired from public life as Jefferson did—refusing flatly to take any further part in governmental affairs and accompanying his retirement and refusal with

[12] Jefferson to Adams, February 28, 1796, *Adams-Jefferson Letters*, I, 259.
[13] Nathan Schachner, *Thomas Jefferson: A Biography* (2 vols. in 1, New York and London, 1951, 1957), 504.

unequivocal statements of determination to remain a private citizen—
and then have allowed himself to become, after a brief lapse of time,
the choice of multitudes for the presidency. Numbers of small land-
owners, country merchants, struggling artisans, and other citizens
sometimes spoken of as the "rabble" matched their purpose to elevate
this man to the highest post in the land with his repeated avowed intention to stay where he was. We cannot plumb the depths of his
nature, but it became apparent to everyone interested that the clamor
of his followers was not vain.

Adams was aware, naturally, of the movement to draft Jefferson and viewed it with some alarm. At the same time he looked
upon the probability of his being chosen as Washington's successor
with mixed feelings. As in Jefferson's case, they were like imperfectly
meshing gears.

After the publication of the "Discourses on Davila," his tortoise-
like withdrawal into the shell of official silence continued through the
debate, public and private, over the Jay Treaty. He succeeded so well
in maintaining the appearance of neutrality that Jefferson commented, "Adams holds his tongue with an address above his character."[14] But when he was put to the test, as he sometimes was through
the necessity of breaking a tie vote in the Senate, he invariably sided
with the party of Hamilton. Because of his past record and present
standing, most Federalists were of the opinion, as Hamilton had been
when Clinton was a vice-presidential candidate, that Adams was the
only man who could set up an adequate bulwark against the threat
of Jefferson.

At times the man in whom these hopes were centered thought that
his chances of occupying the highest post were very slim. He would
then try to make himself believe that the slimmer they were, the
better the outlook for his future. Yet he was far from indifferent. He
was not poisoned by ambition, as he thought Jefferson was, but he
was not free from it. Unlike Jefferson, he had never denied an interest in public life. Once, in writing to Abigail, he included a statement
which might have been omitted if the missive had been intended for

[14] Jefferson to Monroe, September 6, 1795, Jefferson, *Works*, VIII, 188.

other eyes. Reminding her that the time was approaching for a succession, he coyly observed, "I am heir apparent, you know."[15]

He was not inclined to underestimate his abilities and believed that such an "accession," when and if it came, would be most appropriate. Yet there were recurrent yearnings to go back as a permanent resident to the environs of Penn's Hill, matching Jefferson's desire to stay at Monticello. While he was willing, if not eager, to subordinate such yearnings in the event of his being summoned to higher duty, he kept attributing to his contemporary a vitiating desire to realize a great ambition.

The choice of Adams and Jefferson as the 1796 candidates of their respective parties was as inevitable as if it had been foreordained. By an ironical twist of events the two men who had been conspicuous co-champions of American independence were now the principal antagonists in a battle, the principal issue of which would be the continuance or the overthrow of Federalist supremacy.

The points of contrast between that presidential election—the first in our history in which there was a real contest for the top position—and those with which we have become familiar are more numerous than the points of resemblance. There were no preliminary primaries. No nominating conventions were held, no speeches of acceptance delivered by the chosen candidates. No campaign trips were made by either aspirant. No nation-wide publicity was given to their daily doings; no meetings were held in which they were brought face to face; there was nothing remotely resembling a modern television debate. Indeed, from a modern point of view, the engines of propaganda were running in low gear.

In one respect, however, this national election was a prototype of many that have since taken place. Actually, by the standards of the time, there was nothing sluggish about this early movement of political machinery; and much of the excitement connected with it was on a low plane of behavior. Long before the struggle ended, a lively exchange of reckless charges took place. Adams was a tool of the aris-

15 Adams to Mrs. Adams, January 20, 1796, Adams, *Letters Addressed to His Wife*, II, 191.

tocrats, Jefferson of the French government. Adams desired the substance as well as the form of monarchy. Jefferson believed in anarchy and did not believe in God. To their credit, and in line with their conduct four years before, neither Adams nor Jefferson attempted to tarnish the honor or the patriotism of the other. And both of them spent the months just preceding the actual making of the choice by the electors as if the outcome did not concern them very much.

As his custom was, Adams stayed through the summer and fall at his Quincy residence. Not through reports in the current newspapers, but by way of his diary, which he had intermittently neglected, we learn in some detail of his activities in that pre-election period. He superintended the construction of a barn. As his farmer progenitors had done for generations, he watched his barley, clover, and corn crops mature, and exulted in the joy of harvest. He climbed occasionally to the summit of Penn's Hill and surveyed the landscape, eastward to its point of meeting with the ocean—and beyond, in other directions toward other horizons. Usually he attended church on Sunday, and more than once had the minister for a dinner guest. He read his Bible and books about it and renewed acquaintance with Greek and Roman classics. For his stomach's sake he drank regularly a "Jill of Cyder," and when necessity demanded took "balm Tea, Rhubarb, and Salt of Wormwood." At times there were minor annoyances, such as "Muskitoes numerous and busy"; and in late August the weather became excessively warm. One monosyllabic notation in his diary should strike a sympathetic chord in any reader who has sweltered through sultry summer days: "Hot, went not out." But that summer was, he said, the "freest from Care, Anxiety, and Vexation" of any through which he had lived. So contented was he that he christened his home "Peacefield." And while he was greatly interested in the impending election, his attitude towards it seems, on the surface, to have been that of an obscure Yankee breadwinner.[16]

Unlike Adams, Jefferson took a lively interest in the mechanical side of agriculture. He spent hours that summer directing the construction of a threshing machine, using a model which at his request

[16] Adams, *Diary and Autobiography*, III, 226–49.

had been sent over from Scotland. He perfected and put to use a new type of moldboard for plows. Also, he turned to manufacturing on a small scale. On his estate there was established a nail factory, for which there was no counterpart on the Quincy farm.

Like Adams, he was, throughout the growing and harvesting season, the busy manager of an agricultural enterprise. Even his letters dealing with matters of public policy contained frequent references to his wheat, clover, and peas. Like Adams, too, he was, if not entirely carefree, nevertheless happily adjusted to life in his home environment. Children and grandchildren were about him. Prices for farm products were satisfactory. His travels were very limited; persons who wished to see him had to come to his mountain. There were days when, if questioned about it, he might have stated over again that he "hated politics" and reiterated his purpose never to go to the federal capital again as an officeholder. And yet—the thought kept recurring—if by the voters' decision he should be named Vice-President, the duties of that office were not so binding as to prevent his spending the greater part of each year at home.

Time was about to usher in a new year when it was possible to give statistically the outcome as determined in the several state elections. Three near-unknowns in the new electoral college, one in Jefferson's own Virginia, one in North Carolina, and one in Pennsylvania, would cast their ballots for Adams, thus keeping those states from being solidly for the Republican candidate. But the West and the South had given him overwhelming support, and the total count showed that he had come surprisingly close to victory. The "heir apparent" had won out by a narrow lead of three votes.

When Jefferson learned definitely who the second President would be, he wrote a congratulatory letter to him. It was a friendly communication and showed no trace of dissatisfaction with the verdict of the voters. On the contrary, the writer asserted that he had never wished for any result other than the one then assured. And he would not do anything knowingly that might add to the difficulty inherent in the situation in which Adams would soon be placed.

With reference to a dark threat taking form in the nation's pathway, France having replaced England as a potential war enemy, he wrote a statement which, seen in retrospect, has in it a faint hint of prophecy: "I devoutly wish that you will be able to shun for us this war, by which our agriculture, commerce, and credit will be destroyed. . . . If you are," he continued, "the glory will be all your own." Then he ventured to become a bit more personal. "Little incidents" had either just "happened," or had been "contrived," to separate them as they voyaged through life. Notwithstanding those incidents, now, as always—and here he was careful not to express more than he knew to be true—he retained for Adams the "solid esteem of the moments when we were working for our independance."[17]

It would seem that in such a message there was nothing that could harm friendship or be misused to hinder the furtherance of the democratic movement. But the writer was in a quandary. On a former occasion his problem in relation to this infrequent correspondent had been to write or not to write. Now the alternative before him was related but different—to send or not to send what he had written. Would Adams, reading it, suspect some ulterior motive in the sender? Was there a chance that he might make some unwise use of it? After some deliberation, Jefferson decided to send the letter to Madison in Philadelphia, with instructions to keep it or deliver it, according to his own best judgment. Madison straightway thought of several reasons for isolating it in his own desk. But it is probable that he divulged some of its contents orally and that Adams received, by the grapevine route, knowledge of its general drift and purpose.

At any rate, during the interval between his election and his inauguration Adams revealed to at least two men, in some unofficial letter-writing of his own, his hope, amounting almost to expectation, for an amicable *modus operandi* with the incoming Vice-President.

To one of his Massachusetts friends he wrote, under an *entre nous* injunction: "His [Jefferson's] talents and information I know very well, and have ever believed in his honor, integrity, his love of country and his friends." But—and here was the rub—he professed

[17] Jefferson to Adams, December 28, 1796, *Adams–Jefferson Letters*, I, 263.

and proclaimed certain pernicious doctrines and his patronage of such characters as Paine and Freneau was deplorable. However, the Senate, over which he would preside, might very well serve as a corrective institution. His friends with French leanings would certainly continue to flatter him, but that influence could possibly be counterbalanced. In fairly optimistic mood Adams added, "I hope we can keep him steady."[18]

A few weeks later, writing to another Massachusetts friend in whom he did not hesitate to confide, he praised Jefferson as much as he conscientiously could. The Virginia leader's erratic conduct in politics should not be attributed, he stated, to any native perversity, but to an "irritation upon his nerves." He was hopeful that the source of that irritation could be removed. Moreover, considerations of their "ancient friendship," as well as Jefferson's own "good Sense and general good dispositions," would incline him, at the very least, to decorous conduct. He [Adams] as Vice-President had supported Washington unswervingly through all the past eight years. Probably Jefferson could not duplicate that fidelity, but he could, conceivably, approximate it.[19]

These were the cautiously expressed sentiments of one who was, on the whole, thinking constructively about the future rather than regretfully about the past. They reflected a certain partisan bias, but seemed to be held in balance with a bipartisan purpose. On the strength of reports coming to him, Jefferson himself admitted that Adams was giving evidence of an intention to "steer impartially between the parties." As the day set for the assumption of his new duties drew near, the President-elect decided to make an open bid for cooperation to the leader of the opposition party.

During the winter, his previous "unalterable" decision revoked, Jefferson made ready for the first of another series of journeys as a high-ranking officer of the government. One cold day, about two

[18] Adams to Tristram Dalton, January 19, 1797, *Magazine of American History*, Vol. IX (June, 1883), 470–71.

[19] Adams to Gerry, February 20, 1797, *Massachusetts Historical Society Collections*, Vol. 73, p. 331.

weeks before time to take once again an oath of office, he spoke his
farewell to kinfolk and others at home, and started down the mountain road on the first lap of the long pilgrimage. In the family carriage
which transported him as far as Alexandria were stowed some carefully wrapped bones. These had once belonged to a mastodon and had
recently been presented to Jefferson by a Kickapoo Indian chief. In
Philadelphia they would have value as objects for expert scientific
examination. Before the traveler were ten wearying days in carriage
and stagecoach, then a future with a large question mark attached to
it. But, like the man who would be his superior in the new government, he was moderately hopeful.

This was another journey presenting a marked contrast to the first
Vice-President's triumphal progress from Braintree to New York in
the spring of 1789. En route from Monticello there were no organized ovations. Jefferson had taken precautionary measures to forestall
any formal honors out of keeping with the simplicity associated with
his name. For most of the way he succeeded in fulfilling his wish to
travel incognito. Any fellow traveler on the stage going north from
Alexandria, if given an opportunity to glimpse the contents of Jefferson's baggage, might have taken him for an obscure college professor
with a peculiar interest in osteology.

But this mild, soft-spoken gentleman could not prevent one significant demonstration in his honor. As he drew near Philadelphia, some
of his admirers saluted him with a round of cannon fire and a banner
held aloft, on which huge letters spelled out the phrase: "Jefferson
the Friend of the People."

Without delay the Vice-President-elect went to pay his respects to
Adams. The latter was staying at the St. Francis Hotel on Fourth
Street. The call which Jefferson made there was rather short and
formal, but Adams reciprocated with a visit that had more than
social significance.

It was on the day preceding the inaugural ceremonies that the man
about to be President, having partaken, we may guess, of one of the
buckwheat-cake breakfasts for which the St. Francis hostelry was well
known, went to the residence where Madison lived, at which Jeffer-

son was stopping temporarily. There the two of them engaged in serious conversation. Writing some years later about this meeting, Adams stated, "With this gentleman I had lived on terms of intimate friendship for five-and-twenty years."

There was, of course, no direct recording of what the two men had to say to each other on that early March day, but it was important enough in Jefferson's opinion, just as it was in Adams', to justify his writing out, after a lapse of years, a summary of it. In the two accounts there are minor discrepancies, but they largely agree concerning the main thread of the dialogue.

Adams stated his determination to send a mission to France. It was possible, he thought, for the dark cloud of war to be dissipated. He would like very much to appoint Jefferson as a member. However, it might not be very wise, or even constitutional, for the Vice-President to be out of the country for a stay of indefinite length. He was anxious to get Jefferson's opinion on the subject.

The reply was distinctly negative. Jefferson was not primarily concerned with whether or not such an appointment would be wise or constitutional. He had lived long enough in Europe. He had no desire to go back.

Adams then questioned him about the availability of Madison. Was he qualified to serve in such a capacity with Elbridge Gerry and Charles C. Pinckney? And would he be willing to go?

Jefferson expressed no doubt about Madison's fitness, but as to his willingness there was another negative reply. Washington had once tried, without success, to get Madison's consent to serve on a similar mission. But Jefferson agreed, in compliance with Adams' desire, to consult his younger friend on this matter and then report to Adams.

Having finished their interview, the two men parted, "as good friends as we had always lived," according to Adams' account. "But," he frankly added, "we consulted very little together afterwards."[20]

Indeed, not more than four days after this consultation, the situation presented an entirely different aspect.

[20] Adams' report of this conversation appears in his *Works*, IX, 284–85; Jefferson's in his *Works*, I, 334–36.

On the Monday following the inauguration, a number of Washington's friends and admirers gathered at his invitation for a farewell dinner. President Adams and Vice-President Jefferson occupied places of honor reserved for them. When it came time for the guests to depart, the dinner being over and the ceremonial toasts given, Jefferson managed to fall into line with the President. As the two of them walked along the street together, the Vice-President attempted to pick up the thread of their conversation on the preceding Friday. He reported that Madison's reluctance to accept the appointment tentatively suggested by Adams would amount to a refusal if the opportunity were given.

The response to this information was given, so Jefferson recalled, with traces of embarrassment. It was to the effect that, quite apart from Madison's own attitude, he could not be appointed. Certain developments over the week end, which Adams did not explain, had removed Madison from further consideration. In the President's manner there was no resemblance to the affable approach which Jefferson remembered in their previous meeting. The March weather could change in much less time than had elapsed since that friendly encounter. But what could account for the winds of Adams' disposition, variable as they were, veering around to such an extent in so short an interval?

The two men, who had been placed in a unique juxtaposition over the week end, parted at the corner of Market and Fifth streets. It was more than a casual adieu of a pair of companions. It was the end of any prospect of mutual helpfulness along the way which stretched ahead of them. While Jefferson did not realize it at the time, it symbolized the futility of any hope that he may have had, in common with the President, for a working entente between the two parties. We have Jefferson's word for it, along with Adams' candid admission, that never afterward did the two of them consult together on the subject of the pre-inaugural meeting, or to any great extent on any other of the problems confronting the executive head of the country.

What had happened to cause such a sudden and radical change in the attitude of the new President? Why this about-face in respect to a bipartisan approach to the threat of war? A privilege which Jefferson did not have at the time is ours, that of looking behind the scenes and finding the solution to this puzzle.

Some time between the Friday morning and the Monday evening of that week end certain revelations were made to Adams which were to have a direct bearing on the fortunes of his administration. They pointed toward a schism in his own party, narrow at that stage, but one that would widen. It would be incorrect to say that Adams was a Federalist first and a patriot afterwards; his public career negates any such statement. But at this time, yielding to strong partisan pressures, he chose a course of action counter to the one he had contemplated, one which he could easily rationalize as patriotic. One result of that choice was that in the years just ahead he and Jefferson were to be kept farther apart, in all but a physical sense, than they had ever been since the time of their first meeting.

In his account of those first post-inaugural days, Adams states that on one of them Fisher Ames called on him. That brilliant Federalist leader, worn out with years of service, was about to leave the capital to seek recuperation in his New England home. On the occasion of this visit, he used his powers of persuasion, which were still formidable, in an effort to get George Cabot named as a member of the proposed embassy to France. Cabot was the incarnation of hostility to that country, and Adams eventually turned down the plea made for him. But in the course of the discussion it became clear that a veritable hornets' nest would be stirred up if Madison should be appointed one of the government's representatives on this diplomatic venture.

Still more effective in bringing about a change of the presidential mind was the intransigent attitude of most of the members of his cabinet. If this son of the Puritans, who believed in heavenly guidance, had a guardian angel, that celestial attendant must have been off duty as his earthly charge took for his own official advisers those who had served his predecessor. When he turned to them at the very beginning of his administration for counsel about the personnel of the group that would deal with the French leaders, he was brought face to face with a number of political realities which he had not clearly foreseen.

Oliver Wolcott, secretary of the treasury, indicated that if Madison, whom he looked upon as darkly tinged with "Jacobin dye," were named one of the special envoys, the entire cabinet would resign forthwith.

Timothy Pickering, secretary of state, agreed with his Federalist ally. His idealism, such as it was, found frequent expression in the language of democracy, but he was too set in his anti-French bias to go along with Adams in a nonpartisan approach to problems created by the men who were in authority in France.

The Secretary of War, James McHenry, chimed in with Wolcott's thinly veiled threat of a wholesale resignation of cabinet members. Like Pickering, he had no deep-seated hostility to the democratic ideal, but he understood that his bread was buttered and his cake frosted, not by the man who had retained him in his present position, but by the scheming genius in the New York law office, as much as ever determined to exercise the real leadership in the Federalist party.

Recalling the circumstances, when he was far removed from them in time and place, Adams frankly admitted, "I soon found myself shackled."[21]

He was conscious of those shackles as he walked with Jefferson, on that March evening, toward the parting of their ways. They were the source of his evident embarrassment. Because of them he felt compelled to follow a pattern of procedure very different from that which he had in mind when he had talked with Jefferson before his inauguration.

He had not been in office very long when he received from his daughter a letter, part of which was entirely unrelated to domestic matters. As a rule, the feminine members of his family were neither hesitant nor unqualified in the matter of giving him advice that could be called political. Abby wrote, "I fear that the party, who have

[21] Adams, *Works*, IX, 301.

hitherto embarassed the President by their cabals and who have exerted themselves to divide the election, will continue to render it [the presidency] as uncomfortable as possible."[22]

This was indeed a perceptive comment for a lady of the eighteenth century to send to her father, who had lately assumed the responsibilities of the highest executive office. Her observation may have seemed to him very much like a warning, and many men would have looked upon it as meddling, coming as it did from a member of the sex often considered incompetent in areas of government. If Abby's father did not so regard this expression of opinion, he was not willing to admit to her that she might be right. Replying, he forgot about the shackles and boasted, "I am not at all alarmed; I know my countrymen very well."[23]

As an expression of a mood, this statement may have been accurate, but a less explicit one would probably have been more in keeping with his prevailing attitude. Certainly he was no less concerned than he had been when taking the oath of office, as he looked upon interparty and intraparty divisions within the country, associated as they were with a growing peril to the national security from without. The conversations with his unco-operative cabinet members constituted evidence, as did other experiences, that the statesmanlike pronouncements of his inaugural address had not been received with unanimous cordiality. While he has appeared to some critics naïve, he was not so obtuse as to underestimate the force of certain political cross-currents which boded no good for his administration.

Nevertheless, there was some justification for the rather jaunty tone of the letter in which he attempted to reassure his anxious daughter. Most of his fellow citizens were faithful in their adherence to orderly government. More than that, there were certain granite-like strata in the structure of his own character about which he was not ignorant. Further, his essential integrity, his resoluteness, seldom wavering as he pursued his duty, and his loyalties, never wanting

---

[22] Mrs. Abigail Adams Smith to Adams (undated), quoted in Roof, *Colonel William Smith and Lady*, 231.

[23] Adams to Mrs. Abigail Adams Smith (undated), *ibid.*, 232.

when put to a crucial test, were to be important factors in keeping the young nation from becoming embroiled in the cauldron of European conflict, and likewise from degenerating, as it could have done, into a parasitic oligarchy.

Congress was called to meet in special session on May 15. The growing belligerence of the French government, a circumstance which provided propaganda for a "war party" in the United States, seemed to make this session necessary. Jefferson, having been compelled to make his stay in Monticello short, arrived in Philadelphia in ample time to perform his constitutional duty in the Senate. About the same time Abigail rode proudly into the city with her husband, who had gone out as far as Bristol to meet her. The final services which she could render for her mother-in-law had been conscientiously performed. Now, risking again the threats of the Philadelphia climate, she came dutifully to receive the honors and assume the obligations of the second First Lady. On the sixteenth she forwarded this message to her sister: "Today the President meets both Houses at 12 to deliver His speech.... We are indeed as Milton expresses it, 'Thrown on Perilous Times.' "[24]

On that day, Jefferson was alert at his post, which to him was one, in part, for listening and observation. He was figuratively left out on a limb in respect to participation in executive councils. Not so long before, he could have been likened to an eagle in a remote mountain eyrie. That similarity no longer existed. From the perch to which he was now relegated he could get a much closer bird's-eye view of what was going on, and it was an opportunity of which he took full advantage.

In the opinion of the majority of Republicans, the message which the members of Congress heard that day was equivalent to the beating of war drums. Their leader shared uneasily in this estimate of the presidential address. Jefferson believed that his good friend of other years, taking the outbreak of war for granted, was, in fact if not intentionally, stirring up the martial spirit in Congress and throughout the country. With the recollection of this address still vivid in his

[24] Mrs. Adams to Mrs. Cranch, May 16, 1797, *New Letters of Abigail Adams*, 90.

mind, Jefferson told the French consul general in Philadelphia that the President was "vain, suspicious, obstinate, excessively egoistic, not taking advice from any one."[25]

For one whose normal speech was mildly seasoned, this was strong language, even if the chance of its being published seemed remote to him. But he was viewing with genuine alarm Adams' advocacy of measures that would step up preparations for what was publicized as a "defensive" war. At the same time, he was beset with fears for the future of the party embodying his political ideals. These fears were a part of the background for a breach, seemingly as inevitable as it was tragic, in a personal relationship which had hitherto withstood severe strains. Reviewing the circumstances which led, during that spring and summer, to this result, one student of the period has written, "When the choice between the future of his [Jefferson's] party and the future of his friendship presented itself, he chose the former."[26]

But the break, total or nearly so, did not come by deliberate choice on the part of either man. To a greater extent than ever before, the two were caught between opposing forces which would have snapped, or left dangling by a single thread, ties connecting almost any pair of friends anywhere.

There was some lessening of Jefferson's anxiety, perhaps some slight change in his feeling about the President, when the announcement was made, two weeks after the special session of Congress began, that Elbridge Gerry had been given a place on the mission to France, the others named being Charles C. Pinckney and John Marshall. In the Virginian's estimate, Gerry's qualifications were scarcely inferior to those of Madison. The speedy confirmation of this trio by the Senate further brightened the Vice-President's outlook. It might be possible, he thought, to "rub through" the current year without a declaration of war. It was even conceivable that the catastrophe which he feared could be permanently avoided.

[25] *Correspondence of the French Ministers to the United States, 1791–97*, edited by F. J. Turner, American Historical Association *Annual Report*, 1903, II, 1030. The quotation is a translation from the original French.

[26] Stephen C. Kurtz, *The Presidency of John Adams*, (Philadelphia, 1957), 237.

On the other hand, for reasons that seemed good to him, Adams had revised downward his earlier opinion of Jefferson as a statesman who should be consulted. He now thought of the Monticello philosopher as worse than an "impractical dreamer." However good his intentions, he was capable of leading the Republic down the broad way of unchecked democracy to destruction.

Partly responsible for the increasing deterioration of Adams' opinion of Jefferson was the publication, in the same week in which Congress met, of the Mazzei letter. About a year before, on a day which, if not rainy, was certainly not an auspicious one for Jefferson, the former Secretary of State wrote to his former Virginia neighbor, Philip Mazzei, then resident in his native Italy. He felt at liberty to write frankly to this man, separated by several thousand miles from the whirling maelstrom of American politics. He referred to the rise and growth of an "Anglican and monarchical party" and repeated earlier assertions that there was a disposition in high places to copy the "rotten as well as sound parts of the British." Then he placed in his missive this fragment of verbal dynamite: "It would give you a fever were I to name to you the apostates who have gone over to these heresies, men who were Samsons in the field & Solomons in the council, but who have had their heads shorn by the harlot England."[27] When the text of this letter was sent back to the United States and published, with some scathing editorial comments, most of those who read it were sure that Washington was one of the "Samsons" and Adams one of the "Solomons."

The Biblical allusion was only partially accurate, but it was clear that something very uncomplimentary was meant for those obliquely designated as modern counterparts of the ancient Hebrew personages; and to some without partisan bias the language seemed unbecoming in a man who had been a high government official. There were many in Federalist circles to whom the public release of the letter came with the force of an explosive blast. Most prominent among the individuals so shaken were the President and former President.

Adams soon received an additional shock, proceeding from the

[27] Jefferson to Philip Mazzei, April 24, 1796, Jefferson, *Works*, VIII, 240–41.

same source and producing a similar effect. An army officer conveyed to him the substance, as it was alleged, of another letter written by Jefferson. This one was intended for a select group of Republicans, but with respect to unwarranted use made of his private and semi-private letters, this man, who wrote so many of them, was peculiarly, almost mysteriously, unfortunate. Once again, one or more persons, through indiscretion or malevolence, became responsible for leaks of contents. In this particular letter there was some adverse, although not especially harsh, criticism of Adams' conduct of foreign affairs. When these leaks, with a few additions channeled into them for good measure, reached Adams' ears, he reacted as those who knew him best might have expected.

He sent a letter of thanks to the officer, in it using language about Jefferson which had a razor-like edge. While the latter's name was not mentioned, there was no need to do so. In unmistakably clear reference to him, Adams declared that the communication which had just been brought to his notice was "evidence of a mind soured, yet seeking for popularity, and eaten to a honeycomb with ambition." That mind, moreover, was "so inconsiderate as to be capable of going great lengths."[28] No protestations in this letter, as there had been in a few of Adams' earlier ones, of belief in Jefferson's "honor, integrity, his love of country and his friends"! In its entirety, it was a match for Jefferson's oral communication to the French consul general.

It was written two weeks before the twenty-first anniversary of the Declaration of Independence. Plans were then being made for an appropriate recognition. Abigail, feeling obligated to follow a precedent set by the first President and his wife, invited to a holiday reception the members of Congress, also "all the Gentlemen of the City." The man from Monticello, with all the faults attributed to him, was nevertheless one of the "Gentlemen" of the capital, officially outranking all others except Adams. He could not have been bypassed when

---

[28] Adams to Uriah Forrest, June 20, 1797, *Works*, VIII, 546–47. General Forrest had not seen Jefferson's circular letter, but had heard it read and then communicated its contents, as he remembered them, to the President. In the process of transmission there could have been some garbling of the original.

the invitations were given out. Eager as he was to be on his way homeward, and averse as he probably was to attending the function, he had no inclination to defy accepted social conventions. We may reasonably assume that he was present.

For the guests an adequate supply of refreshments—cake, wine, and punch—was provided. The normal procedure of those in attendance was to partake of the collation, either on the lawn or in a first-floor reception room, then to be presented to the President, and afterwards to proceed to the second floor, there to be greeted by the hostess. It is highly probable, therefore, that on this festive occasion Abigail and Jefferson stood face to face for a little while and exchanged surface pleasantries.

In the first few weeks following the announcement of the electoral college vote, Abigail had shared in her husband's hope that relations with the Vice-President might be amicable. She thought that Jefferson's occupancy of the second place in the government could be a means of keeping in line the southern states, inclined, in her opinion, to be "fractious." If he could and would hold tight rein over them, his elevation to the vice-presidency might turn out to be a "fortunate event." And her personal feeling toward him, while lacking the warmth of the early period of their acquaintance, was nevertheless set forth in complimentary terms. "Tho I can not altogether accord with him in politics," she wrote, in that pre-inauguration period, "I believe him to be a man of strict honor and of rare integrity of heart."[29]

But now the total situation presented a different aspect. She had read the Mazzei letter. Her own "good Gentleman" had undoubtedly informed her about the contents of the communication received from the army officer. Quite apart from any influence Jefferson might have been exerting on "fractious" states, his election to the vice-presidency had not turned out to be, in her opinion, a "fortunate event." How could a man of "strict honor" and "rare integrity of heart" stigmatize, even indirectly, as he had done, the great Washington and her own peerless husband with the charge of "political heresy"? She undoubtedly greeted this Fourth of July guest with

[29] Correspondence of Abigail Adams, Massachusetts Historical Society, Adams Manuscripts.

cordiality; but we may be sure that she could do so only by masking some of her feelings about him.

Similarly, if Adams and Jefferson met that day, the greetings exchanged were probably even less effusive than usual. Memories of that other Fourth of July must have stirred within them; but the mutual association that they had experienced in the period of which that date was symbolic seemed like something that belonged to another world. The younger man now looked upon the older one as so much under the influence of chauvinists and warmongers as to render most improbable any lengthy extension of peace with honor. The older man, if he still believed in Jefferson's integrity, now thought of him more than ever as one whose talents were spurred and directed by a relentless and potentially dangerous ambition. Both men, of course, were completely mistaken in these estimates. But in any social encounter which took place on that anniversary or at any time during a long period thereafter, outward tokens of friendship would have belied their real attitude toward each other.

In each of the two families, during those early months of the new regime, a wedding was in the offing. At intervals, when the pressures inseparable from their public status eased somewhat, the two fathers contemplated hopefully, and of course separately, these prospective domestic events. Adams' oldest son and Jefferson's younger daughter had found, each of them, a mate; soon they would be standing before a marriage altar, ready to take the traditional vows.

John Quincy was traveling steadily upward, professionally and otherwise. Having been appointed three years before by President Washington as ambassador to The Netherlands, he had served successfully in that capacity until sent to London to aid in the negotiations which terminated in Jay's Treaty. If he did not meet fully, in his representative role, all that was expected of him in the British capital, he carried on there some private negotiations which he came to regard as highly satisfactory. The other party to these negotiations was Louisa Catherine Johnson, one of seven daughters of the American consul in London.

At first John Quincy's father and mother were inclined to doubt the advisability of his union with a young lady whose mother was an Englishwoman and whose long residence abroad had caused some interested persons to wonder if she were an American citizen. But while the young diplomat formally sought his parents' consent, he believed that he was entitled this time to make his own choice freely and he might have resisted parental interference. On July 26, 1797, while the elder Adams and Abigail were en route from Philadelphia to Quincy, the formal ratification of this son's betrothal agreement took place in the parish house of the Church of All Hallows Barking in London. Thomas Adams, who had gone with his brother to Europe, informed his mother that he had acquired an "amiable and accomplished sister." Both parents of the groom accepted gracefully the *fait accompli*. Abigail, making a snap judgment and thinking no doubt of some contrast shown in Abby's experience, in one of her letters had these words of praise for her new relative: "The Young Lady has much sweetness of Temper and seems to love *as she ought*."[30]

On the whole, however, Jefferson was more pleased with his acquisition of a new son-in-law than John and Abigail were in getting another daughter-in-law.

When he learned early in the summer that Maria had accepted the proposal made by her cousin John Wayles Eppes, he tried to express what he called an "inexpressible pleasure." He did so by writing that if he had searched throughout the entire earth, he could not have found one more to his liking as a mate for her.[31] The couple was married at Monticello the following October, the young bride wearing the gown her mother had worn at the ceremony performed more than a quarter of a century before in which she became the wife of Thomas Jefferson. Along with all the other thrills of the occasion for this bride and groom was that of coming into possession of a luxurious coach and four Thoroughbred horses, the latter from the bluegrass country of Kentucky—the entire outfit the gift of the bride's father.

[30] Mrs. Adams to Mrs. Cranch, October 31, 1797, *New Letters of Abigail Adams*, 110.

[31] Jefferson to Martha Jefferson Randolph, June 8, 1797, Randolph, *Domestic Life*, 245.

Disturbed as Jefferson was by the course taken by the ship of state with Adams at the helm, he had only minimum worries in connection with his household. Now more than previously, but still prematurely, he spoke and wrote of himself as a "patriarch." And there were additional excuses for his doing so. His status as grandfather lacked by one numerical point that of his New England contemporary, but it was well established and was being periodically strengthened. In addition to the young charmer Anne and the sturdy hopeful christened Thomas Jefferson, there was now in that domestic circle a winsome toddler named Ellen. Except for the fact that he was a widower, a state in life to which he had become more or less resigned, this father, grandfather, and father-in-law looked upon himself as a very fortunate family man.

Very different at this time was the President's outlook as the head of an expanding family, one who might also have claimed "patriarchal" standing. Both he and Abigail were concerned more than ever as they reviewed over and over again possibilities in the path of more than one of their children and all their grandchildren. Abby's Colonel was roaming about the frontier regions of New York and Pennsylvania, even farther west. For long stretches of time no one having a family connection with him knew where he was. Abby herself was living in near isolation at East Chester, New York, twenty miles from New York City. No longer having complete custody of her sons, she had with her, for much of the time, only her very young child, Caroline Amelia, the red-head of whom the grandmother wrote shortly after her birth, "She mortifies her mother not a little." But the mother's mortification, caused by the color of the little one's hair, was of short duration. For years grandparents and parents alike had wanted the little Smith boys to have a sister. Now they had one, and, as Abigail further reported, she was a "lovely Girl."[32] But her father's main interests were not, it seemed, those of a parent.

In the same year in which Caroline Amelia was born, her Uncle Charles married one of the Colonel's sisters, thereby making that

---

[32] Mrs. Adams to Mrs. Cranch, June 25, 1795, *New Letters of Abigail Adams*, 85. The third child of Colonel and Mrs. Smith, a son, died in infancy.

young lady Abby's double sister-in-law. They with their baby Susan lived in the city of New York, where the young man was seeking to establish himself in his father's profession. His attainment of the marital state had not been followed by any substantial improvement in his manner of life. The reports about him that came to the President's house in Philadelphia were, more often than not, disappointing. One whose heredity and early environment should have kept him in the path of rectitude appeared, at times, to have an aversion to it. In the opinion of his father and mother, the outlook was not very rosy either for daughter Abby or for son Charles. And they must have wondered sometimes what new and prolonged obligations might devolve upon them in connection with the four innocent grandchildren.

For Adams, the business of administering the government was, of course, more immediately pressing, and it could not be attended to indefinitely at Quincy. After a stay there, prolonged as much as possible, he returned to Philadelphia, even though that year's epidemic was still claiming many lives. He was not disposed to risk his health unnecessarily, but he was more concerned about the war fever, a virulence over which the frosts of winter had no effect and to which he himself was not immune. His address to Congress at the opening of its session in November, while fairly moderate in its summary of foreign relations, indicated that some germs of militarism were active in his system.

Following the wedding festivities at Monticello, Jefferson was busily occupied with duties about his farm and in his mansion, the latter emerging slowly from the dream stage into reality. Although Congress had been called to meet on November 13, he did not resume his duties in connection with it until mid-December. Once again at the seat of government, he professed to look upon it in the same way he had frequently done in the past, as a place of "torments." Yet he could describe these mental afflictions as "splendid torments."

Not long after his arrival in Philadelphia, he and the chief of state, who was treading a very uncertain path but still hoping for the best, entered, with all their fellow countrymen, into the hectic year of 1798.

For many weeks the President, members of his cabinet, and members of Congress waited with varying degrees of impatience for reports from the envoys who had been sent to the French Directors. It was during this interval that Adams entertained a group which included the Vice-President. Following the dinner, the President and his highest-ranking guest had an interesting conversation. For a while they talked, as men and women have done ever since commodities were first bought and sold, about the rising costs of living. Then, according to this guest's report of the interview, they "got on the Constitution." Adams elaborated on the theory he had long held that there was need in the government for a Senate that would not be subject to recall by popular vote. He quoted with approval the statement of a certain writer that all the mischief that tyranny could accomplish in an age would be less than what might easily be unloosed in a night by men—and women—practicing anarchy. Did Jefferson need any proof of that truth? Let him look at France, where mobs had actually done more harm in less than twenty-four hours than despotic rulers had done in twenty or thirty years.

When he got back to his writing desk, Jefferson made some notes of this pronouncement. Doing so, he wondered again how this man with whom he had been talking could banish from his mind, as he seemed to do, the memory of tyrannies associated with the name of George III, out of which had issued the Declaration of Independence. And yet no one, as he once more recalled, had supported that Declaration more vehemently and effectively than this same man. Jefferson, bound by restraints of different kinds, kept this written account, as he did some others that came from his pen in that decade, in his most secret files.[33]

At length there came to the President and the Secretary of State the first dispatches from the trio sent abroad, conveying the information that they had not been properly received. The apprehension which these delayed reports aroused in Adams' mind was increased as later dispatches arrived and were decoded, gradually unfolding a sordid story. It centered around "X," "Y," and "Z," as three in-

[33] For Jefferson's record of statements made by Adams on this occasion, see his *Works*, I, 341–42.

dividuals came to be designated, agents of the wily members of the Directory. Through those intermediaries attempts had been made to bribe the American representatives; when the offered bait was rejected, insult had been added to duplicity. Marshall and Pinckney were officially edged out of the proceedings, while Gerry, regarded as more pliable, was informed that he might hold himself in readiness for possible negotiations in the future.

If Adams had been as eager for war as some of his critics, including Jefferson, believed him to be, he would have released this information voluntarily, omitting no ugly detail, and called on Congress to make a martial declaration. He did send to that body what Jefferson exasperatedly called an "insane message." The gist of it was that the mission to France, through no fault of its personnel, was a failure, and that additional appropriate measures for defense should be taken without delay. But only when the Congress requested that the story sent back by the envoys be transmitted in toto to that body did he allow this highly explosive material to get out of his hands. The next development, which could have been expected, was the general publication of the dispatches.

Those who had been fanning the war spirit now quickened the tempo of their efforts. A slogan leaped like lightning across the country: "Millions for defense but not one cent for tribute." A song entitled "Hail, Columbia," written by a young man in his twenties, became the musical expression of frenzied feelings of vast numbers of people. One spring day several hundred marching men made their way along the streets of the City of Brotherly Love, their destination the President's house. There, in full military regalia, the chubby leader met them. They heard him recite the sins of the degenerate French and predict that Divine vengeance would be wreaked upon the Directory. Within a few days Madison wrote—and here he was certainly expressing Jefferson's opinion as well as his own—that Adams' language on that occasion was "abominable" and "degrading" and out of keeping with the character of the "Revolutionary patriot."[34]

[34] Madison to Jefferson, May 20, 1798, *The Writings of James Madison*, edited

However, in the view of the President, as the man primarily responsible for preserving domestic tranquillity, there was a more immediate threat than that issuing from the quintet who were manipulating the controls in France. The more assertive members of the party of Jefferson and Madison—and their numbers were not negligible—began to counter the parades and speeches of the Federalists with demonstrations of their own, amounting in some cases to actual riot. The times called, Adams believed, for a "Day of Public Humiliation, Fasting and Prayer throughout the United States," and such a day was set aside by presidential proclamation. While at the time appointed many of the church meeting-houses were filled for special services, one suspects that humiliation and fasting were not outstanding features of the day's observance. Before it was ended, Adams, who certainly had not omitted his own devotions, heard that certain French immigrants in the capital were planning, in connivance with some of the native population, a macabre climax to the day's events in the form of conflagrations and possible massacre. Haunted as he was by the fear of mobs, he directed that a quantity of firearms and bullets and powder be carried into the basement of his residence and arrangements made to use them at a moment's notice. On the whole, the conduct of Adams and his aides on that day provides an early example in American history of praising the Lord and passing the ammunition.

The rumors were exaggerated, and the day passed without bloodshed. But throughout the country as well as in the capital tension was reaching epidemic proportions. Jefferson, with a wisdom which some members of his party did not show, kept a cool head. While insisting that a resort to arms was unnecessary, that the path to negotiation with France was still open, he counseled his followers to be moderate in their protests against warlike policies of the government. But he saw many evidences of disregard for his instructions. As spring gave way to summer, he became convinced that what he had long feared—armed conflict with France—would break out in the near

by Gaillard Hunt, (9 vols., New York, 1900–10), VI, 321 cited hereafter as Madison, *Writings*).

future. On a day in June, his mood being especially pessimistic, he wrote to a friend that war was "now inevitable."[35]

The opposition to Adams and the course of action to which he appeared to be committed was more than counterbalanced by a popular support unprecedented in his experience. In his renewed belligerence the Yankee President was riding high on a wave of popularity. It did not measure up to the crest of admiration for Washington several years before; but if there had been at that time a poll of public opinion, it would have shown a conspicuous thrust in that direction. On the other hand, as Adams went up, Jefferson went down. And if the cause to which the latter was so thoroughly devoted did not suffer a setback, it was at least brought to a temporary standstill.

Early in the previous winter's social season, Abigail made brief mention in her correspondence of Jefferson's belated arrival in the city. "The Vice-President is come," she wrote, "and dines here today with 30 other gentleman."[36] The contrast between this factual reference to him and her complimentary notice upon his appearance in New York as secretary of state is noteworthy. No longer did she think of him as an important addition to the social circle. However, in one of those winter months he made what she regarded as a negative contribution. He rejected, as she and her husband did, an invitation to the "Birthnight Ball," arranged in recognition of Washington's birthday. There had been no similar observance of an anniversary of Adams' birth, and Jefferson's refusal to share in a function which she thought, with good reason, seemed disrespectful of the President was something to be added to the credit side. Yet her attitude toward him was only slightly mellowed. Referring to his compliance with the proprieties in this instance, she wrote very confidentially to sister Cranch, "Give the d[evil] his due, but lay no more than he deserves to his Charge."[37]

While this bit of spicy counsel was not directed to Jefferson's de-

[35] Jefferson to Archibald Stuart, June 8, 1798, Jefferson, *Works*, VIII. 437.

[36] Mrs. Adams to Mrs. Cranch, December 12, 1797, *New Letters of Abigail Adams*, 117.

[37] Mrs. Adams to Mrs. Cranch, February 28, 1798, *ibid.*, 137.

tractors throughout the country, some of them began attacking him in print and orally as if he were the incarnation of evil and as if he deserved an even more violent use of vocabulary than they were capable of making. Except for a greater measure of emphasis, this attack, in the form of ridicule, abuse, and vilification, was a repetition of earlier attacks. On the part of some of his less hostile critics there was renewal of allegations that his very diet was reprehensible. He had been raised, it was said, on hoecake, and to that violation of good morals he had added the worse offense of partaking, on occasion, of "fricaseed bullfrogs." More contemptuous in spirit was a toast that evoked a hearty response at a public dinner where a number of high Federalists had gathered. It was worded: "John Adams—may he like Samson slay thousands of Frenchmen with the jawbone of Jefferson."

As has been noted, a precedent had been set by Jefferson himself for using Scripture stories and characters in a way uncomplimentary to political leaders. But he probably never heard of this grim, crude toast which encapsuled the bitter feeling of many who belonged to the party of which Adams was the titular head. At any rate, he had no intention of allowing his jawbone to be used for any such massacre.

A discipline imposed upon him by circumstances while he was secretary of state became necessary again. To the best of his ability he had to steel himself, not only against snide references to his cultural background and political philosophy, but also against occasional slander. Old charges were scraped up again. Some persons were willing to spread once more the filthy untruth that the lanky backwoodsman from the hill country of Virginia was not morally fit for public office or even for polite society.

The victim of these libels and quasi-libels was compelled, during that spring and early summer, to sit helplessly in his presiding chair in the Senate while the legislative mill which would presently turn out the Alien and Sedition Bills kept steadily humming. The former measure empowered the President to seize and deport all persons who were citizens of a country with which war appeared to be imminent. The Sedition Bill, as it finally emerged, provided that anyone charged with "printing, writing, or speaking in a scandalous or malicious way against the government of the United States, either house of Congress, or the President, with the purpose of bringing them into contempt, stirring up sedition, or aiding and abetting a foreign nation in hostile design against the United States" would be subject to prosecution under federal jurisdiction. Penalties deemed suitable were spelled out for those found guilty.

The verbs used in this language were rubber words. Moreover, "scandalous" and "malicious" statements about the Vice-President did not, apparently, come within the purview of those operating this legislative machinery.

Adams had not recommended these measures, but he signed them without delay. He lived long enough, however, to attempt to wash his hands of all responsibility for them. Even as he affixed his signature, as a statesman he must have had doubts concerning their wisdom and as a lawyer must have known that in effect they abrogated (in particular the Sedition Act), the Bill of Rights.

Immediately there began what Jefferson called a "Federalist reign of terror." Government agents got busy and jails were opened to receive prisoners whose common offense was that they had acted "seditiously." A Vermont congressman, several New England editors, and a Philadelphia physician were among the more prominent victims of this "terror." All over the country persons who were friends of freedom as well as foes of treason viewed the proceedings with justified alarm.

The man who carried the weight of leadership for the Republicans, while not overly suspicious by nature, came to believe that some of his private correspondence was opened in search of evidence against him. Also, he was sure that spies had been assigned to watch his movements and report on them. Once in the early summer, as he was going to the outskirts of Philadelphia to visit at the home of a friend, Dr. Logan, a man regarded with suspicion by the Federalists, he took a circuitous route with the idea of circumventing government sleuths. Whether or not he exercised unnecessary caution, he encountered no interference on the way.

In fact, the hated laws did not go into effect until after Jefferson had left Philadelphia for another extended stay at Monticello. Very probably any fear that he had of being subject to physical restraint, either in the capital or at home, was unjustified. Those who were ferreting out individuals suspected of sedition or subversion manifested toward him a discretion not characteristic of their usual procedure. After all, he was Vice-President of the United States, one upon whom many looked as a political Messiah. He remained secure in his person. There were never any fetters about his wrists.

Adams, however, remained shackled in the same sense in which he had been, by his own admission, when the mantle of his high office was a very new garment. And one fact which Jefferson had to face was that the mandatory responsibility for the enforcement of obnoxious legislation rested principally upon the shoulders of one who for many years had held a place in the inner circle of his friends.

Throughout the latter part of the summer and fall Jefferson performed routine duties as a plantation owner and carried out plans for the laying of new floors in his house and for an extensive installation of mantels and moldings. But there were more important matters calling for his attention. He took time to translate into strategic action some purposes which were probably formulated while the way was being paved for the Alien and Sedition Acts to be foisted on the country.

In September he spent more than the usual amount of time at his writing desk, composing, almost as carefully as he had the famous Declaration, what came to be called the "Kentucky Resolutions." The basic principle of these resolves was that the several states, in forming the federal union, did not promise or imply "unlimited submission" to the government so created. From this he adduced the proposition, vulnerable from the point of view of many contemporary and later interpreters, that each state had the right to nullify unconstitutional assumptions of power.

The preparation of this document and communications regarding it with a few trusted friends, principally Madison and Wilson Cary Nicholas, were veiled in secrecy. In this undercover discussion much attention had to be given to the problem of launching the Resolutions, in the most effective way, on the perilous sea for which they were destined. At this juncture, the arrival of John Breckinridge of Kentucky at the Nicholas home for a visit appeared almost as a heaven-sent solution of the problem. Breckinridge had been an Albemarle County neighbor of Jefferson, was a current member of the Kentucky Legislature, and a man who saw eye to eye politically with Jefferson and Nicholas. He readily agreed to introduce the Resolutions in Kentucky's law-making body. The chances for adoption were good, inasmuch as that state was a stronghold of opposition to extreme tactics of the Federalists.

In December this approval was formally given, with the deletion, however, of the author's more radical pronouncements. Likewise, in the same month resolutions of similar tenor, but toned down to a lower scale in comparison with the original document, passed the Virginia Assembly.

Thus it happened that some ideas which had been secretly spoken and written within the walls of Monticello were soon proclaimed in substance from two legislative housetops. They constituted the answer, less provocative and vigorous than Jefferson at first intended, to the Alien and Sedition Acts.

Jefferson's connection with these "Mad Resolutions," as Abigail pointedly described them, was indeed anomalous, since he occupied the next-to-the-top position in the federal government. Years passed before the initial part he played in this early championship of states' rights became generally known. But he was successful in respect to his main objective; notice was served publicly—and on the state level, officially—that infringement of civil rights, even if rationalized and legalized by men in high places, would not be accepted in servile fashion. More than that, as people in the backwoods settlements and in the larger village and city communities heard about the Resolutions, the man whose name above all others was associated with democracy received the lion's share of the credit—and the blame. In the sequel, his over-all gain in popularity more than offset his loss.

On Christmas Day Jefferson arrived in Philadephia again. On the seventh day thereafter, as the first hour of another year approached,

189

two groups, made up largely of artisans and other persons who eked out a modest or precarious living, began separately to march to his place of residence. They chanced to meet, coalesced into one company, and led by a band of musicians continued toward their destination. Arriving there, they gave the Republican leader a round of cheers. Shortly the tall, spare figure appeared in a dimly lit doorway, and there was acknowledgment, as much as this leader's aversion to such demonstrations would permit, of lusty and long-continued applause.

As on the occasion of the previous welcome given to him at the time of his entrance into the capital just prior to his being sworn in as Vice-President, there was more than immediate significance in this holiday-mood ovation. In the night air perceptive ears could have heard—and probably did—some motif-notes of prophecy, fulfilment of which would come in the not too distant future.

Even more important in its bearing on events of the next few months than the documents given the imprimatur of two state legislatures was a process continuing during the summer and early fall in the mind of the President of the United States. In that mind a gradual and very meaningful change was taking place in relation to the issue of war or peace.

It was fortunate rather than otherwise that he spent a long period during this portion of his administration in the comparative quiet of his farm home. Far removed from most of those men who for one reason or another were eager for war at any price, he could assess the entire situation with the maximum calmness of judgment of which he was capable. Even the mosquito that bit Abigail as the couple was about to leave Philadelphia in mid-summer may have helped to start a train of events which led to a reversal of the administration's foreign policy. For to that bite was attributed a malady which, although not diagnosed as yellow fever, nevertheless laid low, and for weeks kept low, the lady who was indeed Adams' better half. In turn, her serious illness prolonged his stay in Quincy, adding to the time in which he could ponder without interference the course to take.

While he lingered at home, he was visited by Gerry, who had just returned from France. This one of his appointed missioners imparted to him some pieces of information which did not fit into the picture assembled for him earlier in the year. Also, written communications from Murray, then American minister at The Hague, who was in close touch with important French officials, were in line with Gerry's moderately optimistic report. In them, as in Gerry's statements, were evidences of a change of heart on the part of Talleyrand and his fellow Directors. The chances for an amicable settlement of the quarrel with the French Republic were apparently better than they were represented to be by some individuals purveying second-hand accounts.

Far less bellicose than when he left Philadelphia, Adams returned late in the fall, wondering whether or not he had been used, to some extent, as a tool, and inclined to be more independent in his decisions.

Meeting with his cabinet, he learned that a few members, while having no intention of being "ghosts," had nevertheless written for him a message on the "state of the union," anticipating that he would relay it without much change to Congress at the beginning of its regular session. He promptly revised certain passages having to do with a possible renewal of negotiations with France; and while this revised version did not lack firmness, on the whole it was more conciliatory than the original script submitted to him.

Washington, who had come all the way from Mt. Vernon in symbolic recognition of his emeritus authority as titular leader of the army being fitted for "defense," occupied a place of honor in the hall where Congress met to hear the message. Resplendent in uniform, he helped to create an aura of special dignity for the occasion. There, too, was Hamilton, likewise in uniform, a major general now, proud in the attainment of a long-nurtured ambition. In the war which he thought, and apparently hoped, would be declared in the near future, only Washington, who was in a class by himself anyhow, would outrank him. Jefferson was not present. His farm, his house, the meetings and correspondence involved in his political strategy—these had taken all the time he had alloted to himself for this stay at home—and more. But Congress could manage very well for a time without a vice-president. After his arrival, having learned the contents of the President's address, he admitted that it was "unlike himself [Adams] in point of moderation."[38]

Having asserted to a degree his independence in the formulating of foreign policy, Adams lapsed into a state of mental distress which continued for weeks. On New Year's Day, just after Jefferson had received the nocturnal greetings of some of his followers in the city, the President served punch and wine to callers. But his mood was far from festive. His prediction, made the preceding fall, that the coming winter would be an extraordinarily dismal one for him, seemed to be in the process of fulfillment. Abigail was far away, in touch with him only by correspondence. Although convalescent, she was still unable to make the journey which would bring her to his side. Moreover, he was troubled, more than he had been hitherto, by ugly doubts. Were there men in his circle of advisers, official and unofficial, who, swayed by ambition or by a perverse spirit of factionalism, might not hesitate to undermine his administration even as Abby had warned him? Such suspicions kept gnawing, with rasping insistence, at his mind. For a time he shunned social functions as much as possible. He became, as he admitted, a "solitudinarian."

It is a thousand pities that during those weeks the President and his Vice-President were kept from experiencing a mutual companionship such as that which had meant much to them in past years when they were not separated by party schisms. Each of them, deprived temporarily of the company of loved ones, needed just such a soul tonic as friendly and unhurried visits with the other would have provided. However, Jefferson did not withdraw into a shell of abject loneliness. He spent a part of his leisure time pleasantly with Dr. Benjamin Rush and a few other congenial contemporaries living in the city. But he was not a very happy man. A letter received from his younger daughter affected him, he declared (borrowing from Ossian), like the "bright beams of the moon on the desolate heath."[39]

[38] Jefferson to Madison, January 3, 1799, Jefferson, *Works*, IX, 3.
[39] Jefferson to Mary Jefferson Eppes, February 7, 1799, Randolph, *Domestic Life*, 256.

And Adams repeatedly insisted, in writing to Abigail, that his state was far from blissful. But any helpful contact between the two exiles, one in his existence as a "solitudinarian," the other on his "desolate heath," was as nearly impossible as if they had been living on separate continents, with no facilities for the exchange of ideas.

In fact, the chasm between them, hollowed out by an avalanche of events beyond their control, was as wide and deep as it had been in the previous year.

Unhappy as he was in his nostalgia and anxiety, Adams never swerved from his determination to do his duty as he saw it. In midwinter there came to him, indirectly but authentically, assurance that the French foreign minister would receive an envoy from the United States as the "representative of a great, free, powerful, and independent nation." This was the only additional cue for action that he needed. Summoning all his reserves of moral strength—and they were considerable—and disregarding his cabinet, he sent to the Senate on February 18 the nomination of Murray as special plenipotentiary.

This act was a clear sign that Hamilton's influence in fashioning government policy was waning. It was also a severe blow to the party which that statesman had created out of inchoate material and, after breathing into it the breath of life, had nurtured over a period of years. Jefferson's first reaction to Adams' firmer grasp of the controls of government machinery could have been that it was too good to be true. Actually, he referred to it, in a letter written on the day after Murray's nomination, as the "event of events."[40]

From this time on until near the end of the administrative period, there was a struggle for supremacy in the Federalist camp which at times almost overshadowed the interparty contest. Straightway every effort was made by offended Federalists in Congress, supported by others outside of it, to block approval of Murray's appointment. The sequel was a compromise, in the form that two other men would be named to serve with Murray and that no further move toward negotiation would be made prior to receiving additional, and even more specific, assurance that the three representatives would be received

[40] Jefferson to Madison, February 19, 1799, Jefferson, *Works*, IX, 52.

with proper dignity and respect. There was no doubt, however, that Adams had won, singlehanded, a victory of great psychological value, and the knowledge of it buoyed up his sagging spirits.

Congress adjourned early in March, and very shortly thereafter the Chief Executive, who had given evidence of a new purpose to live up to that rather unpretentious title, started off once more for Quincy, disregarding hints from cabinet members that he should remain at the seat of government. Not long after his departure Jefferson thought it worth while to copy in his private notebook a statement attributed to one of the more combative of Hamilton's followers. It expressed a hope that the horses pulling Adams' carriage might run away and cause his neck to be broken.[41] But all the horses used were manageable, and Adams got back home with unbroken neck and otherwise in fair physical condition.

Jefferson also traveled home in that spring of 1799 with equal safety and eagerness. Once more in the familiar environment, he could see in every direction special needs requiring immediate attention. The floors in his mansion were now stable, but for part of it there was no roof. He wondered if he would ever get it as habitable and comfortable as he wished. And there was the spring planting—an activity that could not be delayed. In a few months another harvesting season would arrive, and in addition to normal seed-time duties it was necessary to begin preparations for harvesting and storing crops.

Moreover, very important letters were to be written, letters to go north, south, east, even west as far as Kentucky. About a year before he had reminded Madison of the potencies latent in pen and ink. "There never was a moment," he had written, "in which the aid of an able pen was so important to place things in their just attitude."[42] The need for help of this kind had not diminished, and Jefferson, using the instrument more powerful than the sword, continued to match his counsel with his practice. The goal before him was a Republican victory in 1800, and the prize, a lure upon which his eyes were undoubtedly fixed, the Presidency. No general ever mapped strategy

[41] *Ibid.*, I, 352.
[42] Jefferson to Madison, April 12, 1798, *ibid.*, VIII, 404.

or deployed forces with greater shrewdness than he displayed during the long interval between the March adjournment of Congress and his December return to the capital. As much as he could, he banned any publicity which might be used in such fashion as to injure his cause.

At Quincy the salty breezes and the village quiet served again as a natural tonic for the nation's chief executive, whose store of vitality had been depleted, as was usual, during the winter months. Feeling no sense of great pressure, he performed routine presidential duties and awaited the issue of unofficial negotiations in progress overseas. The pace of events was very slow, almost incredibly sluggish from the point of view of a twentieth-century American. The sailing vessels carrying dispatches crept, as it were, across the ocean; and to this natural delay was added the effect of such dilatory tactics as Hamilton and Pickering and other like-minded politicians could employ.

Spring and summer and part of the fall had gone by when Adams started again on a long, tiring journey, with Philadelphia his destination, as it had been many times before. But that city was still held in the recurrent grip of yellow fever, and he was advised to stay away from it until the coming of November's frosts. In fact, the cabinet officials, because of the emergency, had found temporary quarters in Trenton. Thus it came about that the Jersey city was the scene of a decisive showdown that followed between Adams and some of his appointees who intended, if possible, to outmaneuver him.

The President's earlier determination to come, if the way should open, to honorable terms with France had recently been bolstered by tardily renewed gestures made by authorities in that country, more friendly than those which had preceded. Rising from a sickbed in Trenton, on which he had languished for a little while after his arrival there, the ailment being described by him as "almost as bad" as yellow fever, he acted as a man whose hands were entirely free to do his bidding.

There followed a series of conferences with Pickering and other cabinet members, also a meeting with the man to whom most of those members looked, incongruously, for leadership—Hamilton himself.

195

In that meeting there was a head-on collision of opinion, the ultimate effect of which was the collapse of one of the Federalist general's cherished plans.

From his dissident advisers Adams secured reluctant acquiescence to a draft of instructions for the new envoys to France, whom he had already selected. Oliver Ellsworth, chief justice of the United States, and William Davie, governor-elect of North Carolina, were slated to serve with Murray. But while the conversations at Trenton were in progress, Adams, like a foxy and resolute card player, gave no hint of his intention to issue the instructions immediately. When, therefore, Pickering and McHenry and Wolcott learned that orders had just been given for Ellsworth and Davie to sail from Newport, Rhode Island, not later than November 1 (Murray was already in Europe), they were more surprised and frustrated than ever before in their relationship with their nominal leader.

Precisely at this point, in the view of a modern historian, Adams came to the "proudest and most masterful moment in his life."[43] If this judgment be questioned, there can be no doubt that by reason of the action then taken the prospect of armed conflict with America's Revolutionary ally was greatly diminished. The statesman who once helped lead the American colonies into a necessary war with England had reduced to minimum proportions the threat of an unnecessary war with France.

In doing so, he toppled the pillars of Federalism, placing himself in position to be politically obliterated by their eventual overthrow. Unlike Samson, he did not, in the spirit of the toast proposed by certain members of his party, slay thousands with a jawbone; but there is a rough parallel between his encounter at Trenton and the final performance of the Biblical hero at Gaza.

Within a few days he was lamenting to Abigail that throughout his life he had fulfilled his duties "weakly and imperfectly." But he never had less reason for directing such a stricture against himself. Some years after the conclusion of this "cold war" he stated that no epitaph for himself would please him more than the simple declara-

[43] Claude G. Bowers, *Jefferson and Hamilton* (Boston and New York, 1925), 438.

tion that he had, on his own initiative and with assumption of full responsibility, made a move which led to the restoration of harmonious relations with France. Many years after his earthly career ended and just a century after this grave crisis in his administrative experience, American history repeated itself, up to a certain point. Beyond that point came what many now regard as an avoidable war with Spain.

As to the effect which the October confrontation of Adams and his secretaries and its issue had upon Jefferson, the records are not very informative. As a party leader, he would have taken, if he had been on the scene, some satisfaction in the spectacle wherein the foundations of Federalism were subjected to such damaging blows. As a citizen, he was certainly pleased with the gradual waning of a war hysteria which he had consistently deplored. If his earlier characterization of the President as an "obstinate individual" needed no revision, he could scarcely have failed to admit to himself that the weight of that Yankee stubbornness had at last been thrown on the right side of the scales.

When the "black frosts" had minimized the dangers of yellow fever, the victor at Trenton rode into Philadelphia, now in its final year as the federal capital. Abigail, who had come on from Quincy, was with him for two days' travel, part of the distance through rain and mud. The couple looked forward to sharing together one more winter and spring in that city. Jefferson, who was seldom punctilious, did not make his appearance until late in December.

During the final months of their concurrent service in this city where their friendship began, the President and Vice-President followed separate paths, just as they had done since Adams' administration had begun. Jefferson continued to find diversion in the company of friends with whom he had no political quarrel, men who shared with him an interest in philosophy and natural science. But more of his free time, of which he had plenty, was occupied with furtherance of the task to which he had already given a large measure of devotion. By conference and correspondence he kept organizing the Republican forces for the impending presidential campaign.

There were times, as there had been often since he entered public service, when it seemed that his greatest desire was to separate himself from all that party leadership involved. It was during that winter that he wrote to his older daughter, "Politics are such a torment that I would advise every one I love not to mix with them."[44] But it was a torment—and the point merits the emphasis of repetition—from which, as a man whose patriotism was spiced with ambition, he was not willing to escape. In that dual nature of his, where for so long loyalty to his country and his party, with recurring desire to reach a pinnacle of success, contended with domestic yearnings, the latter once more definitely yielded.

Adams experienced no such conflict as he viewed the possibility of being relieved of the office which he held by virtue of a three-vote margin in the electoral college. The death of Washington early in the winter reminded him, as it did others, of the final destination of the paths of glory; and by removing from the scene the greatest cohesive force the Federalists had, it increased the odds in favor of a Republican victory in the coming election. Moreover, there were other factors in the prospect which seemed to warrant a prediction that he would not become a second-term President. By steering too far and too often in the direction to which Hamilton pointed, he had alienated many persons not closely affiliated with either party. His share in responsibility for the Alien and Sedition Acts, although overestimated, had cost him the active support of a sizable number of moderate Federalists, including some in his native New England. At the same time, his ultimate decision for peace at any price short of national honor and security ended his usefulness to influential men who were calling a more martial tune, and made him, in their estimate, definitely expendable. More and more, he and Abigail thought with genuine satisfaction of going back to their own home, in its peaceful, rural setting, and staying there for the rest of their lives.

Ironically, the city on the Delaware never appeared more delightful to them than it did during the closing weeks of their residence there. The cold abated and the snow melted earlier than usual. Abigail, enjoying better health than during most of the time she was

---

[44] Jefferson to Martha Jefferson Randolph, February 11, 1800, Randolph, *Domestic Life*, 262.

in Philadelphia, reveled in the sunshine as the days lengthened. Observing the "verdure of the feilds and the bursting of the Buds," she could almost imagine herself in the well-loved garden at home. It was all so different from that bleak autumn of the first few weeks she had spent in the Philadelphia area.

Moreover, there was less anxiety than there had been in some former seasons about the welfare of Abby and her family. The Colonel, recalled from his wanderings by the threat of war, was now an officer of high rank in the army raised to combat aggressors. Through the winter just preceding he had helped, in a military camp in mid-Jersey, to train troops for the war which the militaristic group still insisted was possible. For much of the time he was there, Caroline Amelia, now in her fourth year, was an important member of the President's household as she had been more than once before. Like another Caroline, the small daughter of a twentieth-century President, she was an object of adoring attention. John and Abigail, who as grandparents were not different from the majority in that category, took special delight in the presence of this one of Abby's little flock. In some ways life was wonderful for them during this latter part of their stay in the Morris manson.

But there was one specter which continued to haunt them. By day and by night it repeated the warning that the young republic, to which they had given unstintedly of their time and talents, might be brought to irretrievable ruin by the Jeffersonians. Unusually disturbing was this warning when news came, early in May, that in the state of New York, marked as having pivotal significance, the party of Jefferson had won a decisive victory. Roused by Aaron Burr, a leader almost as shrewd as the master strategist himself, the Republicans, in an election corresponding roughly to modern presidential primaries, achieved a triumph with ominous meanings for all Federalists who had continued to believe, in spite of all assaults upon it, that their power was safely entrenched. Abigail sadly commented, "Out of all this will arise, something which tho we may be no more, our Children may live to Rue."[45]

[45] Mrs. Adams to Mrs. Cranch, May 5, 1800, *New Letters of Abigail Adams*, 252.

On the day the results of the New York balloting were made known in Philadelphia, Jefferson went to call on the President. His errand was strictly official. But Adams showed no inclination to talk on matters of business. Noticeably affected by what he had just heard and ready to make a premature concession, he greeted his visitor in this fashion: "Well, I understand that you are to beat me in this struggle. I will only say that I will be as faithful a subject as any you will have." (Adams knew, of course, that in the United States one person can not be the "subject" of another, but it appears that he still used, at times, certain words and phrases as if he lived in a land ruled by a monarch.)

Jefferson's reply was that the contest then in progress was not a personal one between Adams and himself. He pointed out that Adams favored one set of principles, while he favored another. If both of them were to die that day, two other names would take the place of theirs. There would be, in such event, no change in the operation of the machinery of the two parties. The motion of that machinery proceeded, not from himself or from Adams, but from the principles. To all of which Adams agreed, with the admission that the political battle should not affect their dispositions toward each other.

If someone familiar with the facts we have been relating could have overheard this conversation, he might have thought that the former friendship of the two men was almost, if not completely, restored. But Jefferson concluded his account of the interview with the observation, "He did not long retain this just view of the subject."[46]

A little later that month two important caucuses were held in Philadelphia. In each of them a candidate for President and one for Vice-President were officially designated. (Because of the constitutional provision that was still in force, the choice for the Vice-Presidential post could not be specific, as it now is.) On the Republican side, no one except Jefferson was considered for first place. With the same unanimity, Burr, hero of the recent skirmish in New York, was

---

[46] Jefferson reported this conversation in a letter to Dr. Benjamin Rush, January 16, 1811, *Works*, XI, 169–70.

agreed upon as Jefferson's "running mate," in modern parlance. In spite of opposition from some quarters, the Federalists picked Adams to succeed himself, and then, in what Jefferson called "hocus-pocus maneuvers," decided to run Charles C. Pinckney for second place.

On one of those springtime days Adams and Jefferson met again, this time at a public dinner. There remained only a very small portion of their joint stay in the city where their first meeting took place. General Henry Lee, one of the company present at this dinner, recalled after an interval of some years that Adams' behavior toward the Vice-President was surprisingly cordial. He told how he ventured to remonstrate with Adams after Jefferson had made his departure. Did he not know that this "friend of the people" was a cunning schemer and that his well-polished manner was a cover for motives that were not too scrupulous? The General apparently did his best to make the point that any show of friendliness toward Jefferson was flirtation with danger.

The phrases used in this unsolicited advice, according to Lee's account, were near duplicates of some which Adams himself had more than once spoken or written, but he was now in the grip of another set of emotions and did not take kindly to the admonition. The General was surprised at the signs of irritation which he witnessed. "He [Adams] observed with warmth," we are informed, "that he believed Mr. Jefferson to be more friendly toward him, than many who professed to be his friends; and that he further believed Mr. Jefferson never had ambition or desire to aspire to any higher distinction than to be his first lieutenant."[47]

This conversation took place near the time of Adams' summary dismissal of Pickering and McHenry. Undoubtedly they were included in the group of men whom he thought of as less friendly to himself than they outwardly appeared. At any rate, if we assume that he was correctly quoted, he denied, in a moment of excitement, assertions he had previously made about Jefferson's ambition. Apparently, if the mercurial rise and fall of his feeling toward Jefferson could have been

[47] *Memoirs of the Administrations of Washington and John Adams,* edited by George Gibbs (New York, 1846), II, 366.

charted graphically, there would have been on the eve of this presidential campaign a noticeable up trend.

Early in the summer, a little more hopeful in spirit than he had been a few weeks before but certainly not beaming with confidence, Adams started on a trip which included stops in some places which he had not previously visited. Among them was the burgeoning new capital in the federal district, also Alexandria, in Jefferson's Virginia. On this journey, an early presidential "swing around the circle," he did not win many friends or influence many people. The blinds of the coach in which he rode out of Philadelphia were drawn—evidence that he wished to be concealed from the public gaze. Later, when in other places he was seen and heard, he did not establish that rapport with the citizenry which for many politicians has been the open sesame to preferment. In the areas which he visited there was a strong tide of opinion running against him, and he was not emotionally equipped to cope with it.

At the time of early harvest, he rejoined Abigail at Quincy. He had been so eager to get there that on some days he had covered, almost incredibly, a distance of fifty miles or more.

Jefferson made his final exit from Philadelphia a few days before the President's semisecret departure. As he rode away from the city where, in what now seemed to him a long-ago time, he won an enduring fame, he did not, we may presume, cast any lingering looks behind. He was eagerly anticipating his forthcoming meeting with Maria, whose health had not been the best during the winter months. Traveling a roundabout way, he went first to her home at Mount Blanco, near Petersburg, and thence brought her to her native place for a few weeks' stay at that more salubrious elevation. There, while the bloom of springtime lingered, ensued another unhurried family reunion. It was good for the spirit of this partially reluctant candidate to be home again. There was no place like it. And yet the little city in the making along the Potomac, representing what it did, appealed to him as it has to many other political leaders in our American history.

As he followed once more the familiar routine of a family man and plantation manager, he must have thought often of what he had seen and heard and done since going for the first time as a delegate to the Continental Congress; also, of the long, tangled skein of events, with its twisting and incomplete patterns, shaped by the forces of history during that quarter-century interval. Looking forward, he faced the probability that he would be chosen president of the country and thus given a mandate to take over the reins of government from his former friend. But the country was at peace, and the outlook bright for that political ideal which he had been proclaiming. In a broad reference to the next "chapter of events" he had recently informed one of his correspondents, "I am in the habit of turning over its next leaf with hope."[48]

He had supervised, directly and indirectly, preliminary work for the coming struggle. Now that he had withdrawn to the quiet of his little mountain, his role would still be like that of a general. Surveying from that eminence all sectors of the battle, he would give signals for charges and all the logistic movements that might seem necessary. There would be other demands upon his time, but he would continue to inspire with that magic which he possessed in rare degree. As a deist and a democrat, he fully understood that the outcome was, and should be, beyond his complete control. He was content to let the hand of Providence operate through the American electorate.

[48] Jefferson to Mrs. Angelica Church, January 21, 1800, Randolph, *Domestic Life*, 260.

CHAPTER V

Tumult along the Potomac

W ITHOUT POMP OR CEREMONY John Adams arrived in Washington on November 1, 1800. As rotund and obese as ever but with shoulders sagging under the weight of invisible cares, he rode in to the permanent capital to fill out the few months remaining of his term of office. In his retinue there were only a servant and a secretary, the former mounted on a horse which kept near to the lumbering vehicle, the latter seated with him and sharing the frequent bumps which the ride provided. Of pageantry, which on some former occasions had been arranged in his honor, there was not a trace.

Even the house which was being built as a residence for him and his successors in the presidential office offered a cheerless prospect. Outwardly it appeared magnificent in contrast to the hutlike structures which housed many of the city's inhabitants, but inside it gave the impression of being barely habitable. Many of the rooms were not yet plastered, and in those which had been, there lurked an ague-breeding damp. There was a "great scarcity of firewood, not a single apartment finished, and the unfinished East Room was used to hang the family washing."[1] Moving into this house after living in the Morris mansion, Adams was scarcely an object of envy. But he established himself as comfortably as possible, and began waiting for Abigail's arrival with even more eagerness than usual.

She had stayed in Quincy for about two weeks after he left, probably because of serious illness in the home of one of her sisters. One day, while on the last stage of her journey to the new capital, she and her traveling companions were lost for a while in woods not far from

---

[1] W. B. Bryan, *A History of the National Capital* (2 vols., New York, 1914–16), I, 376.

Baltimore, but were fortunate enough to find their way before nightfall to the home of Major and Mrs. Snowden, whose acquaintance
Abigail had made in Philadelphia. There they remained overnight.
It did not detract from the First Lady's appreciation of the generous
hospitality that this host and hostess provided that they were, as she
reported, "true federal characters." Early in the afternoon of the next
day, riding in the chariot sent out from Washington to convey her the
last few miles, she arrived at her destination. She described it as a
"castle of a House." But she noted that all the near landscape was
"wild, a wilderness."[2]

The thought of living within the walls of this huge "castle" for a
while, even if it were only a few months, appealed to her as little as it
did to her husband, but the two of them took full possession, and
Abigail soon turned the place into something like a home. There was
a more cheerful glow in each of the thirteen fires without which the
big house, at that time of year, would not have been livable. For Abigail's harassed spouse the burdens of life were appreciably lessened.

Jefferson made his entry into the crude little settlement on November 27. Congress had already convened, meeting in the recently completed north wing of the edifice that crowned Capital Hill. There, a
few days before, Adams had delivered in person what could have been
called his "swan song" as President. The object of a greater interest
than he had been on the occasion of his former appearances as Vice-
President, Jefferson took his place, once more tardily, at the vantage
post which by constitutional provision had been his for almost four
years. He had found a temporary home at the boardinghouse of
Conrad and McMunn, south of the Capitol and separated from it by
a distance over which his long legs could take him in a very few minutes. It was the most pretentious place of its kind in the unfamiliar
seat of government. The meals served there, however, were not like
those to which he was accustomed at home.

Thus for another period, and for the last time, the couple from
Quincy and the widower from Monticello were housed in the same

[2] Mrs. Adams to Mrs. Cranch, November 21, 1800, *New Letters of Abigail
Adams*, 256–57.

city, exiles from home in response to a call which each of them was bound to heed. Many a time during that late fall and the winter following Jefferson must have looked out over the wide, swampy plain that stretched toward the unfinished house in which his former friends were living, and wondered what shape the future would take.

By the time government officials and those members of their families who had embarked on the venture with them were in the process of getting adjusted, after the manner of pioneers, to the new environment, presidential electors had been chosen in most of the states. While the final outcome remained in doubt, Jefferson and his followers had good reason for thinking that a majority of voters throughout the country had registered a preference for him as President.

In the campaign which preceded, issues were beclouded with even greater animus than that shown four years before. On the face of it a contest between Federalists and Republicans, actually it was a three-way clash, Hamilton and many of his "regulars" being even more eager to shelve the official leader of their party than they were to defeat the "visionary" of Monticello. It developed into a scramble for electoral votes which, in terms of sheer virulence on the part of some of its participants, has seldom been duplicated in American history.

Visiting New England in the early summer, Hamilton began attempts to divert popular support from Adams to the South Carolinian who was ostensibly the party's choice for Vice-President. Jefferson could have agreed with one statement which Hamilton made on this tour, that a revolution would be the consequence if Pinckney were not elected. But the revolution which Jefferson envisioned was not to be brought about by a military coup; rather a peaceful, orderly, and thoroughgoing shift in control of all the processes of the federal government.

In the late summer and fall Hamilton continued the efforts to carry out his purpose, for the most part by semisecret machinations. The President, however, did not remain ignorant of the stratagems directed against him. Yet there was no viciousness for which he was directly responsible. Only those who knew him best were aware of his growing preference for Jefferson as his successor, if the alternative were anyone indebted for the honor to a man who had sometimes used him as a puppet.

As between Adams and Jefferson, Hamilton's choice was the Republican leader against whom he had often stood in bitter opposition. "I will never be responsible for him [Adams] by my direct support," he said, "even though the consequence should be the election of Jefferson. If we must have an *enemy* at the head of the government, let it be one whom we can oppose, and for whom we are not responsible."[3]

Not long after Hamilton's appearances at New England hustings, a report was widely circulated that the man whom both Adams and Hamilton, by a strange irony, would prefer, under certain circumstances, for the presidency was irrevocably out of the picture.

It was late in June when a news item, so called, went out from Monticello to the effect that one of Jefferson's Negro servants, who allegedly bore the name of Thomas Jefferson, had died. This report did not travel far before being twisted, intentionally or otherwise, into the misinformation that Jefferson himself had expired. On the last day of the month a Baltimore newspaper printed the following statement, with some reservation, however, about its authenticity: "The man in whom is centered the feelings and happiness of the American people is no more."[4]

For several days thereafter similar items appeared in Philadelphia and New York papers, in a few cases the accompanying reservation being very mild. On July 9 the *Columbian Centinel* of Boston, a staunch Federalist organ, printed the story, raising no question regarding its truth and refraining from any praise of the man who was supposedly dead and buried. Very probably Adams read the item, and, if he did, certainly shared in the prevailing relief that followed the publication, two days later, of the truth. By the time Jefferson learned that the rumor had spread throughout a large part of the country, in some places as a fact, there was no need for him to dismiss it as being greatly exaggerated, but he was inclined to look upon the printing of the unverified report as a deliberate attempt at deception

[3] Hamilton to Theodore Sedgwick, May 10, 1800, Hamilton, *Works*, X, 375.
[4] *Baltimore American*, June 30, 1800.

on the part of a few men whose regret would not have been over-whelming if the original report had been correct. "I am very much indebted to my enemies," he wrote, "for proving by their recitals of my death that I have friends."[5]

It was fortunate for the cause of democracy, to which no major victory could yet be credited, that Thomas Jefferson remained very much alive during that campaign. Without him the ultimate success of the "bloodless revolution," as he described it, would have been as questionable as the earlier one, in which blood was freely spilled, would have been without George Washington.

While it was in progress, he very seldom got farther from his mountaintop residence than the limits of a short canter on his favorite mount. He spent long hours at his writing desk, devoting many of them, we may suppose, to the preparation of his comprehensive *Manual for Parliamentary Practise*. This was a self-imposed task issuing out of his experience as presiding officer of the Senate. More-over, scarcely a day went by when he did not share in the ordinary seasonal activity of a farmer. On the twenty-fourth anniversary of the Declaration of Independence he helped finish the harvesting of a record wheat crop. A casual observer of his daily routine unfamiliar with current happenings would never have supposed that he had more than an average stake in a contest which was claiming the atten-tion of multitudes, all the way from the Canadian border to the Georgia swamps.

But long experience had brought the unobtrusive magic of his leadership to a point near perfection, and throughout the summer and fall he made good use of it. "He knew how," one of his modern admirers has stated, "to lengthen the fuse far from the point of explosion."[6] And in many parts of the country there were "explo-

[5] Jefferson to Pierre Samuel du Pont de Nemours, July 26, 1800, *Correspondence between Thos. Jefferson and Pierre Samuel du Pont de Nemours, 1798–1817*, edited by Dumas Malone, (Boston and New York, 1930), 18. The full story of the spread of this false rumor is told in Charles Warren's *Odd Byways in American History*, (Cambridge, 1942), 127–35.

[6] Claude G. Bowers, "Jefferson, Master Politician," *Virginia Quarterly Review*, Vol. II (July 1926), 331.

sions" set off, on his initiative, by long-range connections. The pent-up forces of many who had caught his vision were being released in ways that promised—or threatened, depending on the point of view—the overthrow of the party that had hitherto held control.

It is not strange, therefore, that Jefferson began to feel once more the brunt of hostile criticism on the part of some men whose power and prestige were being so directly menaced. Hamilton, engrossed as he was with his main objective, continued to denounce democracy and belabor its exponents. His natural distrust of what was later called "government of the people, by the people, and for the people" had developed into an antipathy which was almost bitter. Less prominent Federalists used all means of propaganda to convince others that Jefferson was still tainted with "Jacobinism," a poison brewed, they kept on insisting, from roots grown in the cultural soil of France. And it was from this sector that there came the most unscrupulous and malicious attacks of the entire struggle.

A few of the more rabid followers of Hamilton refurbished and released vicious canards about Jefferson the man and the citizen. Undisturbed by the fact that their charges had no substantial basis, they contended that he was personally unfit to be President and was presumptuous in allowing himself to be named as a candidate for the office. Although wounded in spirit by repeated slanders, the object of them remained steadfast in the determination to let his past life and record be the only public answer.

But it was the charge of outright godlessness rather than that of moral turpitude or of utter incompetence as a "dreamer" and a man under the influence of an alien culture that the more vocal of the Federalist pamphleteers and pulpiteers emphasized as the major count in their indictment. There have been other presidential campaigns in which a candidate has been attacked because of his religious affiliation, but it was Jefferson's fate to be subjected to verbal abuse on the ground that he had no religion at all. It was bad enough to be a "fanatic in politics"; it was worse to be an "atheist in religion." Hamilton had coupled these allegations,[7] and many parish ministers took up

[7] Hamilton to Jay, May 7, 1800, Hamilton, *Works*, X, 372. In the sentence from

the latter charge and repeated it so frequently that Jefferson, while unwilling to answer his detractors openly, nevertheless semiprivately accused these accusers of scheming to obtain the "establishment of a particular form of Christianity thro the U.S." To one believing, as he did, in religious freedom as thoroughly as in civil liberty, such an establishment would be intolerable. In the midst of the struggle, where for so many so much seemed to be at stake, he prepared a statement which later came to public attention and has outlasted anything else written or spoken during its progress: "I have sworn upon the altar of God, eternal hostility against any form of tyranny over the mind of man."[8]

While the outcry against Jefferson as an alleged atheist came from all directions, it came most often from Adams' New England; but Adams himself, for whose Puritan ancestors God had been the recognized Creator and Lord of their lives and was the object of his own veneration, took no part in it. He knew very well that there was no basis of truth in sermons and tracts portraying Jefferson as a godless man lacking in moral integrity. While he did not publicly express disapproval of such tactics, as an honest man he must have been disturbed by the extensive use made of them.

His appearance of detachment from the contest was almost on a par with that of his nominal opponent. After the early summer tour on which he visited the "city of great expectations" on the Potomac, he was the guest of honor at a few ceremonial occasions in Cambridge and Boston; but for the most of the time in which campaign propaganda, true and false, was being channeled out to the voters, he tarried quietly in and around his comparatively secluded farmhouse. As in many previous summers, he was, on the basis of outward appearance, only a moderately successful farmer with a better than average education, having no interests other than his hay and corn and oats and livestock, and, of course, his books and his family.

---

which the phrases are quoted Hamilton did not refer to Jefferson by name, but the context makes it clear that he had Jefferson in mind.

[8] Jefferson to Rush, September 23, 1800, Jefferson, *Works*, IX, 148. This sentence is inscribed, in letters two feet high, on a circular frieze within the Jefferson Memorial in Washington, D.C.

Adams, too, was a natural target for criticism, some of it malevolent, although scarcely ever on the ground that his religious beliefs were unorthodox, or that he was morally deficient. From the Republican front came repetitions of charges often made against him since he returned from foreign duties. All possible variations of the theme that he favored a form of government modeled on the British monarchy, were advanced. Only a deep-dyed "Angloman," it was argued, would have endorsed the Alien and Sedition Bills. And while those legislative mistakes were nearing the edge of oblivion as far as enforcement was concerned, Adams' part in their inception and the use he made of them provided ammunition for the militant hosts of democracy.

The leader who had been most influential in the framing and adoption of the Kentucky and Virginia Resolutions did not openly discourage this form of attack, but at one point in the campaign word came down from Monticello headquarters to key workers that they should turn the attention of voters to the alleged "vast" expenditures and extravagant practices of Adams and his subordinates in office. Thus the issue of "big spending" became one of the focal points of controversy, as it has many times since in such contests.

The shrewdness of the Republican candidate as a tactician was not matched by Hamilton, who, while still the master mind on the Federalist side, was giving evidence of some slackening of his prowess. Concerned as he was to oust Adams and get in his place someone more consistent in practicing principles of "sound government," he manifested more zeal than wisdom. And he became the leading participant in a performance which backfired, affecting the final result in a way opposite to that which was intended.

In the early fall, as the day of decision in the several states was rapidly approaching, he prepared and had printed a fifty-page pamphlet, in the form of a letter, to which was given the title, *The Public Conduct and Character of John Adams, Esq., President of the United States*.[9] Its thesis was that the conduct of the said President had been such as to retard rather than advance the welfare of the country and

[9] This pamphlet is published in Hamilton, *Works*, VII, 309–64.

that his character, while not lacking in patriotism and not barren in respect to good motives, nevertheless had "great intrinsic defects" which made him unfit for the high office he was occupying. Hamilton's plan to have this pamphlet circulated exclusively among his influential personal friends went wrong. In some manner Burr obtained a copy not long after the printer's ink had dried and forthwith arranged to have certain passages relevant to his purpose published in journals of his own party. In some places the effect, as in the case of the Mazzei letter, was like that of a devastating physical shock.

Adams' determination not to tangle with Hamilton in a public exhibition of anger almost cracked, but for one whose ire sometimes seemed uncontrollable, he withstood the inner pressure surprisingly well. In private letters he expressed indignation in incisive terms, but for a record of wider circulation he persuaded himself to postpone defense to a later date. Not always an astute judge of the fitness of things, he was certainly correct at this time in believing that an immediate reply would be out of order. To one friend he wrote: "It would take a large volume to answer him [Hamilton] completely. I have not time, and if I had, I would not employ it in such work while I am in public office. The public indignation he has excited is punishment enough."[10]

It is certain that there was widespread indignation, but there is some uncertainty about the extent Jefferson shared in it. We know that he studiously avoided any public approval of the statements made in the pamphlet, although he agreed with some of them. In line with his policy in the preceding presidential campaign, he refused to make an issue of Adams' personality and character. Credit belongs to both men for refraining from any attempt to defame or belittle character, and for abstaining from controversy unrelated to the issues of policy which divided the two political parties.

Jefferson viewed the "revolution," as he kept thinking of it, with growing satisfaction and optimism. In the early fall he remarked that even in Connecticut, a state which he thought of as "clergy-ridden," the movement was progressing "with very unexpected rapidity." In

[10] Adams to Dr. Ogden, December 3, 1800, Adams, *Works*, IX, 576.

many of the other states, such amateurish samplings of public opinion as his field workers could make were encouraging. One of the Republican stalwarts in Virginia visited Jefferson's home county several weeks before the election and soon afterward reported to a correspondent, "I have sunk into perfect security since I have reconnoitred ye state of our forces and the weakness of the enemy."[11] If the party standard-bearer did not lapse into such overconfidence, he was fairly certain, as indeed he had been for some time, that the country was returning, like a prodigal, from the far country to which he felt it had strayed.

Early in December, Jefferson in his Washington boardinghouse and Adams in the great "Castle" which he had the dubious privilege of occupying first of all began getting the election returns which they had been eagerly awaiting. Brought in as rapidly as the steeds of post riders could travel, the early reports indicated that there would be no landslide, but the two principal contenders had reason to believe that within a few days a definite result could be announced, so that each could discern the nature of his immediate future.

Among the states reporting early was Jefferson's Virginia. He could not have hoped for a more sweeping victory there. Approximately four out of every five votes in the general election had gone his way. Similar reports came up through the mountain passes from Kentucky and Tennessee. From the opposite direction came the news, surprising very few, that in New York all the electoral votes would be given to the Republican candidate.

Entirely different were the results in New England. That bastion of Federalism stood firm. The manipulations of Hamilton which were calculated to undermine Adams in the area where he was known best had been completely unsuccessful. Even Connecticut, about which Jefferson had been hopeful, went along with its sister states of the region. New Jersey and Delaware lined up solidly with New England, while in Pennsylvania, Maryland, and North Carolina there were divisions.

[11] M. H. Woodfin, "Contemporary Opinion in Virginia of Thomas Jefferson," in *Essays in Honor of William E. Dodd* (Chicago, 1935), 59–60.

To all observers—and many indeed were nervously watching—it appeared near the middle of December as a neck-and-neck race. At that time the outcome seemed to depend on the tidings from South Carolina, which were delayed. When at last they were received, a Washington paper, in a story faintly resembling a modern news "flash," informed its readers that the electors chosen by the South Carolina legislature would be favorable, without exception, to Jefferson and Burr, and went on to declare, "Mr. Jefferson may, therefore, be considered as our future President."[12]

The newspaper was, of course, correct in this statement, but the contest was not over; more than the shouting remained. There were hurdles, some of them quite formidable, to be crossed before the official announcement of the winner could be made. In less than a week it was known that an "absolute parity," in Jefferson's phrasing, existed between Burr and himself. To each of them, according to the best calculation, were credited seventy-three of the coveted electoral tallies. Therefore, the House of Representatives would have to decide whether Adams would be succeeded by the Monticello statesman or by the New York lawyer colonel, who had been slated, as definitely as possible in the clumsy constitutional procedure then followed, for the vice-presidency.

A "lame duck" now, although the phrase had not yet been coined, Adams heard these later returns with the appearance of unconcern. From his barren residence on Pennsylvania Avenue came no statement admitting defeat or expressing interest, but after the certainty of his rejection was established, he revealed in private correspondence some portion of his feelings about the two men between whom the choice of his successor was yet to be made. Writing to Gerry, he declared that if Jefferson were elevated to the presidency, it would be "nothing wonderful"—a concession that might be interpreted as a subtle, left-hand compliment to his erstwhile friend. But the spectacle of Burr, a "dexterous gentleman" rising "like a balloon filled with inflammable air" over the heads of others, some Federalists and some Republicans, whose talents as leaders had been demonstrated

[12] *National Intelligencer* (Washington), December 12, 1800.

and whose experiences in the councils of government had been extensive even though misdirected in some cases—that, indeed, was astonishing.[13]

Jefferson naturally considered the possibility of having one or more helpful discussions with Adams in the event of a decision favorable to himself in the House of Representatives. In the time that would elapse before the day appointed for turning over the reins of government, the retiring President would have opportunity to do more than a little mischief. Jefferson was troubled with some misgivings; the temperamental Adams might do just that. Writing to his chief lieutenant, he revealed his intention, when and if his victory was assured, to "aim at a candid understanding with Mr. A. . . . I hope to induce in him dispositions liberal and accommodating."[14] Here we may anticipate to the extent of stating that this hope was dispelled by developments that were only partially foreseen. The President was not responsible for all of these. But nothing could have been farther from Jefferson's wishes, as the most likely choice for President and then as President-elect, than the course of action followed by "Mr. A." during this closing phase of his administration.

Most disturbing were certain rumors spreading like threatening tentacles. Apparently well founded, they were to the effect that a group of Federalist partisans, smarting under the blow they had sustained, were determined to thwart the will of the majority of voters. It was whispered, and later more openly stated, that these men would use force if necessary to put someone of their own choosing in the top executive position. This threat, with the counterthreats it induced, seriously affected the habitual serenity of the philosopher statesman. There were others, also, who shared his fear that soon there might be a tumult along the Potomac which would in some ways resemble the interracial clashes of which they had heard, fairly common in the recent history of frontier settlements beyond the Alleghenies.

These were some of the unprecedented features in the posture of

[13] Adams to Gerry, December 30, 1800, Adams, *Works*, IX, 577–78.
[14] Jefferson to Madison, December 19, 1800, Jefferson, *Works*, IX, 159–60.

public affairs as a new year, and with it a new century, arrived. On January 1, Adams, assisted by Abigail, was host at a full-dress reception in the mansion which in a few more years would be called the "White House." Over the winter roads the callers came, among them men who had shared the frustrations and the accomplishments of the administration that had failed to win a vote of confidence, also a few who were to have a part in the new government. It is natural to assume that among the latter was the principal designer of a model that was the first of its kind in American history, a political party soon to be subjected to the test of experience.

Indeed, the probabilities add up to approximate certainty that Adams and Jefferson, also the latter and Abigail, on the opening day of the nineteenth century stood once more face to face. For those who derive satisfaction in thinking, with some play of imagination, about meetings under unusual circumstances of well-known personalities of the past, this one, unreported but presumably actual, affords ample scope for such an exercise. One may picture the man still President, wearing a black velvet suit and contrasting white waistcoat, the ensemble fitted out with such conventional accessories as powdered wig and brightly polished knee and shoe buckles, exchanging civilities with his one-time intimate friend, now the voters' choice as his successor. Close to that picture would be one of the mistress of the dreary mansion extending a formal greeting to the personable gentleman whom she once described with adulatory superlatives, and receiving from him the polite verbal tokens appropriate to the occasion.[15]

Accepting the evidence that such meetings took place on that day and considering the likelihood that it was the last of many social functions in which they were brought together, we cannot but wonder what they said and thought at the time. If they conversed at any length, to what extent did they speak of their past associations? And were there any fleeting conjectures, silent or spoken, about the future, as it might affect their personal relationships? Nothing has been recorded which would give any clue to the answers to such questions.

[15] Brief mention of this reception is made in Bess Furman, *White House Profile* (Indianapolis, 1951), 29.

As the new year advanced, social amenities in government circles were virtually halted, and the attention of most Washington residents, official and otherwise, was centered in the procedures still necessary for the election of a new President. If there were some who believed that the choice was, in one sense, in the lap of the gods, they knew that in a more immediate way it belonged to mortals thrust into a potentially explosive situation. Nor were the local inhabitants alone in experiencing mingled excitement and anxiety. From far and near came a horde of visitors, the curious and the concerned, overtaxing sleeping accommodations in the new settlement. These outsiders joined with many interested persons living in the little city in observing as well as they could the preparations for an extraordinary function of government.

It was a time for intrigue—much of it sinister and all of it centered about members of the House of Representatives. As the day appointed for decision, February 11, drew near, there was a new angle to the threat which had aroused Jefferson's apprehension after the fact of a tie between Burr and himself was established. A report circulated that if the Federalist scheme to make Burr President failed, a law would be passed declaring by *fiat* that John Marshall, lately made Chief Justice by President Adams, would be the next chief executive. Along more than one "grapevine" route came the word that if such an attempt were made, troops would be marched into the federal city under orders of Republican governors and force would be used to prevent any illegal usurpation of power.

Jefferson and a number of other citizens interested in an orderly transition were less sure than they had been early in the winter, when victory was hailed prematurely, that the "revolution" would be bloodless.

Day after day, as the tense interval shortened, Adams persisted in his attitude of aloofness. If he had chosen to use it, the weight of prestige belonging to his office, along with that which he could privately exert, might have been sufficient to avert the prolonged struggle that followed. But a chance visitor from some remote corner of the earth, personally unconcerned about the outcome, could scarcely have appeared less interested. There was no evidence, for the time being, of any willingness on his part to accept gracefully one certainty that lingered among many doubts—that his candidacy to succeed himself had been unsuccessful.

Physically he seemed in better condition than he had been at many times since as "heir apparent" the succession had devolved upon him. Abigail, whose eyes were keen to detect any symptoms of bodily disorder, reported in mid-winter that he had enjoyed good health since moving into the drafty mansion. And after she started back to Quincy, preceding him by a few weeks, he sent to her this assuring word: "I sleep the better for having the shutters open, and all goes on well."[16] But it is probable that another factor in his situation contributed more to the restfulness of the presidential slumbers than opening window-shutters at night and letting in fresh air—a new-fangled notion. Chagrined as he was because of the election results, he knew that a heavy burden of care would soon be lifted from him. Composing himself for the night, he may have told himself that he had no responsibility for what might happen on the hill beyond the muddy terrain bordering the street marked on the blueprints as Pennsylvanie Avenue. Perhaps he dreamed peacefully, on some of those February nights, of the scenes of his youth and early manhood.

Nature was in one of her tempestuous moods as members of Congress assembled on February 11 for the proceedings that signalized the beginning of the end of this long campaign. Snow gales swept along the streets and threw up a white screen about the Capitol. Representatives of the states and of the people, having battled their way through the storm, entered the chamber of the upper house and at the stroke of noon subsided into comparative silence. Shortly the formal certification of election returns began. In expressionless tones, such as might have come from a reading clerk, Vice-President Jefferson announced the results state by state, and then calmly declared that, there being a tie, it became the duty of those elected directly by the people to make a choice.

The men who now shouldered this onerous responsibility filed

[16] Adams to Mrs. Adams, February 16, 1801, Adams, *Letters Addressed to His Wife*, II, 269.

soberly back to their desks. They were preceded by their Speaker, huge Theodore Sedgwick, whose strong attachment to the Federalist party made it difficult for him to be an impartial presiding officer. His face flushed as up the aisle a group of men assisted invalid Joseph Nicholson, a Republican member from Maryland. Rather than miss his part in the drama of that day, he was risking his life, fever-ridden as he was. By his side was his wife, in charge of arrangements to make him as comfortable as possible and prepared to give him his prescribed medicine. The hardy pair was ready to make a lengthy stay, if necessary. It was not generally expected that this battle of ballots would be brief.

The voting was by states, and no one could be declared winner until he acquired a majority in at least nine of the state units. The result of the first ballot confirmed predictions. The tellers announced it: eight of the component units were for Jefferson, six for Burr; Vermont and Maryland each reported a tie. In his physical weakness, Nicholson was using a leverage of power to keep Maryland from going to the "dexterous gentleman" who was at this stage, by a strange irony, the hope of a number of conniving Federalists.

The polling of the members continued throughout the afternoon, the ranks on both sides holding fast and unbroken. With the approach of the winter night, the fury of the physical elements outside abated, but there was no sign of an end to this struggle within the darkening chamber. Presently servants lit the candles in the wall sconces and placed tapers on the desks.

All night long and for hours after daylight came, the increasingly weary but unflinchingly resolute representatives stayed at their posts, marking down their choices at intervals. Twenty-four hours and thirty ballots after the first test of strength, these men, who had become in large degree custodians of the nation's immediate future, gave themselves a much-needed respite until the following day.

On that day and on the Saturday and Monday following, actual balloting was reduced to a minimum, allowing time for lengthy parleys in suspense-filled rooms; but there was no immediate change in the voting. After nearly a week of wire-pulling and nerve-fraying and temper-ruffling the count remained the same as that reported by the tellers at the conclusion of the first ballot: eight states for Jefferson, six for Burr, and two void because of a tie.

On one of those days Jefferson called on the President. "We conversed," as he phrased it later in a reminiscent narrative, "on the state of things." Adams was reminded by his caller that the "state of things" was not good. The plot being incubated by a few irreconcilable Federalists might hatch any day, even any hour. In that event, an interregnum would be declared and chief executive power lodged in Marshall or some very "dark horse" illegally chosen. The sequel to this action, Jefferson intimated, might well be anarchy, a reign of lawlessness endangering life and property throughout the country. Adams could use his influence, so he was told, to frustrate a purpose conceived in desperation by certain members of his own party. As tactfully as he could, Jefferson pointed out that considerations more important than partisan ones should constrain the President to take some positive action.

Then, according to Jefferson, Adams "grew warm." If this warmth did not mount to the feverish height reached in a few outbursts on previous occasions, it was of sufficient intensity to surprise, if not to shock, the visitor. That visitor was addressed with a frankness that went far in the direction of vehemence. Nothing like it had happened in innumerable conversations between the two men throughout their long acquaintance.

Adams bluntly declared that Jefferson should give assurance to the right persons that his election would not be followed by certain exercises of power which the Federalists greatly feared, such as wholesale dismissal of officeholders and initiation of policies which would affect the navy adversely or might threaten the nation's financial security. The implication was that the giving of such promises would insure a speedy break of the deadlock.

This sentiment was delivered, it appears, more in the manner of a lawyer arguing before a jury than in that of a friend pleading with a friend. Jefferson's rejoinder was that he could not enter upon the presidency with his hands tied by specific commitments: "I will not come into the government by capitulation. I will not enter on it, but in perfect freedom to follow the dictates of my own judgment"—so he quoted himself. Adams' next remark, probably not soft spoken, was that things would then have to take their own course. Immediately Jefferson changed the subject, and as soon and as gracefully as he could, he took his departure.

According to his report of this conversation and its abrupt ending, it was the first time that the two of them had parted with "anything like dissatisfaction."[17] Perhaps it was the last time that they spoke to each other. There is no record of any meeting between them thereafter.

Jefferson's plea did not produce any visible results. Whether Adams influenced his caller in telling him what he ought do remains doubtful. Much that happened in the Capitol's side rooms during the days of ineffectual balloting was never made public. But sometime during the week end that brought a lull in the struggle, General Samuel Smith, acting as intermediary between leading Federalists and Jefferson, obtained from the latter what were regarded as assurances substantially the same as those which the President had urged him to give. Word was passed around to representatives of the party still in power that Jefferson had privately "capitulated" at those points where, up to that time, he had been uncompromising.[18]

As side lights upon the situation in which our two leading characters were involved, it seems fitting to interject here a few observations about the conduct of Hamilton and of Burr and some of his supporters in this critical period. The outstanding Federalist genius used his influence, directly and indirectly, to prevent the election of the man he called the "Catiline of America." Definite proof is lacking, but it seems most probable that he helped to swing a few votes to the candidate whom he said he ought to hate, on whom he had pinned the labels of "fanatic" and "atheist." He based this preference on the ground that "private consideration" should be subordinated to

[17] Jefferson wrote his recollections of this meeting in a letter to Rush, January 16, 1811, Jefferson, *Works*, XI,170–71.

[18] For a brief but authentic record of moves made during the final days of the struggle leading up to the election of Jefferson, see Schachner, *Jefferson*, 658.

the "public good." And he appears in a much better light in this emergency than at certain other points in his career.

Burr was not lacking in the arts of intrigue, and may well have sought to capitalize on the opportunity which the situation presented. He had assured Jefferson, while returns coming in from the various states indicated that the margin of victory for the winner would be close, that neither he nor any of his friends would attempt to divert to himself a vote that was not his. If later, when the chance of capturing the big prize seemed better, he made any tempting overtures to members of the House of Representatives, they were ultimately without effect.

Least credit-worthy of all who played roles in this drama were members of that small group of partisans who postponed as long as possible acceptance of the majority decision of the electorate. Whether or not Adams could have influenced them to take a more reasonable course, these "extremists" offer, in the words of a competent critic, "one of the most flagrant examples of putting the interests of party above those of country."[19]

Their intransigence finally gave way not only because of reports that Jefferson had yielded on certain matters of policy, but also under pressure of some of the facts confronting them. One such fact was the presence and attitude of crowds hovering about the Capitol, unofficial representatives of average citizens. The die-hards became aware that tolerance of the long delay was running out. Daily the threat of mob action became greater. On the thirty-sixth ballot, taken on Tuesday the seventeenth, the Federalist from Vermont withdrew, and the one from Maryland put in a blank piece of paper. Accordingly, those states went into Jefferson's column. As the other twelve states kept their respective lines, the burly Speaker was forced to announce the culminating result: ten states for Jefferson, four for Burr, and two left, by their own volition, out of the count.

Now, most certainly, the next President would be Thomas Jefferson, the next Vice-President Aaron Burr. Almost immediately, Jeff-

[19] Dumas Malone, *Jefferson and the Ordeal of Liberty* (Vol. III of *Jefferson and His Time*, Boston, 1962), 502.

ersonians began celebrating the triumph of their candidate in all the ways their ingenuity could contrive. As the dusk of the February day that brought that triumph descended, windows along New Jersey "Avenue" and other lanes of traffic glowed with festive lights. Later in the evening some of the celebrants joined in a series of toasts which included one expressing the wish, in the spirit of generous victors, that the public might long remember the patriotic services of John Adams.[20] In other cities, especially those in which Republicans were numerous, arrival of the couriers bringing the eagerly awaited news was followed by the ringing of bells, the firing of salutes, and in some taverns and homes extraordinarily convivial demonstrations.

But the news came to Abigail as a harbinger of evil. She was in Philadelphia, en route home, when the tidings reached that city. She heard the bells of Christ Church adding their volume to celebration of the election of "an infidel," as she referred to Jefferson in writing to the man she had left behind.[21] While still in Washington, having little doubt of the outcome, she had made clear her feeling about it in terms that echoed those used recently in many pulpits. "Have we any claim to the favour or protection of Providence," she inquired rhetorically of her sister, "when we have against warning, admonition and advise Chosen as our Chief Majestrate a man who makes no pretentions to the belief of an all wise and suprem Governour of the World, ordering or directing or overruling the events which take place in it?"[22]

Grounded in the faith as she was, she may have found it difficult to believe that the "suprem Governour" had ordered, or was overruling, this particular event.

But as she continued her last lengthy journey, she could not forget the farewell call this "infidel" had made on her. He had been especially friendly. In his conversation there was the same charm which she remembered from the early years of her acquaintance with him.

[20] *National Intelligencer* (Washington), February 20, 1801.

[21] Mrs. Adams to Adams, February 21, 1801 (Massachusetts Historical Society, Adams *Papers*) quoted in Smith, *John Adams*, II, 1062.

[22] Mrs. Adams to Mrs. Cranch, February 7, 1801, *New Letters of Abigail Adams*, 266.

He inquired solicitously about John Quincy and assured her of his continuing willingness to render any possible service to the absent diplomat or to any member of the Adams family. These remarks of her visitor did not assuage her fears for the public welfare, but they revived in her, for the time, a feeling of moderate friendliness toward him.[23]

Compelled now to fend for himself in the "home of the Presidents," Adams became once more a recluse, yielding to moods of mingled bitterness and pessimism. He was more than ever the victim of forebodings unrelated to religious bias. Actually, the impression he had given to observers in the weeks just preceding, of a lack of interest in the current excitement, was false. He had done all in his power, including the appointment of Marshall as Chief Justice, to minimize the evils which, as he previewed the course of events, might accumulate when "visionary schemes" and "fluctuating theories" were put into practice. In the few days of authority left to him he continued to forestall as much as he could the calamities which he feared would be unloosed following the impending innovation in government.

Congress had passed a bill, and he had signed it, providing for the setting up of district courts to supplement the Supreme Court. Undoubtedly the machinery originally authorized for the administration of judicial functions was already inadequate. But Jefferson thought, correctly or incorrectly, that back of the installation of new machinery at that time was a determination that Federalists should wield some power in the new era. After the event of February 17 more than a few of the members of Adams' party were as adamant as the President himself in the intention to do everything possible to protect themselves in the deluge of misfortunes which might descend upon them and upon the country after March 4. And those of that number who were in Congress watched for opportunities to make the most of the power advantage which was still theirs.

[23] Mrs. Adams to Thomas Boylston Adams, February 3, 1801 (Massachusetts Historical Society, Adams Papers), quoted in Smith, *John Adams*, 1061. See also letter of Mrs. Adams to Jefferson, October 25, 1804, *Adams-Jefferson Letters*, I, 281.

There was no lack of opportunity of this kind for the men who sat in the upper house. Throughout the last days of his tenure, on up to the evening preceding Jefferson's inauguration, Adams kept sending to the Senate nominations for federal offices, including the newly created judgeships. The individuals so named were persons about whom there was no suspicion of sympathy with the "radical" Republicans. Confirmations followed as regularly as if they were dollars being rung up on a cash register. Even some of the President's good friends disapproved as they watched him bestow governmental "plums" upon men whose chief qualification, in many cases, was their party loyalty. As was natural, his political adversaries directed new and sharp shafts of criticism toward him. Albert Gallatin, an ardent Jeffersonian, but freer from bias than many other contemporary observers, wrote to his wife that she could have no idea of the "meanness, indecency, almost insanity" which characterized Adams' official conduct at the time.[24]

On the day after the House of Representatives reached an ultimate decision, Jefferson, communicating with Madison, stated with some restraint, "Mr. A. embarrasses us."[25] A few weeks later, the embarrassment having developed into something like bitterness, his protests regarding these actions of "Mr. A" became more emphatic. He had been "indecent" in piling up nominations "after he knew they were not for himself, till 9 o'clock of the night, at 12 o'clock of which he was to go out of office."[26] In another letter he also labeled as an "outrage on decency" the making of these appointments, "crowded in with whip and spur from the 12th of Dec., when the event of the election was known."[27]

It was the first time in their long acquaintance that Jefferson had harbored a deep personal resentment against Adams. And while after a time he made little or no room for it, he continued to believe that the outgoing President had taken unfair advantage of him.

[24] Albert Gallatin to Mrs. Gallatin, March 5, 1801, Henry Adams, *Life of Albert Gallatin* (Philadelphia, 1880), 265.

[25] Jefferson to Madison, February 18, 1801, Jefferson, *Works*, IX, 183.

[26] Jefferson to Rush, March 24, 1801, *ibid.*, IX, 230–31.

[27] Jefferson to Henry Knox, March 27, 1801, *ibid.*, IX, 237.

By almost complete agreement of those competent to judge, he was justified in feeling and believing as he did. Charles Francis Adams, who was sparing in adverse criticism of his grandfather, admitted in his biographical narrative that these appointments of "sound" Federalists constituted a "stretch of authority," in no way to be thought of as a "safe measure" in popular government.[28]

In general, Adams' administration of his office in those closing weeks was not very praiseworthy. Associated with his feverish haste to salvage something from the wreckage of his party was the continuing bitterness caused by his political defeat. But a very worthy constraint helped to shape his course of action. Being John Adams, he was motivated by what he deemed patriotic considerations even more than by personal pique or partisan attachment.

Madison protested that the President in his official behavior did not "manifest a very squeamish regard to the Constitution."[29] But if all the facts had been generally known, Madison himself and Jefferson as well could have been charged with a similar lack of "squeamishness." Early in that winter, when the "Father of the Constitution" and the author of the Declaration of Independence were troubled with apprehensions about the "dissolution of the government and the danger of anarchy," the two of them agreed upon, and were prepared to endorse publicly, a proposal that was entirely outside the pale of constitutionality. It was to the effect that, if the situation should become more acutely critical, the two candidates whose votes were tied would summon jointly the newly elected Congress and then place upon the lower house the responsibility of electing a President.[30] As the retiring President and his successor had done during the years of the Revolution and throughout all the intervening period, they shared now in a primary concern for the perpetuity of the Republic.

Most fortunately, the ship of state was not wrecked upon reefs of any kind. And the Constitution, which was soon to undergo some

---

[28] Adams, *Works*, I, 620.

[29] Madison to Jefferson, February 28, 1801, Madison, *Writings*, VI, 417.

[30] See Jefferson's letter to Tench Coxe, December 31, 1800, *Works*, IX, 162–63, and Madison's letter to Jefferson, January 10, 1801, Madison, *Writings*, VI, 410–16.

repair work, continued to be the sheet anchor of American liberties. Moreover, when the passage of a little time had given Adams and Jefferson a better perspective, each became more generous in assessing the other's motives throughout the period just reviewed.

Adams' actual exit from public life was scarcely graceful. It was probably before the cock crowed on the morning of March 4 that he denied by his actions claims upon him that were justifiable on the basis of precedent and of propriety. When daylight came, he had started on the final one of his many long journeys, his coach threading a muddy way toward Baltimore—and Quincy far beyond. He would have no part in the ceremonies connected with the triumph of the man whom an ungrateful people had preferred to himself.

He and Jefferson were not to see each other this side of eternity, but there was yet much to be added to the record of their mutual dealings. Some parts of that uncompleted story would extend beyond the limit of ordinary probability. On that March day those of their contemporaries who were interested in the course of events on the government level might well have predicted that each of these men would live out the remainder of his life without any friendly recognition of the other. In such prediction they would have been very much mistaken.

"One of the most interesting scenes a free people can ever witness," as it was described by an observer, was enacted within the walls of the Capitol at the hour of noon on that March 4.[31] Jefferson, having walked the few hundred yards from his boardinghouse, was ushered into the Senate chamber, a room too small to accommodate comfortably the fortunate persons who managed to secure admission. After sitting for a few emotion-packed moments in the chair which he had recently occupied as Vice-President, he rose and proceeded to read his carefully prepared address. He did so in low tones, scarcely audible to those in the rear of the assembly room.

In this inaugural statement, couched in simple, eloquent phrases, there was no mention, even indirectly, of his predecessor, now removed from the scene as far as eight hours or more of arduous travel

[31] Mrs. Samuel Harrison Smith to Miss Susan B. Smith, March 4, 1801, *First Forty Years of Washington Society*, edited by Gaillard Hunt (New York, 1906), 25.

could take him. There was acknowledgment of the blessings of an overruling Providence who takes delight, the speaker affirmed, in the "happiness of man and his greater happiness hereafter." (This was a subtle disavowal of the label of infidel with which Abigail and many others of his opponents had tagged him.) To close up the "circle of our felicities," the new President said, it was necessary only to maintain a "wise and frugal government" which would "restrain men from injuring one another," refuse to take "from the mouth of labor the bread it has earned," and in general leave the people of the country to the unregulated pursuit of peaceful objectives. Linked with these broad statements of policy was the not-too-accurate flourish: "We are all Republicans; we are all Federalists." This was a natural effusion for such a man to indulge in at such a time. But those who could give close attention got the impression, as it was intended they should, that citizens who differed with Jefferson politically would be treated justly. Most of his hearers looked upon him as one who had brought them and their fellow citizens to the verge of a Promised Land—a feat that more than compensated for his limitations as an orator.[32]

The personal felicities of the man who on this occasion publicized his faith and purpose were almost full-orbed, more nearly so than at any time since he became a widower.

Each of his daughters was living happily after her marriage, at least with as few disruptions of marital bliss as the average wife experiences. On the same level of President Jefferson's satisfactions were the accumulating "honors of grandfatherhood," a phrase he was to use in private speech and correspondence. Although Maria had lost her first-born, her sister had added to the tally of the younger generation of Randolphs. The child named Cornelia was almost old enough now to romp with her older sisters and her brother. For them and his daughters this "patriarch's" affection, almost feminine in its nature, remained unchanged. And the blessings which their reciprocal love brought to him were as immeasurable as they had ever been.

To few men, indeed, have the bonuses of Providence been given

[32] Jefferson, *Works*, IX, 195, 197.

in greater number than to this beneficiary as he came to a pinnacle in his career—a pinnacle which he had been viewing, in the manner of a mountain climber, for years. His spirit, of course, was not free from scars, marks made by personal bereavement and by party strife, but there was scarcely a trace of open wounds. In bountiful measure he was enjoying not only honors pertaining to the venerable head of a family clan, but also those of an eminently successful leader of men.

In contrast, the shortage of domestic felicities on Adams' part was greater than ever before. Astrologers of the time might well have attempted to prove, by making use of their zodiacal charts, that planetary influences were especially baleful at this time for the rejected leader. The indisputable fact was that the "slings and arrows of outrageous fortune" were being hurled toward him in great number as he approached the end of his long public service.

Many of them were responsible for worry, privation, and grief centering about members of his family. One of the fears that had beset him was that the change in government might place John Quincy's career in jeopardy. Either in ignorance or disregard of Jefferson's assurance to Abigail that he would help her son in any way possible, the father sent word to that son, then serving as minister plenipotentiary in Prussia, to relinquish his mission and return home. The message, which amounted to an order, was intended to circumvent a summary dismissal, an action which Adams seemed to think his successor might take.

Moreover, there were times during that winter season, as there had been for years, when thoughts about the fortunes of Abby and her brood of children came like a fusillade from an "outrageous" enemy. No appreciable improvement could be seen in the prospects of his daughter and her sons and daughter. It seemed to him that such a dutiful lady, offspring of a couple who could have claimed for themselves the virtues of their Puritan forebears, deserved something better in the form of a home than she had received. He did the best he could for her in his official capacity by nominating the Colonel as surveyor of the District of New York—an action to which the pliant Senate gave assent. But he had little hope that this act of helpfulness would bring about any permanent change in his son-in-law's improvident ways.

For the unmarried son, Thomas, the future, if not bright with promise, was at least free from threatening clouds. He was slowly establishing himself professionally, and, while less brilliant than some other members of the family circle, was a man of steady habits. But for some time there had been no opportunity for that father-son companionship which had often been helpful to both of them in Philadelphia. When Abigail bade her husband good-bye and started homeward in response to his own urging, there were left with him only the servants and, on occasion, a small group of advisers. Many times in the past Adams could have witnessed to the truth of the Scripture affirmation, "It is not good for man to be alone"; but never could he have done so more heartily than during his last days as President.

Worst of all in this well-filled category of troubles was a bereavement that came in one of those winter months. Death claimed the young man Charles.

Nothing had happened in recent years to indicate that this middle one of his three sons might, after all, fulfill the promise of his youth. He kept going the hard way taken by transgressors who allow reason and judgment to be dethroned by liquor. Neither his marriage nor the birth of two daughters availed to stay him in a course which led downhill, physically and morally, and terminated in his untimely death. It was while his father and mother were together in Washington that news of his passing arrived. In the spirit of David lamenting over Absalom, the stricken father wrote to Thomas, "Oh that I had died for him if that would have relieved him from his faults as well as his disease."[33]

As he took French leave of the Washington scene and as, in his own words, he "trotted the bogs five hundred miles" northeastward, he was still reeling from the impact of defeat in the late contest, also that of domestic tragedy. And in respect to his country's future there were

[33] Adams to Thomas Boylston Adams, December 17, 1800 (Massachusetts Historical Society, Adams Papers) quoted in Smith, *John Adams*, II, 1053.

lingering doubts and dreads. He looked forward, as he had never done before in many journeyings, to the peace and security of home.

There is an interesting bit of history, more personal than general, that takes the form of an epilogue to the narrative of the campaign of 1800 and of the tumultuous crisis which followed.

In his haste to get out of Washington, Adams left behind a few papers which he had carefully laid away. Certainly he would have taken them if the circumstances attending his departure had been normal, but this oversight became indirectly the occasion for conveying his good wishes to the "friend of the people," whom he had ceased to think of as his own friend.

On the first Saturday night after Jefferson was sworn in, the papers which had been overlooked were handed to him. It was evident that they belonged to Adams and were of a personal nature. Straightway he forwarded them to their owner and with them a note of explanation. Stiffly enough, the note began: "Th: Jefferson presents his respects to Mr. Adams." Then followed a brief statement of the occasion for it and a polite conclusion, formally affirming his "high consideration and respect."[34]

On one of the days which kept Adams indoors because of a "northeaster" shortly after his return home, this note and the accompanying papers were delivered to him. His acknowledgment, phrased in less formal terms than Jefferson had used, contained no hint of asperity. He explained that the papers related to the funeral of Charles. In the "flower of his days," this one of his own flesh and blood had been "cutt off," not by the "whim of Providence" but by tragic human willfulness; as he stated it, by "causes which have been the greatest Grief of my heart and the deepest affliction of my Life." Then he remembered that Jefferson, not having a son, could never experience an identical bereavement, but he could not withhold the expression of a sincere wish, that nothing "in any degree resembling" his own loss would ever happen to his associate and former companion.

Strangely enough, if one may judge on the basis of this almost friendly communication, those fears for his country's welfare which

---

[34] Jefferson to Adams, March 8, 1801, *Adams-Jefferson Letters*, I, 264.

only a few weeks before had troubled Adams had disappeared. As if they had been lost somewhere in the bogs between Washington and Peacefield, there was in this bit of writing no suggestion that they now disturbed his peace of mind. Even in his own New England he could report a "perfect Tranquility" on the part of the people, in contrast to the violence of the physical elements, which had continued day after day since he returned home. In respect to the federal union, he was surprisingly optimistic. Perhaps he reflected that while the chance to do so was his, he had done much to safeguard its future. At any rate, he concluded, "I See nothing to obscure your prospect of a quiet and prosperous Administration, which I heartily wish you."[35] One gets the impression that Adams was trying subtly to make some amends for his disregard of the amenities on March 4.

The real Adams, refreshed physically and mentally, was beginning to look more objectively on the picture within the frame of which he had been for years conspicuously included. Jefferson, not naturally inclined to nurture grudges, was soon thinking more kindly of his former comrade in patriotic service. But neither of them could foresee, just as none of their acquaintances could, how the fabric of their lives would be further intertwined, as on an extended loom, in the years that lay ahead.

[35] Adams to Jefferson, March 24, 1801, *ibid.*

CHAPTER VI

The Patriarchs

O N NEW YEAR's DAY, 1812, Adams spent a part of his time writing a letter to Jefferson. It was the first direct communication between them in more than a decade. The antecedent circumstances suggest that this act may have issued from a resolution made in keeping with a common custom of attempting to improve one's mode of life as a new calendar year begins.

It was a rather delicate task for a man who had made his full share of fumbles in the game of life. On the whole, he performed it admirably, his achievement being on a par with occasional successes belonging to that part of his career which was devoted to diplomatic labors.

We have seen this scion of the Puritans sensitive, in varied situations, to the call of duty. Now he felt morally obligated to take the initiative in getting personal relations between his former friend and himself back on the old footing. But there was nothing abject or apologetic about the approach he made.

He had already sent to Jefferson, or was about to send, two volumes containing lectures which John Quincy Adams had delivered a few years before at Harvard College. Probably the choice of this particular peace offering, if such it could be called, was not made at random; rather, by a deliberate intention, to be mildly and indirectly reproachful. Certainly some paternal pride was involved. John Quincy's father had never forgotten that the writer of these lectures was removed from a federal office in consequence of a general order issued by Jefferson as President.[1] Now he whimsically referred to his

---

[1] Upon returning from Europe in the spring of 1801, the younger Adams obtained from a federal judge a position as commissioner of bankruptcy. It was his removal from this office, although effected without Jefferson's direct knowledge and approval, that widened the break between his parents and their former friend. See page 240 below.

little gift as "two Pieces of Homespun." He followed this bit of description with what could have been interpreted as a verbal thrust, not exactly playful. The manufacturer of this "Homespun" had "*in his youth*"[2] been honored by Jefferson's attention and kindness.

To the paragraph about the contents of the package which Jefferson would shortly receive were added two others. One of them contained a few items of information about other members of the Adams family. The other conveyed the felicitations of the season. "I wish you Sir," he wrote, "many happy New Years and that you may enter the next and many succeeding Years with as many animating Prospects for the Public as those at present before Us."[3] If Abigail had been called upon to use her talents as a letter writer in the composition of this missive—a supposition that must be ruled out altogether—the gesture of reconciliation could not have been made in a better way.

Exactly one month later Adams was sitting by a fireside in his home, sharing its comfort with the middle-aged lady for whom his usual form of address at this time was "my daughter Smith," the Abby of earlier years. A servant came in with the mail. In the bundle was a letter postmarked "Milton, 23 Jany 1812." About the handwriting on the outside was something familiar. Surely, Adams thought, no one but Jefferson could have written that address, an opinion in which "Daughter Smith" concurred when the letter was handed to her. But how had it happened that the name "Milton" was stamped on the exterior of a letter from far-off Virginia, if it really came from there? And that was only part of the puzzle. It was hard to believe that in less than two weeks a person living not far from Boston could hear directly, especially at that season of the year, from anyone living a considerable distance south of the Potomac.

The little mystery was soon cleared up. Virginia also had its Milton, a little hamlet on the Rivanna River a few miles east of Monticello; and, as Adams learned, it was the outgoing point for some of Jefferson's correspondence. As for the remarkable speed with which

2 Italics mine.
3 Adams to Jefferson, January 1, 1812, *Adams-Jefferson Letters*, II, 290.

the letter came through, there was a simple explanation: The government postal system had become more efficient.

Adams was pleased with the speed-up in the transmission of mail. It would facilitate communication with any distant friend. But the tone of Jefferson's response, more than the promptness of it, strengthened the resolution Adams had begun to carry out. There was no longer any doubt about the Sage of Monticello's willingness to resume, as much as geography would permit, the cordial relationship which had once meant so much to both of them. In his response there was not a word hinting at bitterness of spirit. The specimens of "Homespun" had not yet arrived, but there was expression of thanks for them. Massachusetts, he admitted, could produce better goods of this kind than Virginia.

If Adams ever chuckled, he must have done so when he read that admission. It is even conceivable that "Daughter Smith" heard him say, "I would like to see Jefferson when he learns what that 'Homespun' really is." But as he read on, that same "felicity of expression" which he had once given as a reason for insisting that Jefferson write the Declaration of Independence struck him. Again the words came like the tread of a marching army, advancing, however, on a friendly mission: "A letter from you calls up recollections dear to my mind. It carries me back to the time when, beset with difficulties and dangers, we were fellow-laborers in the same cause. . . . Laboring always at the same oar, with some wave ever ahead threatening to overwhelm us and yet passing harmless under our bark, we knew not how, we rode through the storm with heart and hand, and made a happy port."[4]

Thus, in this initial exchange there was something more than polite generalities. As these retired statesmen began a correspondence unique in its content and in the setting which history provided for it, there was an approximate equivalent to a warm handclasp. Adams told Jefferson in his letter of New Year's Day that his esteem for him had been long and sincere, and subscribed himself "your Friend and Servant." Jefferson concluded his reply with this statement: "No circumstances . . . have suspended for one moment my sincere esteem

---

[4] Jefferson to Adams, January 21, 1812, *ibid.*, II, 291.

for you; and I now salute you with unchanged affection and respect." Both men seemed more concerned with conveying heart-felt sentiments than with literal exactness.

And so it came to pass that the two of them who, in the younger man's figure, had once been fellow-oarsmen renewed their contact with each other. Of course, neither could foresee the length of the earthly span that yet remained for him, but now they had more to live for. Ere long letters were passing between them with a greater frequency than at any time since they had corresponded about pirates, whale oil, tobacco, bankers, loans, a constitution, and a revolution, a quarter of a century before.

Preceding this reconciliation and having a remote connection with it were some letter exchanges in which Jefferson was one of the principals. For a time Adams had only partial knowledge of these communications, in some of which much was wrtten about him. All of them add to the interest with which the few who are familiar with the story view it in retrospect.

Jefferson's younger daughter, the "Polly" who as a child had been taken to Paris against her will and as a young woman was known formally for a few years as Mrs. John W. Eppes, like her mother lacked the physical stamina which makes for longevity. While she was still a rather youthful matron, those who knew her best began to fear that her days on earth were numbered.

In the second winter of Jefferson's occupancy of the President's house, she and her sister spent some time with him there. This joint visit was a happy event in the life of a man compelled to spend much of his time away from home. But neither of the daughters could establish a permanent residence in the federal capital. As the next winter season drew near, an approaching "blessed event" for each of them made it advisable for them to forego life with father in the President's mansion. When Martha's time came, she and the "new bantling," as the grandfather referred to the latest addition, emerged from the experience with normally healthy prospects; but the later appearance of Polly's "little Maria" was followed by the mother's rapid decline.

Yielding to her father's insistence, Mrs. Eppes, along with her husband and small son, had transferred residence to Edgehill—only four miles from Monticello. One day in the early spring of 1804, she was carried on a litter to her native place in the hope that the change might be beneficial. But there was a pallor in her cheeks that remained unaffected by Monticello's vernal breezes, and the medical help available could not for very long ward off a blow which had the aspect of inevitability. On an April morning Maria died. Thus the family circle was narrowed still farther.

For hours her father, who had come home early in that month, sat alone with his grief. We are told that for much of the time in the days that followed there was an open Bible in his hands. Gone forever were some of the fondest hopes that the human spirit can cherish. This was the fifth time that death had snatched away a loved member of his family. Thinking of how for many years he had been the fond father of two daughters, he gave this expression to his bereavement: "Others may lose of their abundance, but I, of my want, have lost even the half of all I had. My evening prospects now hang on the thread of a single life."[5]

As the ensuing weeks went by, many letters of condolence came to his desk. Among them was one from Quincy. The writer was not the man who, had there been no interruption of their friendship, would have been prompt in sending assurances of sympathy. When the news of Maria's death reached John and Abigail, the former resisted any inclination he may have had to write to the father who was going through a valley shadowed in the same manner as the one which he himself had traversed not many years before. But his wife could not maintain a stolid silence. She could not erase the memory of the rebellious, motherless child she had befriended years ago. Now those recollections constrained her to an action against which one part of her nature probably protested. For the first time in many years she wrote to Jefferson.

As charitably and compassionately as she could, she assured him that the news had caused her to mourn with him "most sincerely."

[5] Jefferson to Gov. Page, June, 1804, Randolph, *Domestic Life*, 302.

She called his attention to the fact that she, too, had tasted the "bitter cup." "How closely entwined around a parents heart," she wrote, "are those chords which bind the filial to the parental bosom." And she assured him of her "ardent wish" that he might have the comfort which comes from the "only source calculated to heal the wounded heart—a firm belief in the Being: perfections and attributes of God." Whether or not she still considered Jefferson an atheist, she thought it appropriate to recommend to him the consolations of religion.

The sting in her letter was reserved for its close. Very pointedly she concluded with the statement that she had *once* taken pleasure in subscribing herself as Jefferson's friend.[6]

In his reply, Jefferson apparently made no attempt to hide his mingled emotions. He begged her to believe that nothing had ever happened to cause any lessening of his esteem for her character. Always he had valued her friendship and "fully reciprocated" it.

Having gone this far in the effort to get back in the lady's good graces, he proceeded to discuss at some length his relations with her husband. There was only one act of Adams' public life which he had thought of as being "personally unkind" toward himself. The appointments Adams had made during the closing days of his administration, a few of them even on the final night, elevating to responsible positions some of his own political enemies, could not be sanctioned by "common justice"; but after brooding over that unkindness for some time, he had come to think of it as "something for friendship to forgive." "I forgave it cordially," he assured her, and stated that he still had for Adams a "uniform and high measure of respect and good will."[7]

It may be admitted that Jefferson was unusually tactless in mentioning this bit of past history in replying to a communication of sympathy. His excuse for doing so was that he felt the need of "being unbosomed." While his forgiveness was undoubtedly genuine, the recollection of these appointments still rankled. The opportunity to express his feelings about them was too good to be wasted.

[6] Mrs. Adams to Jefferson, May 20, 1804, *Adams-Jefferson Letters*, I, 269.
[7] Jefferson to Mrs. Adams, June 13, 1804, *ibid.*, I, 270.

If he did not anticipate that this part of his letter would ruffle the Quincy matron, his failure to do so would seem strange, in view of his long acquaintance with her. It would have been unnatural for her to let this criticism of her husband, tempered though it was with benevolent sentiments, go unanswered. Her retort was prompt and vigorous. In making the appointments to which Jefferson objected, her John had been motivated, she maintained, only by considerations of what was best for the country. Moreover, she argued, evidently in ignorance of some of the facts, that at the time the appointments were made, there was no certainty that Jefferson would be chosen President. Was that not a proof that "personal unkindness" was not intended? Having explained to her own satisfaction the conduct at which Jefferson had taken umbrage, she launched an offensive of her own. She, too, had something to forgive.

A man named Callender, whose talent for making scurrilous accusations had earned for him a jail sentence during the Adams administration, was pardoned by Jefferson within a few months after he became President. Since Adams was a special target for Callender's venom, loyal Abigail now leaped at the opportunity to let Jefferson know what she thought of this action. Callender, she declared, was a "wretch," a "serpent," a "viper." The remission of a part of the penalty imposed upon him was, she insisted, a "public approbation of his conduct." She wrote indignantly: "Sir, [the pardon of Callender] severed the bonds of former Friendship and place you in a light very different from what I once viewd you in."[8]

Jefferson's reply to this charge was, in part, a masterpiece of finesse. No one more than himself deplored the "scurrilities" of which certain writers and printers, some of them Republicans, others Federalists, were guilty. He had always been incapable of such conduct himself, had never stooped to approval of it. The same was true of Mr. Adams, to whose personal worth he himself had given consistent testimony. But, strangely enough, he did not admit having any knowledge of Callender's share in publicizing libels about the former President. He had pardoned all who were prosecuted and convicted

---

[8] Mrs. Adams to Jefferson, July 1, 1804, *ibid.*, I, 271–74.

under the pretended "Sedition Law." At this point he became very direct. That law was a "nullity," a violation of the Constitution as palpable as if "Congress had ordered us to fall down and worship a golden image." Quite candidly he informed his critic that this wholesale pardon was without reference to whether the beneficiaries of it were wretches or not. The only question which concerned him was this: Were they sufferers under the unwarranted and despised statute?

Abigail's legal acumen, which, as has been noted, her husband earlier recognized by giving her the sobriquet of "Portia," was still active. In her next letter she very astutely made a point which a constitutional lawyer might have emphasized. Did he, she asked, have any power as "Chief Majestrate" to annul a law because he did not like it? If he had, there was no difference, she argued, between a "republican and a despotic Government." For her that question was merely rhetorical. She held to the opinion that the "power which makes a Law, is alone competent to the repeal," and that decision regarding a law's validity "devolved upon the suprem Judges of the Nation." Jefferson's rejoinder was the Constitution itself gives the chief executive the power to pardon, and that nothing in that instrument permits judges to interfere with the exercise of that power in respect to violations of statutes which he considers to be null and void.

Although she was by no means the loser in this argument, Abigail was ready by this time to end it. She did so with the sarcastic comment that Jefferson had exculpated himself, in his own judgment, from all blame in connection with the Callender affair.

But she had another account to settle with him, if possible. She turned to a grievance involving maternal rather than conjugal pride. Why had Jefferson, early in his administration, removed John Quincy from a position to which he had been duly appointed? The effect of this action upon her was like that of a "barbed arrow"; and it was all the sharper because of the solemn assurance given her, on the occasion of that final visit in Washington, that he would do everything in his power for herself and for members of her family. The answer was that he never had any knowledge that her son held the position, that when, in a transfer from state to federal authority, the power of making nominations of the kind was given to him, he would have preferred John Quincy over a number of others suggested for the post. Abigail accepted his explanation at its face value, but rather tartly remarked that a part of his defense was what lawyers would call a "quible."[9]

In this correspondence between the former First Lady and the current head of the nation, the latter was given every reason to think that her opinion of him had been revised downward. It is not surprising that he got the impression that she would never again think of him as a "candid and benevolent Friend." With one exception, her references to friendship between them were phrased in the past tense. The exception was made, oddly enough and rather obliquely, in the letter containing caustic comments about the pardon of Callender. It was in the form of a Scripture quotation: "Faithful are the wounds of a Friend." In other contexts a suppressed magnanimity came up toward the surface only to be submerged again. But while this candid exchange did not result in a *rapprochement*, the effects were salutary for both correspondents. For Abigail as well as for Jefferson it was an "unbosoming" process, giving her a measure of relief. The net result in terms of better feelings could have been registered at a few points above zero.

Nevertheless, this give-and-take may well be described as a verbal duel, not nearly as well known, however, as another duel, in which bullets were used, that took place that same year. From it we get clearly the picture of a lady contestant, loyal in utmost degree to husband and son. Something splendidly feminine prompted her to write about actual or fancied injustices inflicted upon her men folk. Her readiness and zeal in lauding the record and merits of these members of her family deserve ample commendation.

Adams remained in ignorance, presumably blissful, of this airing of disagreements until it was halted. (Abigail finally let Jefferson

[9] Letters in this exchange, subsequent to those already cited, were written by Jefferson, July 22 and September 11, 1804, and by Mrs. Adams, August 18 and October 25, 1804.

know that she did not care to go on with it, and he acceded to the lady's prerogative in respect to the last word.) One evening late in the fall of that year she brought a sheaf of letters, three from Jefferson and copies of four of her own, and put the little collection before her spouse. She asked him to read all of them. He did so, but if, when he finished, he said anything to her about them, we have no way of knowing. He did scrawl, presumably for the benefit of any chance reader, this brief memorandum on a blank space in the letter which closed the series: "I have no comment to make upon it [the correspondence] at this time and in this place."[10]

Once in a while this ordinarily communicative, sometimes voluble man was very sphinx-like.

After Jefferson's retirement to private life, there came a chain of circumstances, only a few of which appear to have been fortuitous, terminating in the reconciliation of the two former Presidents.

During the years in which they were out of touch with each other, Adams' feeling toward his Virginia contemporary gradually mellowed. The progress began, as has been noted, soon after his return to Massachusetts. It may have been hastened by his reading of the correspondence on which he refused to comment, and certainly continued in response to the more generous impulses of his nature. In a letter which was partly autobiographical, written as he looked back upon a span of life which then covered almost three-quarters of a century, he had this to say about an emotion which had often shaken him: "Anger never rested in the bosom."[11] In this bit of self-analysis there was no great stretching of the truth. Moreover, as he advanced in years, unlike some who came to the stage of senescence, even temporary lapses in the matter of charitable judgments became very rare.

One wonders, however, if the restoration of the broken tie would have been effected without the patient, persistent efforts on the part of the Philadelphia healer, Dr. Benjamin Rush.

This good physician, known more for his contributions in the field of medical science than as a signer of the Declaration of Indepen-

---

[10] This note is dated November 19, 1804, *Adams-Jefferson Letters*, I, 282.
[11] Adams to Skelton Jones, March 11, 1809, Adams, *Works*, IX, 613.

dence, began giving his attention, in a special way, to the Adams-Jefferson rupture, one demanding a skill which he had not acquired in his professional training.

He had been fairly intimate with the two men during some of the sessions of the Continental Congress, and with Jefferson especially throughout the Washington administrations. For several years, following a period in which there was no contact between them, he kept in touch with Adams by correspondence. At the time Jefferson retired permanently to Monticello, the estrangement between these former presidents, for each of whom he had profound admiration, weighed upon him as a heavy burden. Might he not repair this long-continued, regrettable breach? Surely it was worth trying. He believed that no one was better fitted than himself for the task. He thought of it as definitely humanitarian, no less than any other tasks in which he was engaged.

As the first step toward his objective, he sent Adams an account of a dream which actually was a figment of his imagination. According to this whimsy, he had been delighted to read, in the course of one of his recent slumbers, a page of the history of the United States, on which was written: "Among the most extraordinary events of this year 1809 was the renewal of the friendship and intercourse between Mr. John Adams and Mr. Jefferson, the two ex-Presidents of the United States." This statement was followed by a recital of factual details of their respective careers. Then the "dream" dipped again into the future, as dreams sometimes do. In November, 1809, Mr. Adams, taking the initiative, addressed a friendly letter to Mr. Jefferson and received from him an equally friendly reply. The history that Rush conjured up, as he indulged his fantasy, ended in this fashion: "These gentlemen sunk into the grave nearly at the same time, full of years and rich in the gratitude and praises of their country, (for they outlived the heterogeneous parties that were opposed to them), and to their numerous merits and honors posterity has added that they were rival friends."[12]

[12] Rush to Adams, October 17, 1809, *Letters of Benjamin Rush*, edited by L. H. Butterfield, (2 vols., Princeton, 1951), II, 1021–22. There was no clairvoyance in

Adams could not take offense at this benevolent make-believe, and without much delay he informed Rush of his wish that the Doctor should continue to dream "all day and all Night." His only objection to the dream was that it could not be called history, but, he added, "It may be prophecy."[13]

He was not willing, however, to admit that this possibility might be a proximate one, and time went on without any inclination or desire for the prophecy to be fulfilled. As a medical practitioner, however, Rush had never given up his patients easily. When it became evident that further approaches on his part were desirable, he made them.

In one letter he wrote what Adams called a "panegyric." The old man admitted that while he was an "indurated stoic," tears welled up in his eyes as he read these words of a perceptive judge of his associates: "You stand nearly alone in never having had your *integrity* called into question, or even suspected. Friends and enemies agree in believing you an honest man."[14] Adams, who always took delight in a fair appraisal of his virtues, may have been softened by this one for further moves which Rush had in mind. And he was susceptible to Rush's admonition concerning the briefness of the time remaining to him. It would be better for him to make his entrance into the next world reconciled with all his fellow men.

Rush assumed correctly that his chief difficulty as a mediator was with Adams' hesitancy rather than any reluctance on Jefferson's part. But, in earnest as he was, he did not direct all his efforts toward the more temperamental of the two men with whom he was dealing. He hinted broadly to his friend in Virginia that some attempt should be made to renew the long-interrupted relationship between himself and Adams. Jefferson countered with the assertion that he did not lack the desire, but believed himself to be under no obligation to do more than he had done. He even forwarded to Rush copies of the letters in which he had clashed verbally with Abigail. Having no

the statement that "these gentlemen" would go to their respective graves at "nearly the same time," but in view of what actually happened, the prediction is noteworthy.

[13] Adams to Rush, October 25, 1809, *ibid.*, II, 1023n.

[14] Rush to Adams, August 20, 1811, *ibid.*, II, 1096.

doubt that her husband knew what she had written and received in that interchange, he felt that if amicable relations were to be restored, the next step should be taken toward, rather than by, himself.

Meantime, another series of incidents took place of which Rush had no knowledge but which had the effect of hastening the result he was so eager to bring about. In the summer of 1811 two well-known Virginians, Edward Coles and his brother John, friends and neighbors of Jefferson, visited some of the New England states. Before they left home, Jefferson wrote several letters of introduction for them, including a letter to John Adams.

When this pair arrived in Quincy, they were received hospitably at Peacefield. No southerner could have been more cordial than the portly head of the household. During their overnight stay the visitors spent much time listening to their host as he talked about men and events, including one man and certain events of particular interest to them.

Many of the remarks which the now garrulous former President made about his former colleague were, from the standpoint of the two tourists, surprisingly complimentary. Yes, there had been times when Jefferson's conduct had been a source of vexation to him, and he cited instances, but he had put them all in the past. No trace of lingering antagonism could be detected as the two brothers listened to one great man talk about another. Before the visit ended, Adams, in a characteristic outburst of emotion, declared, "I always loved Jefferson, and still love him."[15]

This admission was too good for the travelers to keep to themselves, and at the first opportunity they relayed it to Jefferson. In many years nothing originating outside his own domestic circle had given him as much satisfaction. When he next wrote to Rush, he declared that he had never withdrawn "from the society of any man on account of a difference in organization and experience," and added, "I wish therefore, but for an apposite occasion to express to Mr. Adams

[15] An account of this visit is given in a letter from Edward Coles to Henry S. Randall, May 11, 1857, published in Randall's *The Life of Thomas Jefferson* (3 vols., Philadelphia, 1858), III, 639–40.

my unchanged affection for him." He left no doubt, however, that Mrs. Adams was excepted from this "fusion of mutual affections."[16]

Thereupon the Philadelphia humanitarian quickened the tempo of his efforts. He carefully edited the letter just received, deleting from it passages not appropriate to his purpose, and sent it, in the revised form, to Adams. With it went a copy of his own renewed plea, the original of which was already on the way to Monticello. It was worded in lofty oratorical style: "Fellow-laborers in erecting the great fabric of American independence—fellow-sufferers in the calumnies and falsehoods of party rage—fellow-heirs of the gratitude and affection of posterity—and fellow-passengers in a stage that must shortly convey you into the presence of a Judge with whom the forgiveness and love of enemies is a condition of acceptance; embrace, embrace each other. Bedew your letters of reconciliation with tears of affection and joy."[17]

Rush had never written such a prescription before. It certainly called for extraordinary ingredients. But it was one which his patient scarcely needed. Very soon there came another first-hand report, more encouraging than any yet received.

On Christmas Day, the spirit of good will toward men welling up within him, as we may assume, Adams wrote to his doctor friend, partially hiding his conciliatory disposition with a coyness which seemed to invite another florid exhortation. He accused Rush of "teasing" Jefferson to make a friendly gesture, and then proceeded to tease Rush himself. After all, what important differences had there been between Jefferson's practices and his own? Jefferson (and Rush, too) had been in favor of "liberty and straight hair"; in his own opinion, "Curled hair was as republican as straight." And Rush might recall that while he [Adams] as chief executive usually dined a "large company once or twice a week," his successor "dined a dozen every day." He conceded that in some other ways his ideas had not coincided with Jefferson's, but denied that there had been any war between

[16] Jefferson to Rush, December 5, 1811, Jefferson, *Works*, XI, 175n.
[17] Rush to Adams, December 16, 1811, *Letters of Rush*, II, 1110.

them. Therefore, as he wrote, "there can be no room for negotiations of peace."

The persiflage in which Adams indulged in this letter was, of course, apparent. But on the same page he became serious and alluded again to the reminders about human mortality Rush had used as a prod for mending a broken friendship and doing so quickly. Many times in moods of hypochondria, Adams had been sure that he would not live to the age of which he could now boast. Even at this time he could scarcely believe that he would reach the fourscore mark. He declared, perhaps with some regret, to Rush, "I am soon to die. I know it and shall not soon forget it."

Then he concluded this semiplayful, semisober communication in baffling style. With tongue in cheek, he asked, what point was there in Jefferson and himself writing to each other? What would the two of them have to offer in such an exchange except a mutual admonition to get ready for heaven? From that state of bliss, he added, with a pleasing confidence about their common destination, neither of them could be far distant.

And yet it might not be long before Rush's desire would be fulfilled. Possibly he and Jefferson would get into friendly touch with each other right here on earth. Time and chance, perhaps even "design," might bring about, in the near future, the beginning of correspondence between them.[18]

As a matter of fact, the "design" was already in the back of Adams' mind, and Rush was not so obtuse as to miss the evidence of it. So matters stood as the dawn of a new year approached. There seems to be, therefore, a valid basis for our assumption that Adams thought of the coming calendar change as an "apposite occasion," in Jefferson's phrase, for taking the initial step toward restoration of a friendship that had been stricken by near fatal blows.

Rush's part in bringing about the reconciliation was by no means the least of his many public and private services, but it turned out that there was not much time left for him. In the year following that

---

[18] Adams to Rush, December 25, 1811, Adams, *Works*, X, 10–12.

at whose beginning Adams made his friendly overture, the Philadelphia physician, unable to cure himself, passed from earthly life. While he died prematurely, as it seems, it was fortunate that he was spared long enough to be permitted to write "Cured" at the end of the records of this case.

At this point in their lives, both Adams and Jefferson were enjoying a boon which they frequently coveted in ther officeholding years. Peacefield and Monticello meant as much to their owners as Mt. Vernon had to Washington; and as the "Father of his Country" had done upon retirement, they, too, in turn, went home to stay. Enjoying a fair measure of health and physical comfort, holding earthly honors of a kind won by only a few, the second and third Presidents of the United States were making the most of their "golden years," which, as they often thought, were being portioned out to them in generous measure.

A few months after renewing contact with Jefferson, Adams wrote to another one of his friends that no other part of his long life had brought him as many genuine satisfactions as the eleven years elapsed since the burdens of office were lifted from his shoulders. It is possible for any interested person to learn in some detail the nature of those satisfactions. Now and then we may get, through the medium of his correspondence and Abigail's, rather intimate glimpses of his way of life, no longer the transplanted city-dweller, but one breathing, all the year round, the air of his native place.

Sometimes there were games of whist with relatives or neighbors. Occasionally the spacious living room was filled with guests, kinfolk and others; and the host, more evenly jovial than when he was a public official, shared in the general good cheer. Nearly every good day there was a walk, on some days for a distance of three or four miles. Frequently there were carriage rides along the main street of the village, with side trips toward the western hills or by the salt marshes in the direction of the ocean. On Sundays he went, as a rule, to church and sat through a sermon; he had been, as he said, a "church-going animal" all his life. And there were more hours than at any time since his boyhood that he could spend with books—the best inanimate friends that he had. Volumes of history, biography, government, not infrequently those dealing with ultimate concerns—he would hold them, one after another, in unsteady hands, sometimes for hours at a stretch, and devote himself to them.

As for Jefferson in his mountaintop sanctuary, life likewise moved along with as much smoothness as could be expected. He had recently recovered from a severe attack of rheumatism, but he was able again to ride horseback over his acres. The encroachments of advancing age meant for him, among other deprivations, fewer hours in the saddle; but on the whole he was physically well favored. Like Adams, he continued to read omnivorously. Whenever he wished, especially on days when the weather was not propitious for outdoor pursuits, he could choose for browsing or perusal any one of 6,500 volumes in his library, said to be the finest private collection of its kind in America at that time. He could well boast of a "considerable activity of body and mind." There were times when the peaceful flow of events was interrupted by a surfeit of visitors, many of them comparative strangers. To some extent it was possible to reduce the number of these invasions and at the same time find a relaxing change by retreating to his Poplar Forest possession, a four-thousand-acre estate located nearly one hundred miles southwest of his home.

There, during his time as President, he had supervised the building of a residence, architecturally simple but amply comfortable. For years his migrations to this quiet spot, usually in the company of one or more members of his family, were fairly regular. In addition to relieving him temporarily of the strain of dealing with the recurring influx of visitors, withdrawal to Poplar Forest made possible more leisure for his books. It was, in general, an Indian-summer time of life that he was enjoying, very much in realization of the hopeful anticipations which helped sustain his spirit during the years of more strenuous activity.

Since her marriage, Martha had been presenting him with grandchildren at a rate which fairly well guaranteed that the family line would not become extinct. There were nine of them to her credit when Adams' New Year's letter arrived at Monticello. One had already "promoted" Jefferson, as he put it, to the grade of great-grandfather-hood. Also, in the line of succession was the lamented Maria's son, who was now nearing adolescence.

Of the seven older ones of Martha's flock, six were girls (including the one who had died in very early infancy). But about the middle of Jefferson's tenure as President, Nature changed her procedure, and in the next four years the arriving grandchildren were all boys. It made no difference to him; and when he came home at the completion of his public career, the prattle of young children was heard as much as ever. It was as pleasing to him as any music he had ever heard.

Long afterward, one of the quintet of older granddaughters, to whom Jefferson referred as the "sisterhood," put into writing some of her memories of life with grandfather. Her account gives us a picture of the domestic setting surrounding her mother's father about the time that he and Adams figuratively clasped hands in renewed friendship.

She tells how, in the early part of winter evenings, daylight having begun to fade, all family members would often gather about the living-room fireplace and play games. Grandfather knew a great many himself and would take an active part. Also, he was willing to learn new games which had been brought to the attention of the young sisters and brothers and introduced by them into this entertain-ment. All too soon the fun-filled time would be over. Then servants would bring in candles, Grandfather would pick up his book, and usually the younger children old enough to read would follow his example. But sometimes, when there was snow to shovel, out they would go to make paths and perhaps frolic in the snow.[19]

All the year round there were seasonal sports interspersed between the necessary and usually agreeable chores. Here was a household in which a former President and his immediate descendants lived in more than average happiness and contentment. There was much to compensate for the grievous personal losses which the "patriarch" of the family had sustained in earlier periods of his life.

[19] Virginia J. Triste, in a letter written at Servan, France, May 26, 1839, Randolph, *Domestic Life*, 347.

The grandfather at Quincy was also fortunate in having a goodly number of children's children. All together, the count at this point was thirteen. Two, the older sons of John Quincy and Eliza, had been left behind in the care of relatives when their parents started on a journey to Russia, to which country the father was appointed as United States ambassador. They stayed at intervals in the old house by the Quincy turnpike, playing with resident or visiting cousins and helping with farm chores. Among the older cousins were Susanna and Abigail, daughters of Charles and Sarah; for most of the time since their father's death, the grandparents had made a home for them, a duty forced by circumstances but willingly accepted. Their Uncle Thomas had finally married, and in his native town was rearing a good-sized brood of children. Once in a while, and especially on holidays, there were at the "President's house" informal family reunions, with children romping, their elders visiting, and all sharing the delights of a New England festal board. Adams could not yet boast that he was a great-grandfather, but with pardonable pride he could write about the sons and daughters of his own children: "They are all good Boys and Girls . . . and are the solace of my Age."[20]

But, like any cluster of circumstances that affect human beings, those which now confronted the aging former President and his wife were not ideal. The fortunes of their son-in-law had declined to a low point. When relieved of the government post which he had held for a time, he turned again to the way of the speculator, and along that way he and Abby had come to the privations of the wilderness. By necessity rather than choice they had established a residence in the Chenango valley of New York. Now and then Abigail referred to this region as the "valley," a word that had for her, it seems, some sinister connotations. Adams himself, more tolerant of human frailty than at times in the past, was inclined now to pity the unfortunate rather than blame the transgressor. In the brief mention of his family made in the New Year's Day letter, he told Jefferson that the veteran of the Revolution who had married his daughter was being compelled to seek a livelihood in ways beneath his talents and merits.

[20] Adams to Jefferson, February 3, 1812, *Adams-Jefferson Letters*, II, 296.

A recent development added much to the Adams' anxiety for their daughter. Abby's health was far from good. As she busied herself with the task of making a home in the pioneer settlement, there was a loss of bodily stamina which could not be charged against the change in her manner of life. It became clear after a time that a cancerous growth was sapping her vitality. In the summer of 1811 she went back to her parents' home in the hope that better medical care available there might help. Months of treatment followed, including, on the strong recommendation of Dr. Rush, submission to surgery. Dark forebodings kept coming to the elderly couple at Peacefield.

Of less importance, but by no means negligible, were depressing thoughts caused by John Quincy's long-continued absence. The latter was still at the court of the Czar in St. Petersburg, half a world away; how much longer it might be necessary for him to represent his country on a continent reeling under the impact of Napoleon's movements, no one knew. Like many other elderly individuals, his father felt keenly the need of having those of his own flesh and blood comparatively near him. It had not been easy for him when he was younger to be separated by a wide ocean from members of his family; it was most difficult now. A little while after he and Jefferson got back on what might be described as speaking terms, he wrote, in a letter to another of his associates of former years, "I know not how we shall get him [John Quincy] home, although that is the dearest wish of my heart."[21]

Here, then, is the picture before us: two highly honored and eminent grandfathers, both unusual makers of history, men for whom the cup of life had held much joy and some sorrow and now contained a mixture different from any in it before, beginning once more to open their minds and hearts to each other. Mentally they were as alert as ever. In neither was there a trace of dotage or senility. They had plenty of leisure and a large store of common memories upon which they could draw. A long-thwarted desire, on the part of each of them, for the renewal of their "ancient friendship" was to be fulfilled, as well as it could be for two elderly men living, in the first quarter of

21 Adams to William Plumer, March 28, 1813, Adams, *Works*, X, 36.

the nineteenth century, several hundred miles apart. There was nothing to hinder what followed—a correspondence in many ways more remarkable than any other conducted between great political leaders in our history.

"It does not seem possible," a twentieth-century writer has stated, "that anyone who has curiosity about the inside of two old heads could fail to find a lark in these letters."[22] Now, as we turn our attention to them again, we may expect to find that kind of a lark.

The "two pieces of Homespun" which Adams sent to Jefferson as a good-will token were soon matched by a similar gift, one that was "homemade" in Virginia. While Jefferson was President, Edward Livingston, who practiced law in New Orleans, instituted a suit against him, claiming $100,000 damages, contending that losses in that amount were sustained as the result of an act authorized by the executive. This act dispossessed the plaintiff of certain properties in Louisiana which had been turned over to him in payment of lawyer's fees. The government's rebuttal was that these properties were still under its direct control. Some fine legal points were involved, and the case was pending in the courts for some time. After the claim was dismissed on the ground that the court had no jurisdiction since Jefferson was not a resident of Louisiana, he had his rather extensive brief printed and circulated as a "public service." This was the document sent to Adams as a reciprocal "homespun" offering. It was delivered one spring day in 1812.

Adams was as capable as ever in his judgment of lawyers' pleas. He read this one with even more than professional interest. He had unqualified praise for it. He informed lawyer Jefferson that he had never read a more "masterly" pamphlet. In every particular it was "worthy of the Mind that composed and the pen that committed it to writing."[23]

Jefferson had been almost as complimentary in writing about the Massachusetts product recently added to his collection. The younger

---

[22] *Correspondence of John Adams and Thomas Jefferson, 1812–1826*, edited by Paul Wilstach (Indianapolis, 1925), 14 (cited hereafter as *Correspondence*).

[23] Adams to Jefferson, May 3, 1812, *Adams-Jefferson Letters*, II, 302.

253

Adams' lectures pleased him immensely. In them there was, as he put it, "that display of imagination which constitutes excellence in Belles-lettres."[24]

The two men had made a propitious beginning in manifestations of good will. If their first letters in this long sequence were not "bedewed with tears of affection and joy," as Rush in his declamatory flourish had requested, they were at least adorned with a few verbal bouquets betokening admiration of valuable "homespun" gifts.

At first Adams appeared to proceed rather gingerly in suggesting subjects for their discussion. To write about "Politics" in the preliminary exchanges might be like lovers, reconciled after a quarrel, beginning to rake over old coals. But whether deliberately or not, he turned to an unrelated subject, one he believed to be on the list of Jefferson's interests—prophets and prophecies in general and an Indian prophet, Tesnkwatawa, in particular. At that time this individual, a brother of the Indian chief Tecumseh, was attracting a share of public attention, but he had never been either a Federalist or a Republican. What did Jefferson know about him, and about others who claimed to be able to foretell future events in detail?

Jefferson responded fully to the inquiry about the Wabash prophet, of whom he had learned much while serving as President. A few weeks later, in another letter, having been asked for specific information about the traditions and culture of the earlier inhabitants of America, he supplied several items of fact and speculation. At the same time, declaring that his interest in and "commiseration" for the Indians had been lifelong, he recalled for Adams' benefit a bright, moonlit night many years before when he had heard a great Cherokee orator speak to his people. The impression made upon the young white listener was one of utmost awe, leading to veneration. Adams replied that he, too, from his childhood had felt "commiseration" for the red people, and mentioned some of his contacts with them. Often, as a boy, he told Jefferson, he had visited the wigwam of a Punkapaug, (or Neponsit) family, located less than a mile from his

[24] Jefferson to Adams, April 20, 1812, *ibid.*, II, 298.

father's house. Invariably he was treated on such occasions with berries and fruit.

For more than a year, these correspondents kept reverting, as if their special interest had been anthropology, to the question of where these American aborigines came from and to discussion about their ways of life. Then Adams, who had brought up the subject, rather inconsistently declared that he did not care where they came from or how. With more than a trace of impishness he set forth a theory which, he wrote, was as good as any. It was that the prodigal son of the New Testament story in the course of his "Amours" made a trip to the western continent in one of "Mother Carey's Eggshels," and in the new world became the ancestor of a new race. Upon reading this bit of nonsense, Jefferson decided, as we may infer, that he and Adams had written enough about the Indians.

Among the other subjects introduced by Adams in the first phase of their renewed correspondence was, in his phrasing, the "Character Life and death of a Gentleman whose name was Wollaston." This man was the original leader of a small colony established in Massachusetts not long after the Pilgrims came. After a time he migrated to Virginia and was succeeded by Thomas Morton, whose reputation was shady. During the latter's regime pagan celebrations took place on what was at first called Mount Wollaston and was later rechristened "Mount Dagon" by the "Separatists," and eventually came to be known as "Merrymount." By way of explaining his interest in Wollaston, Adams wrote, "This Hill is in my Farm."[25]

Jefferson found in his library some material about Wollaston and Morton and forwarded a considerable portion of it. He even copied verbatim a lengthy extract from a history of the early settlements in Massachusetts. And he promised to send any additional details that he might discover.

It was not to be expected that Adams would be satisfied as a correspondent with long excursions in the field of ethnic origins and culture or that of early colonial history. If it was by deliberate intention that

[25] Adams to Jefferson, October 12, 1812, *ibid.*, II, 315.

he steered clear of political subjects in the first few of his letters in this series, very soon and rather abruptly he ventured into that area. On the same page in which Jefferson read praise of his argument in the Livingston case, he was confronted with these forthright statements: "In the Measures of Administration I have never agreed with you or Mr. Madison. . . . I have never approved of Non Importations, Non Intercourses, or Embargoes for more than Six Weeks. . . . I have never approved and never can approve of the Repeal of the Taxes, the Repeal of the Judiciary System, or the Neglect of the Navy."[26]

Adams received no indication that Jefferson ever noticed these strictures. For some time the latter kept hewing closely to nonpolitical lines.

Probably neither man expected that they would communicate indefinitely without resort to controversial topics. At any rate, in the summer of 1813 some unfortunate circumstances brought about a few exchanges of another kind, in which the two former antagonists seemed to be skirting the edge of another disrupting experience.

One day the Quincy booklover, browsing through a volume of memoirs which had recently come into his possession, found published in it a letter written by Jefferson soon after he became President. In it he criticized, in confidence he thought, persons whom he called "barbarians" in politics and religion, men who in planning for the future always looked backward to their ancestors. Moreover, that slant of vision, Jefferson contended, was common. "The President himself," so he had written, had declared in one of his formal answers to addresses, "We were never to expect to go beyond them [ancestors] in real Science."[27]

This bit of writing affected Adams very much like a sharp object scraping the raw edges of a wound. Jefferson had come close to calling him a "barbarian." In a letter in which his criticism was quoted, Adams asked, "What President is meant?" But he had no doubt of the answer, and rather testily remarked (perhaps he would have

---

[26] Adams to Jefferson, May 1, 1812, *ibid.*, II, 301.
[27] Quoted in Adams' letter to Jefferson, June 10, 1813, *ibid.*, II, 327.

shouted if he had been speaking instead of writing) : "The Sentiment you have attributed to me . . . I totally disclaim and demand in the French sense of the word demand of you the proof."[28]

Jefferson replied with characteristic suavity, but not without traces of tactlessness. He explained that the publication of the private letter which Adams had found was the "grossest abuse of confidence," another "instance of inconsistency, as well as of infidelity." And the allusion to the "President" contained in it was not directed to Adams personally, but to men who were his secret enemies. It had just "happened" that the President expressed pithily and (as the inference seems to be) with a lack of sincerity an idea held by some Federalists. This was not an apology which would mollify a man who appeared to be close to anger; but having made his defense, Jefferson backed away from the subject with the declaration that he would have no further part in such discussion. He concluded by asserting that, no matter how different Adams' opinions might be from his own, he would always receive them with "liberality and indulgence."[29]

Very shortly he had opportunity to make good on that promise.

Adams did not press his "French" demand and dismissed the matter which had vexed him with a brief, temperate lecture on the immutability of "General Principles" of Christianity and of English and American liberty. But another source of irritation had appeared. In the same letter in which Jefferson had absolved Adams of all blame for the statement made in answer to a formal address, he wrote that the "terrorism" to which Philadelphia and other American cities were subjected more than once during the Washington and Adams administrations was actually felt "by one party only"—i.e., the Federalist party.

Addressing his friend as if he were face-to-face with him, the staunch believer in strong centralization of governmental power used some very plain language. As far back as 1787, "Chaises Rebellion" in Massachusetts had shaken the pillars of American freedom, but Jefferson had given no sign of being disturbed. In 1793, only the

[28] *Ibid.*
[29] Jefferson to Adams, June 15, 1813, *ibid.*, II, 331–33.

"Yellow Fever" had prevented, as many believed, a "Total Revolution in Government." "You certainly never felt the Terrorism," Adams charged. When, a few years later, on the evening of what he proudly called "my Fast Day," Philadelphia streets were filled with a dangerous mob, where was the author of the Declaration of Independence? Very probably "fast asleep in philosophical Tranquillity."[30] It was clearly implied that no credit belonged to Jefferson for being calm at such times. Adams did not cite as a parallel Nero's fiddling while Rome burned, but probably he would have approved that comparison.

The Virginia philosopher's "liberality and indulgence" were sufficient to take these criticisms without any show of offense or attempt at defense. Later in the summer, when he got around to answering a dozen letters which had come that season from Quincy, he wrote, with a tiny flavor of sarcasm, that he had read them all "with infinite delight."

By this time these two "wise old heads" had found many topics on which to touch and several others which elicited what Jefferson called his "senile garrulity" and Adams his "senectutal loquacity." The former, beginning one of his letters, likened himself to the woodcutter in one of Theocritus' poems who, gazing at thousands of trees on Mount Ida, exclaimed, "What first shall I gather?" Adams replied that he experienced the same kind of perplexity. Sitting down to write to his friend, he could not see "Wood for Trees." But in this forest of topics there was one small "tree" which they did not think of approaching—the one which Adams had earlier mentioned as the sole object likely to claim their attention. Never did either of them feel any necessity of exhorting the other to get ready for heaven.

Even as nature slowly knits a bone fracture, so benevolent forces working upon and within them had completely restored their friendship. Even when he was irritated and being rubbed the wrong way by statements made by Jefferson years before, the older man wrote that

---

[30] Adams to Jefferson, June 30, 1813, *ibid.*, II, 346–47. The "Fast Day" mentioned by Adams was one which he publicly proclaimed as President, on April 25, 1799.

he had loved this friend "for Eight and thirty Years" and that he would be his friend "for Life." Jefferson, always less effusive, nevertheless kept reciprocating with assurances of respect and affection. If it had been possible for Rush to make a supplementary and final checkup in the summer of 1813, he would have been entirely satisfied.

The death of the man who had been the principal agent in the reconciliation of Adams and Jefferson brought a sense of great personal loss to each of them. While neither alluded to the real good this benefactor had done for them as individuals, they could never forget it. And they were not unmindful of the contribution he had made to their generation and to posterity. "A better man than Rush could not have left us," Jefferson wrote to Adams, who offered this tribute: "I know of no Character living or dead, who has done more real good in America."[31]

The group of patriotic colleagues to which they belonged in the years of Revolution was now reduced to a very small number. Only a handful was left of those who had affixed their signatures to the great Declaration of 1776. Moreover, the invasions of Death were constantly diminishnig the number of relatives and neighbors. John and Abigail were particularly bereft at this period, as one after another of their kinspeople and fellow villagers were taken from them. About the time that the news of Rush's death was received at Peacefield, there came a letter from far-off St. Petersburg informing them that a granddaughter whom they had never seen had succumbed to some infant complaint.[32] And when one of Thomas Boylston's small children died, the grandfather openly wept, expressing wonder that he had been spared so long, while this rose was "cropped in the bud."

Worst of all the bereavements that came to this "household of afflictions," a designation temporarily applied to it, was the death of Abby. In August, 1813, she breathed her last, leaving, as Jefferson's Maria had done, a little family still in need of her ministrations. On

---

[31] Adams to Jefferson, June 11, 1813, *ibid.*, II, 328. Jefferson's comment, "A better man," *etc.*, is in his letter to Adams, May 27, 1813, *ibid.*, II, 323.

[32] Louisa Catherine Adams, of whom her father wrote that she was "lovely as a seraph on earth," died in infancy.

the day following her passing, her father coupled an announcement of it to his friend Jefferson with a brief, tender eulogy. The latter's expression of sympathy was equally brief, but heartfelt. With the reminder that he himself had been similarly stricken was the comforting declaration that "time and silence" were helpful "medicine." And he placed before his familiar signature the more than friendly phrase, "Ever affectionately yours."

Interspersed between the sorrows that John and Abigail experienced were happy, blessed events. Among them was one rarer at that time, in domestic annals, than it is now.

In October, 1814, on a day when yellow and scarlet leaves were falling back to Mother Earth, the most venerable pair of this New England clan came to an important milestone, their golden wedding anniversary. At home, in what afterwards came to be called the "House of Golden Weddings," they observed the jubilee. There was, it seems, very little outside notice of the event. It is not on record that Jefferson sent them felicitations. Probably his attention was never called to the day's significance. But to them it was, of course, an occasion for special rejoicing. With so many long-time friends gone, they were still spared to each other. And there was left a goodly number of their kindred, most of whom were in fairly close touch with them. Also, Thomas Jefferson once more occupied a place in their circle of friends, for by this time the severed ends of another strand in the relationship which we have been tracing were reunited.

In one of the early letters of this correspondence, Adams, following the direction of his "better half," forwarded her "ancient respect and regards." Although in the letters that kept coming from Monticello there was little to indicate that the writer was aware of Abigail's existence, her own inner monitor was active. It was not fitting, that voice kept saying, for her to remain unreconciled down to the end of her life with this man who was once more on good terms with her husband. Shortly before Abby's death, she let Jefferson know directly that there were no longer any hard feelings on her part. On a page which Adams had partially filled, one that was to go to Jefferson, there was written in a feminine hand a short, revealing message. In that manner, and with a trace of shyness, she opened a door of communication which she had closed nine years before. Her regards for her "old Friend" were still cherished; they had been preserved through all the "changes and v[ic]issitudes of their past."[33] It was evident that the incidents which had provoked acid comments now resembled dead batteries, no longer capable of charging emotions.

There was no trace of restraint in Jefferson's reply. It was phrased in the same free and easy style which marked the letters written when she lived in Grosvenor Square and he in the Hotel de Langeac. His affection and respect for her were, he wrote, unchanged "under all circumstances of health or sickness, of blessing or affliction." In the same vein he added that his prayer was that the "hand of time and providence" might press lightly on her till her own wishes would withdraw her "from all mortal feeling."[34]

The country for whose independence Adams and Jefferson had struggled was now a lusty young adult in the family of nations. But for these three individuals the span of life had stretched out to the borderland, or beyond, of old age. One of them was nearing eighty. One of the other two had passed, the other was approaching, three-score and ten. In the brief time remaining for this unique, three-way relationship, all intervening barriers, save that of distance, were surmounted. It was a result made possible, in Abigail's way of putting it, because memories of the past had been purified of all their "dross."

Having made important history themselves, these former Presidents kept up a keen interest in national affairs and the men who were directing them. No longer involved directly, they were both free from former inhibitions in writing about men and events. Adams became quite forward in airing his opinions of the second war with the mother country and the political issues centering around it.

One-half of New England's population was opposed to this conflict, and here and there within its borders was a spirit of remonstrance which carried the threat of secession. The patriot of Quincy, who

---

[33] Postscript to letter, Adams to Jefferson, July 15, 1813, *Adams-Jefferson Letters*, II, 358.

[34] Jefferson to Mrs. Adams, August 22, 1813, *ibid.*, II, 367.

looked upon the federal union with father-like affection, viewed this development with alarm and eventually anger. On a day when the specter of secession was haunting him, a young visitor became, along with Abigail who was serenely knitting, a captive audience for a speech in which the war policy of the Madison administration was upheld as vigorously as it ever was in the halls of Congress. The young man afterwards reported that his elderly host became excited as he orated. Gesturing with all his energy, he exclaimed that George Cabot, a leader of the New England opposition, had nursed a closely-buttoned ambition which at last was bursting out of bounds. "He wants to be President of New England," the speaker declared in tremulous voice.[35]

In better control of his emotions than at the time of this outburst, Adams nevertheless made no attempt to hide his feelings when writing to Jefferson about the "absurd and pathetic" behavior of Cabot and other extremists. He alleged that in the Kentucky and Virginia Resolutions there was precedent for moves then being made in the direction of disunion. More than that, some of those "Measures of Administration" which Jefferson initiated and carried out had given "much Apology" for the war itself. In the same spirit, he implied that there was a causal connection between a "total Neglect" of "Maritime Protection and Defense" and the hostilities in which the country was then engaged.

Jefferson must have winced at these thrusts, but he continued his policy of refraining from countermoves. In respect to the prosecution of the war, he believed as earnestly as Adams did that vigorous action was necessary. As he phrased it, the "gauntlet must ever be hurled" against illegal interference with American vessels engaged in commerce and against violations of treaty agreements relating to the fishing industry. After the treaty of peace was signed, with its general vindication of American rights, he exulted in this fashion in a letter to Adams: "Peace, God bless it! has returned to put us all again into a

---

[35] *Life, Letters, and Journals of George Ticknor*, edited by G. S. Hilliard, Mrs. Ticknor, and Miss Ticknor (2 vols., Boston, 1877), I, 13.

course of lawful and laudable pursuits."[36] Adams also hailed the return of peace, and at the same time, following his tendency to exaggeration, claimed that no period in the history of the country was more glorious than the one in which this conflict was fought and won.

It was natural, of course, for these two observers to direct attention to the more devastating wars in Europe. Occasionally they shared their thinking about the "little Corsican" who was providing material for lurid pages of history. Jefferson's earlier evaluation of Napoleon as a man who possessed at least a few elements of greatness had given way to the conviction that he was a colossal enemy of mankind. Elba and later St. Helena were names suggesting to him the just retribution of tyrants. For this usurper of the rights of man he came to have little if any sympathy.

Adams' opinion of him was not particularly favorable, but compared with Jefferson's it was almost charitable. "Bona" was a "military fanatic," to be sure. But he was great, at least as nearly so as "any of the Conquerors." And could he really be called a "Usurper"? Was not his elevation to the post of emperor of France as legitimate as Washington's election to the "Chair of the States"? (Here, it would seem, is another outcropping of a long fault of jealousy.) If it were admitted that Napolean was a usurper, it must be conceded, so his argument ran, that John Bull was "as unfeeling, as unprincipled, more powerful, had shed more blood." When the shadows of final defeat closed in and encompassed the "Autocrator," something akin to pity touched Adams' pen as he wrote to Jefferson: "Poor Bonaparte! Poor Devil! What has and what will become of him? Going the way of King Theodore, Alexander Caesar, Charles 12th, Oliver Cro[m]well, Wat Tyler, and Jack Cade; *i.e.*, to a bad End."[37]

But the interest of these two commentators in events that led up to and followed Waterloo, even in those on the domestic scene which

---

[36] Jefferson to Adams, June 10, 1815, *Adams-Jefferson Letters*, II, 441.

[37] Adams to Jefferson, August 24, 1815, *ibid.*, II, 455. See also his letter to Jefferson, July 16, 1814. For Jefferson's estimate of Bonaparte, see his letters to Adams, July 5, 1814, and August 10–11, 1815.

were evoking public discussion, was more nearly peripheral than central. Neither of them had much to write to the other about the election of 1816, the retirement of Madison, and the accession of Monroe to the presidency. Adams did tell his friend that he felt some pity for Madison, who had no children or grandchildren of his own to cheer him in his old age. If he knew the extent to which "Dolley" provided compensation for this lack, he made no mention of it. But in the same connection he made another of his sweeping generalizations. The administration of Jefferson's younger friend had "acquired more glory, and established more Union" than his own and those of Washington and Jefferson put together. On Jefferson's part, silence about the change in government, involving especially his two fellow Virginians, was almost complete.

Quite naturally, there was for both men a major shift of attention and concern as they advanced in this later stage of their lives. After corresponding for some time on a wide variety of subjects having only temporary interest, they turned more frequently to discussion, in depth, of certain underlying principles about which great philosophers and, to a lesser extent, average men and women have spoken and written.

In July, 1813, Adams wrote that before death claimed Jefferson and himself, they should attempt to explain themselves to each other. He believed, with good reason, that he knew certain books he owned better than he knew his friend and that Jefferson might have a similar feeling. He was practically obsessed with the notion that only a little time was left to him for doing anything appropriate or advisable. He closed one of his letters to Jefferson that summer season by stating that he hoped to meet him at no distant time "in another Country." A few weeks later he included in another letter the solemn exaggeration that "only a few Hours," indeed only "a few moments," of mortal life remained to him.

This was an imaginary situation which, as has been pointed out, he envisioned from time to time. But in 1813 a distressing palsy condition, already of long duration, gave him some excuse if not reason for predicting his imminent demise. While this delusion was not as common in Jefferson's thinking, he was by no means insensitive to the swiftness with which time was hurrying him to the border of that other country which Adams had mentioned. The correspondence continued without any admonition from either side to get ready for heaven. But Jefferson was responsive to his friend's suggestion that, pending arrival at their final destination, they should try to explain to each other why they were what they were.

As a matter of fact, both of them, during the year and a half preceding, had occasionally made attempts to clarify and justify their opinions, about matters of more than immediate significance—a process intended to be self-explanatory. Adams had just restated some of his ideas about the fundamentals of civil government. Within that frame of reference, he mentioned two "Ladies" who in an ancient Greek allegory were known as "Aristocracy" and "Democracy." With a slight trace of bitterness he asserted that his defense, in one way or another, of the former of those "Ladies" (i.e., the natural aristocrats) "laid the foundation of that immense Unpopula[ri]ty which fell like the Tower of Siloam" upon him.

Replying, Jefferson neither approved nor protested this appraisal of developments, but he did endeavor to dispel any uncertainty that might still be lingering in Adams' mind regarding the differences in their theories. Adams favored a system in which men of good talents and breeding would have a secure place in co-ordinate branches of government, not subject directly to the people and thereby protecting the general public against the dangers which he thought were inherent in majority rule. Jefferson's own preference was for the method "exactly provided" by the federal constitution as well as by the constitutions of the several states. As it should be, voters, selecting their representatives in free elections, could separate the "aristoi" from the "pseudo-aristoi." In general, they could be trusted to do so with wisdom. In other words, the "Lady" of his choice was the one who had received the approbation of the Founding Fathers, and under her direction the country they both loved would be secure.

This new statement of his long-held faith was made, he declared, with no thought of stirring up controversy. Both he and Adams were too old to change their opinions. His only reason for setting forth these views again, and doing so at some length, proceeded from Adams' suggestion that before it was too late they should get clearer ideas, mutually, of their thinking on subjects such as the one he was presently discussing.

The older man's reaction to this exposition was in the most friendly spirit. It came, however, as was to be expected, with utmost candor. There could be no doubt that this veteran of the political wars still looked upon Jefferson's faith in an informed electorate as visionary, if not dangerous. Without qualification, and in apparent contradiction to some of his previous utterances, he asserted, "Mankind have not yet discovered any remedy against irresistable Corruption in Elections to Offices of great Power and Profit, but making them hereditary."[38]

Actually, on this issue the two correspondents understood each other very well, and they became content to leave the final judgment to posterity.

There was another "tree" which by this time was getting a large share of their attention, the one labeled "religion." They realized that to get a good understanding of any person without knowledge of the beliefs that govern his actions is difficult, if not impossible. Already they had filled some pages with their ideas about God and His ways with men. Not long before Abby died, they resumed the discussion with a freshness like that shown, we may assume, by the Grecian woodcutter as in the early morning he approached his task on Mount Ida.

For more than sixty years, said Adams, he had been "attentive to this great Subject." He had arrived at one negative conclusion—that there was never more than one being who could understand the universe (obviously its Creator). And he tossed off lightly a comment that it was nothing other than wicked for "insects" (i.e., human beings) to pretend to grasp its meaning. But "insects" like himself

[38] Adams to Jefferson, November 15, 1813, *ibid.*, II, 401. See also his letters to Jefferson, July 13 and September 2, 1813, and Jefferson's letter to Adams, October 28, 1813. The machinery of the Electoral College provided for in the United States Constitution to guard against dangers inherent, as was commonly believed, in direct choice by the voters has, of course, never been discarded.

could pursue their investigations. While he was not so wicked as to claim understanding of the mysteries of the creation, he became voluble in theorizing and in relaying ideas of some original thinkers.

He had delved into the writings of philosophers and of more serious poets of ancient times. He had made some acquaintance, too, with the works of medieval theologians, such as Erasmus, Vives, Cardinal Barronius, and Canus. He was more familiar with the treatises of Dr. Joseph Priestley, an unorthodox English clergyman and scholar, then deceased, who for some years had been his friend and also a fairly close associate of Jefferson's. Under the influence of these and other writers he had come to hold some beliefs which many who shared the Puritan heritage with him looked upon as heretical. Among them was the belief that in non-biblical literature of the pre-Christian era there was much of equal value with the best of the Old Testament; also the idea that ancient "Christianism" was debased by inventions of "Greeks, Romans, Hebrews, and Christian Factions."

As if his distant correspondent had become a one-man jury and himself once more a practicing lawyer arguing an important case, he set forth his personal creed with forensic zeal. Could anyone produce evidence to convince this hypothetical juror that God, for the purpose of His own glory, brought into existence millions of human beings with the intention of letting them be wretched and miserable forever? Is the One who sits on the throne of the Universe vain? Does He demand to be tickled with adulation? Is the taste of vengeance sweet to Him? But away with all inquiries of that kind—it was as if the man pleading were waving his arms in an oratorical gesture. Let his Maker pardon him for venturing to ask, even rhetorically, such "Aweful Questions." This, on the positive side, was his religion, let Calvinistic and Athanasian divines think of it as they pleased: the love of God and His creation, benevolence to all His creatures, joy and exaltation in his own existence, even if it did seem to be only a *Molecule Organique* in the universe.

One could remark that Jefferson's response to this summation was a favorable verdict; to do so, however, would be to make an understatement.

The Virginian, an amateur theologian who felt the tug of super-worldly mysteries more than many men do, had organized his thoughts about them more systematically than his partner in this adventure in self-disclosure. He wrote no bulky volumes on the subject, but his reflections on it were long continued, and from them had issued a few remarkable pamphlets, limited in their circulation; also the letter to Dr. Rush, heretofore noted, containing a sketchy outline of his views and with it the memorable dictum about his eternal hostility "against any form of tyranny over the mind of man."[39] By agreement between the writer and the doctor, this letter was for a long time kept in secret files. Throughout the years Jefferson served as President he thought much, but said little and wrote nothing for general circulation, about the "great Subject." There were still many people in the country who thought of him as an infidel, if not as an enemy of all religion. He had no desire to stir up the smoldering fire of religious controversy, with himself likely to be placed once again on a griddle held over the blaze that would result.

Now, however, as an important part of the process of explaining himself, he could write freely to Adams. It was not even necessary for him to make any *entre nous* specifications.

It was Jefferson's belief that Christianity, in the form in which it was minted by the Prophet of Galilee, came nearer being pure gold than any other such system known to man. Most unfortunately, however, during the course of a few centuries it was corrupted by narrow-minded and power-hungry churchmen. Under the influence of Dr. Priestley, just as Adams was, he had prepared, primarily for his own satisfaction, a *Syllabus of an Estimate of the Merit of the Doctrines of Jesus, Compared with Those of Others*. More recently he had gone through the gospel records in the New Testament, not literally with a knife, or pair of scissors, but with the equivalent of an editor's blue pencil, crossing out what seemed to him *addenda* tacked on for no good purpose and retaining what he considered *ipsissima verba* of the Founder and the historical, as contrasted with legendary, accounts of

---

[39] Jefferson to Rush, September 23, 1800, Jefferson, *Works*, IX, 148–49. See page 210 above.

His deeds. It was a process which he likened to picking out "diamonds in a dunghill." The result, in printed form, was a booklet which he entitled *The Philosophy of Jesus of Nazareth*. In it, he maintained, were set forth "pure and unsophisticated doctrines, such as were professed and acted upon by the *unlettered* apostles, the Apostolic fathers, and the Christians of the first century."[40]

He spelled out these ideas for Adams' benefit. The latter in return expressed his admiration of Jefferson's "Employment, in selecting the Philosophy and Divinity of Jesus and separating it from all intermixtures."[41] If he had better eyes and nerves, he wrote, he would engage in a similar undertaking himself. At this point the two men understood one another, in relation to the general subject, about as well as any two human beings can. There was confirmation of what each of them had believed for some time, that on the deepest level of human interest their views were quite similar, however much they differed on other levels.

Usually in their letters they glided easily from one topic to another. But some time after they began, more or less deliberately, to "explain themselves," Adams introduced a subject for discussion with the suddenness of a thunderclap out of a clear sky.

He had been reading some of the volumes of Baron de Grimm's *Literary Correspondence*. The period of which the Baron wrote was that of Adams' young manhood. More than any other books he had read as an old man, these stirred up memories of certain persons who were once among his acquaintances. Also, as if by magic, incidents that had faded out of his recollection flashed back into clear focus before him. It was something like living over again a part of his early life. Since that could not actually happen, conditions being as they are, he put to himself the question: If the impossible could become possible and he were given a chance to retrace his course of fourscore years, would he welcome it?

And so it came about that one day, having "nibbed" his pen, he began a letter to his friend by inquiring, "Would you go back to your

[40] Jefferson to Adams, October 12, 1813, *Adams-Jefferson Letters*, II, 384.
[41] Adams to Jefferson, November 14, 1813, *ibid.*, II, 396.

Cradle and live over again Your 70 Years? He admitted anticipating what he called a "New England" answer—another question, "Would you live your 80 Years over again?"[42] He pretended that he was "frivolous" in propounding such a query. But, sober-minded thinker that he was, he had never been more serious.

It has been suggested that the broaching of this subject may be likened, not to a clap of thunder, but to the unexpected popping of a "cork out of a wine bottle," and that the sparkle of the letters that followed was "not wholly unlike champagne."[43] Certainly there were many flashes of insight as these elderly men turned their attention to the intrinsic value of human existence.

In the letter which initiated this part of their correspondence, resembling indeed the talk of temperate men lingering over glasses of champagne, Adams replied neither "yes" nor "no" to the question which he first asked himself. His pen raced along with hurried comments about some men of whom the Baron had written, and then he wrote out what amounted to a broad hint regarding the answer which he held in reserve. This world, so it was stated, is "sublime," "beautiful," "very benevolent," and except as it is made otherwise by the fault of human beings, "happy."

The response which Jefferson made to Adams' queries in the next letter from Monticello was scarcely a "New England" one. On the whole, the writer found life worth living. Unlike many people he knew, he possessed a "sanguine temperament." Using, as he had before, a nautical metaphor, he wrote, "I steer my bark with Hope in the lead, leaving Fear astern." He admitted that his hopes were not always fulfilled. But, he argued, those who allow Fear to be "in the lead" just as often find out that there was no good reason for their forebodings.

Of course, he observed, there are even in the happiest lives "terrible convulsions." He knew what it meant to be tossed about by them, as in a whirlpool. Nor could he understand of what use grief, common as it is, can be in the over-all economy of human existence.

[42] Adams to Jefferson, March 2, 1816, *ibid.*, II, 464.
[43] *Correspondence*, 120.

Here was something for "pathologists" to explain if they could. But all the debits that can be listed under that and similar headings are more than balanced by the good proceeding out of a general "principle of benevolence."[44]

Having stated these views, Jefferson turned temporarily to other subjects. But his friend was not inclined to dismiss this topic hastily. He had been brooding over an alternative closely related to the one he "frivolously" submitted, and just as imaginary: making the trip through life a second time, or going on—somewhere. Other subjects of the same nature intrigued him. The next time he wrote to Jefferson he improvised a make-believe dialog between them. It is in the form of question and answers, the assumption being that Jefferson was conducting the inquiry and he himself giving his opinions, including those about the question which he had previously posed.

Would he agree to live his eighty years over again? Although he did not put it in this precise form, his answer was unequivocal, and in substance was, yes, a thousand times yes.

Would he agree to live his eighty years over again forever and ever? The prospect of annihilation would terrify him almost as much. In other words, no, a thousand times no.

Would he prefer to live his eighty years over again as an alternative to accepting an offer of a better life in a future state? Again, an unqualified no.

Would he live those same eighty years again rather than go to something worse in a future state, just for the sake of trying something new? Yes, indeed.

Sitting there at his desk, this man, who had several earthly years yet before him, juggled with these fanciful alternatives. Then, facing reality again, he added another question to his list: How may one estimate the value of human life? What should be the guiding standards? To such inquiries his reply was, "I know not." But he reaffirmed that, like Jefferson, he saw much that was good in life, and with him shared the hope that there was something better ahead. "I admire your Navigation," the Sage of Quincy wrote to the Sage of Monti-

[44] Jefferson to Adams, April 8, 1816, *ibid.*, II, 467.

cello, "and should like to sail with you either in your Bark or my own, along side of yours: Hope with her gay ensign displayed at the prow; fear with her Hobgoblins behind the Stern."[45]

After some time Jefferson acknowledged receiving this and another "philosophical" letter written by Adams. As if, while on long horse-back rides or in the seclusion of his study, he had been more carefully weighing the value of human existence in the balance of his own judgment, he wrote again about his attitude toward reliving, if it were possible, his natural life.

He was not quite so sure now of a willingness to accept an offer to do so. If his own wishes regarding the conditions were consulted, he would certainly make some important reservations. He would not want, for a second helping, as many as threescore years and ten. As to the years between twenty-five and sixty, yes. Perhaps he would take a few under the lower figure, but none over the higher. The prospect of bodily decay is gloomy; and the very thought of living on physically, with little mind or none at all, is of "all human contemplations the most abhorrent." Now, at seventy-three, he was "ripe for leaving all this year, this day, this hour."[46]

These observations were set down on a summer night which may not have been one of his good nights. Perhaps the twinges of rheumatism were unusually severe. Actually, both he and his fellow philosopher accepted in good spirit the necessity of going forward rather than back. And they continued to voyage with hope at the prow. Adams brought this portion of their correspondence to a close by predicting that they would soon meet and be "better Friends than ever."

Picking up a thread which Jefferson had left dangling in giving his first answer to the "frivolous" question, he proceeded to elaborate on the uses of grief. The man who long before thought, for a little while, that he might become a minister poured out on paper words that could have been spoken appropriately from a pulpit. It is not possible, he pointed out, to dissociate pleasure from pain. The capacity for enjoy-

[45] Adams to Jefferson, May 3, 1816, *ibid.*, II, 471.
[46] Jefferson to Adams, August 1, 1816, *ibid.*, II, 483–84.

ment carries with it the likelihood of suffering. If the question *why* be pressed, this partial clarification of the problem is reasonable: grief induces serious reflection, sharpens the understanding, softens the heart, and elevates men to a "Superiority over all human Events." More than this, the wise old man conceded, is scarcely possible by way of explanation. Full enlightenment can be given only by Omniscience. He completed his sermonic essay with the remark that we should "fabricate all the good We can out of all inevitable Evils" and acquire that patience and resignation which lead toward "hapiness of life."

The opinion of the one who received the benefit of this homiletic product was that by it the possibilities for discussion had been exhausted. But Adams was not yet ready to dismiss the broad subject. Within a few weeks he was asking for his friend's opinion on another aspect of it. He wrote, "I will tease you with another Question. What have been the *Abuses* of Grief?"

But this was not so much a teasing of Jefferson, or even a request for an opinion, as it was one more opening for the flow of his own thoughts. How often, he reflected as he wrote, had this sentiment been made to serve unworthy purposes. He cited as one example the "howl" that followed the death of Washington, an event which the "Hyperfederalists" capitalized, according to his view, in order to get more favorable attention to their pet "Funding and Banking Systems." At the same time, other men who had served their country well were cast into the "Background and Shade." (Adams' nature was not yet free from the virus of jealousy, it being especially active when he thought of his illustrious predecessor). He claimed that in more recent years there had been instances of "Mock Funerals" and "Printed Panegyrics," and that they were clear cases of the prostitution of grief by crafty men. Concurrently there had been repetitions of failure to give due honor, at the time of their passing, to some leaders with splendid records of achievement.[47]

Jefferson gave a figurative nod of approval to this argument, one presented without any theological reference. Then he turned his

[47] Adams to Jefferson, September 3, 1816, *ibid.*, II, 487–88.

attention and that of his correspondent to topics in which he was more interested.

About this time word was sent out from some of the post offices along the route between Quincy and Monticello that the two super-annuated Americans were writing frequently to each other. One day Jefferson was surpised, and a bit disturbed, to receive a printer's suggestion that the letters be published. Hearing of this directly from Jefferson, Adams dryly commented that no one had asked him for his letters with such a purpose in mind. We can only guess what his response to such a solicitation would have been.

We do know that his partner in correspondence turned a deaf ear to the proposition. Nevertheless, he, and Adams also, scrupulously filed away the letters as they came. And the unnamed printer was the forerunner of many other persons, publishers and readers, who in the intervening years have shown the same kind of interest. Nothing belonging to the future could be more certain than the eventual publication of what these men wrote in the attempt to explain themselves, and in the sharing of their thoughts about men and events of their times and other times, and in the giving of such answers as they could to some age-old questions. They could not have failed to understand that their correspondence would be of interest and value to coming generations.

More than ever like the swinging of a pendulum, life was oscillating, at this time, for John and Abigail, between extremes of good and evil fortune. The death of Robert Treat Paine and of Elbridge Gerry severed more of the visible links that connected them with the Revolution. Twice in the same month Adams lamented, a bit inaccurately but understandably, "I am left alone."[48] Moreover, Abigail's sister, the only one left to her, Eliza Shaw Peabody, and Dr. Cotton Tufts, a good friend and neighbor, joined the number of intimate companions who had been called from earth. Grieving as they did, Abigail and her husband accepted these dispensations, as they had earlier

[48] Adams to Jefferson, December 11, 1814, *ibid.*, II, 440. He expressed the same feeling in his letter to Jefferson, December 20, 1814, ibid., II, 441.

bereavements, with pious resignation. In a letter to one of her friends Abigail repeated, not in a spirit of complaint but realistically, an observation made by another, that in the case of those who live to old age, "string after string is severed from the heart, until finally there is scarcely anything left to resign but Breath."[49]

Her own health, never rugged, was precarious at intervals as she neared her seventieth birthday and then for a while lived on "borrowed time." Occasionally she expressed surprise, just as her spouse frequently did in respect to himself, that her tenure of life was drawn out to such an extent. She had lived through many cold New England winters and then greeted recurring springtimes with a fair amount of vigor; but now the return of each cold season meant the beginning of a perceptible depletion of her physical resources. At times she suspected, uneasily, the truth that her John would outlive her. Yet she thought of it as an additional mercy of kind Providence that she was spared for many years to help care for her "dearest friend."

In general, his bodily ailments at this time were less serious than her own. Among minor complaints was one that he spelled out as "Hickups." For it he used a remedy which he learned from no less a personage than Plato—a sufficient quantity of snuff to induce sneezing. More distressing were failing eyesight and the palsy which he described as a "quiveration," ailments which limited the range of his activity.

Abigail's ministrations to him were faithfully continued, long after her strength was outmatched by her devotion. Each morning when she could be up and around she saw to it that his tankard of hard cider and all his food and drink requirements were ready for him at breakfast. When guests came, she took her place, if at all possible, at the dining table, and helped, just as in former years, to dispense hospitality.

In that period of parallel physical decline, necessity as well as inclination caused them to stay close to each other, neither venturing very far from the well-loved homestead. While in the years of his

[49] Mrs. Adams to Mercy Warren, May 5, 1814, *Warren-Adams Letters, 1743–1814,* (2 vols., Boston, 1917–25), II, 392.

maturity Adams had been a seasoned traveler, he now thought of a journey even to neighboring Boston as almost too difficult to undertake. An invitation that came in his late seventies for a "little jaunt to Plymouth" to visit his old friend Mercy Warren brought this response: "Three score and nine years have reduced me to the situation, the temper and humor of Mr. Selden, who Clarendon says, would not have slept out of his own bed for any office the king could have given him."[50]

But this couple, who never had lacked the genuinely good things of life, was still blessed in substantial measure. In addition to having each other, John and Abigail continued to have near them for long periods some of their children's children. If now and then they posed problems, more often they brought comfort and satisfaction. After her mother's death and until she left to make a home of her own, Caroline was a member of the Quincy household. Susan and Abigail, daughters of the lamented Charles, were there, too, until they, in turn, married. Even after John Quincy and Eliza's older boys left to join their parents, who had been transferred to London, several of their cousins spent many hours playing and working in the "President's" spacious residence. The numerous offspring of lawyer Thomas brightened many a day for grandfather and grandmother. Adams did not complain when "four pretty little creatures" disarranged papers on his writing table, for, as he explained, they gave him much of his enjoyment.

Not long after the golden wedding anniversary, he and Abigail attained the advanced status of great-grandparents. Adams, like Jefferson, took a patriarchal pride in the number of his descendants. As that number increased, he boasted to one of his friends—not Jefferson, but in a manner that family head would have appreciated—"I have grandchildren and greatgrandchildren multiplying like the seed of Abraham. You have no idea of the prolific quality of the New England Adamses."[51] Even more than in middle life, he counted his blessings, interspersed as they were with afflictions. Once, while bur-

[50] Adams to Mercy Warren, August 17, 1814, *ibid.*, II, 396.
[51] Adams to F. A. Vanderkempt, July 13, 1815, Adams, *Works*, X, 196.

dened with sorrow, he wrote to his brother-in-law, the Reverened Mr. Peabody, "I yet delight and rejoice in life."[52]

At this time the widower at Monticello, although handicapped by age, could number among his blessings, as Adams could not, sufficient strength for working steadily at a variety of occupations. There was much to occupy his well-ordered time. Following the havoc wrought to the Library of Congress in connection with the attack of a British army on the national capital, he offered his own splendid collection to Congress in order to alleviate the loss as much as possible. For it he received from the federal government the sum of $23,950, a portion of which he used to clear up accumulated debts. But, as he informed Adams, he could not live without books. And the labor of cataloguing and disposing of one library was followed by the efforts necessary to accumulate and put in order another one, smaller but not insignificant.

This was only a minor part of multiple activities on his agenda, at one time or another, as a former President. The manager of his estate remarked, some time after Jefferson came home to stay, that only twice had he found him idle in his room, once when he was suffering with a toothache and once with neuralgia. The demands on his time and energy in connection with diverse agricultural and industrial enterprises continued to be insistent. As he had throughout most of his lifetime, he spent many hours at his writing desk, accepting as an obligation the task of keeping up his end of a heavy correspondence. In addition, there were as many visitors as ever at the southern plantation. Inevitably they involved a drain on the owner's time as well as his financial resources, and not infrequently they sorely tried his patience.

There were, however, some welcome guests. Among them were two impressionable young men from Boston, George Ticknor and Francis G. Gray. The former was that visitor at the Adams mansion who heard, along with Abigail, the former President's emphatic denunciation of the New England "Hyperfederalists." Since this was a

---

[52] Adams to Rev. Stephen Peabody, April 21, 1815 (Massachusetts Historical Society, Adams *Papers*) quoted in Smith, *John Adams*, II, 1114.

part of his recent experience, it was possible for him to bring to interested residents in the other mansion first-hand reports of the couple
who had entertained and, to some extent, awed him. Likewise, the
two young men, after returning to New England, could easily picture
for this couple, better than it could be done by the best of letters, life
at Monticello. To their recent host Adams reported, "Tickner and
Gray were highly delighted with their Visit; charmed with the
whole Family."[53]

The two travelers, we learn, were especially impressed by the
charms of Jefferson's granddaughter Ellen, just a few years younger
than themselves. It seems probable that their description of that
young lady set in motion a train of circumstances that led to her going,
some years later, to Boston as a bride. Certainly John and Abigail, on
the strength of glowing accounts to which they listened, became more
personally interested in this one of the Jefferson household, whom, of
course, they had never seen. The Quincy grandfather, closing one of
his letters of this period, sent his compliments to Mrs. Randolph and
all her children, singling out for special mention her "Daughter
Ellen." A few months later Abigail informed the other grandfather
that the "Northern Travellers" kept repeating Ellen's praises. They
were so happy to "have become acquainted with her."

After her own reconciliation with her husband's friend, Abigail
had been moving toward the high point of attachment reached when
they lived in Paris. In the winter of 1815–16 she had appended, in
her own handwriting, this postscript to one of Adams' letters: "Mrs.
Adams adds her affectionate regards, and a wish that distance did not
seperate Souls congenial." Now, filling out a sheet of her own to be
sent to that "congenial" soul, she admitted being tempted to wish
herself twenty years younger. She could then visit in person the
"phylosopher of Monticello." As if nothing had ever happened to
strain their relationship to the breaking point, she told him that their
"continued Friendship" was one of the pleasures of her life.[54]

[53] Adams to Jefferson, June 20, 1815, *Adams-Jefferson Letters*, II, 446.
[54] Mrs. Adams to Jefferson, December 15, 1816, *ibid.*, II, 500.

Gallantly, just as he had done more than once in those years when the only barrier between them was the distance between Paris and London, Jefferson reciprocated this more than respectful expression. He assured her that if he, too, could count backward a score of years, he and Ellen would very soon "pay homage personally to Quincy." But like all others they must travel forward rather than backward in time; their next meeting would have to be in a country where so many of their friends had gone. Old people like themselves could not expect the "master of the feast" to set the good things of earth before them forever. Even if it could be done, it would be a "leaden iteration" to see continually what they had seen, to "taste the tasted," to keep on year after year decanting "another vintage."[55]

In the brief earthly time now left to Abigail there were more of the delectable experiences to which Jefferson alluded; and with them, as before, were mingled occasional visitations of sorrow. Three years after Abby's passing, Colonel Smith's checkered career ended. The old folks, whose son-in-law he was, forgot his vices as well as they could, recalled his virtues, and lamented with Caroline and her brothers, who were thus left parentless.

A few more seasons came and went, and then, near the center of one of them, there was a special event, adding one more to the list of blessings for which John and Abigail were devoutly thankful. It was in midsummer, 1817, that John Quincy and Louisa and the sons who for a time had been with them in Europe came back to their native land. His career as a diplomat having been terminated, the younger Adams was now about to enter on his new duties as secretary of state. As Washington called Jefferson to that post while he was serving as minister to France, so President Monroe had summoned Ambassador Adams from England to take the same position.

What a day it was, a bright, sunny one in that penultimate year of Abigail's life, when this son and his wife and their sons were greeted at the threshold of Peacefield. They had traveled by sailing packet and special stage from New York, where their ocean voyage

[55] Jefferson to Mrs. Adams, January 11, 1817, *ibid.*, II, 504.

ended. John Quincy remarked that getting back to the scene of his boyhood and finding his father and mother in "perfect health," as he described it, was "inexpressible" happiness. It was nothing less than that for his parents. At times their hopes of seeing him again had been very dim. A few days after his return, he and his father were together at a public dinner—a community welcome to the son, whose public service, while far from complete, had already been conspicuous and constructive.

Within a few weeks Jefferson wrote from the solitudes of Poplar Forest, "I congratulate Mrs. Adams and yourself on the return of your excellent and distinguished son and our country still more on such a minister of their foreign affairs."[56] He had no background of experience which would help him to share fully in the joy which this reunion brought to his friends, but that lack did not detract from the sincerity and warmth of his congratulations.

The next winter was the last of such seasons that these parents were to spend together. One may appropriately picture the family as being snowbound when, in one of the cold weeks, Adams wrote to another of his friends that some in that home circle were reading to him every evening from Wirt's *Life of Patrick Henry*. He probably became acquainted with other books in that fashion, and we may well believe that Abigail took her turn in this gracious ministry.

Certainly she continued with that activity for which she had a special aptitude, the writing of letters. At ten o'clock one night she began writing to her beloved Caroline. She had recently composed seven other letters, some of them no doubt that very evening. In all that she wrote during that final year there was that same homely wisdom, feminine delicacy of touch mingled with equally feminine forthrightness, and adroitness of expression that may be found throughout earlier letters.

Writing to Jefferson what turned out to be her last letter to him, she closed with a reference to herself as his "old and steady Friend." His reply, likewise the final communication she was to receive from him, tendered her the "homage" of his "constant respect and attach-

[56] Jefferson to Adams, September 8, 1817, *ibid.*, II, 521.

ment." He also conveyed the wish that she and Mr. Adams might still have "long years of health and happiness."[57]

It would have meant much to him by way of satisfaction if he could have been with the little group that gathered in the parlor of the Quincy farmhouse one day in the spring that followed the winter in which Adams reported the special ministrations to himself, unable as he was to read by candlelight. One of the guests about the tea table on that occasion wrote soon afterward that the former President appeared hale and vigorous for a man of his years, that while he was still afflicted with "quiverations," he could "carry a cup of tea to his lips without spilling a drop from tremor."[58] Less alert physically, Abigail nevertheless took her part as hostess in a manner similar to that which delighted visitors invited to Monticello.

If Adams at that time could handle a cup of tea with some dexterity, he could not use a pen without pain or fatigue. In contrast to the avalanche of letters directed to his Virginia friend a few years before, only two were written to him in the spring and summer of 1818. Jefferson himself let months go by without sending a line to Adams, not because of any weakening of the ties which bound them, but because of an "extreme debility." For some time he was forced to reduce all his correspondence to the barest minimum.

For both men that year was one that put their native optimism to grueling tests. To Adams it brought the greatest bereavement of his life. On a day in October, so agitated that he did not date his letter correctly, he scrawled out a one-page message which he directed to be sent to his "dear Friend." It contained these tidings: "The dear Partner of my Life, for fifty four Years as a Wife and for many Years more as a Lover, now Lyes in extremis, forbidden to speak or be spoken to."[59] After a rather prolonged period of unusual good health, Abigail had suffered a stroke. It came without much warning, and was soon followed by a complication in the form of typhoid fever.

[57] Jefferson to Mrs. Adams, May 15, 1817, *ibid.*, II, 514. The letter to which this was a reply was dated April 29, 1817, *ibid.*, II, 511.

[58] George Bancroft, "An Incident in the Life of John Adams, *Century Magazine*, July, 1887.

[59] Adams to Jefferson, October 20, 1818, *Adams-Jefferson Letters*, II, 529.

Eight days after her husband's missive was dispatched, she breathed her last, having done all for her family, her friends, and her country that lay within the wide scope of her talents and affections.

Jefferson, still convalescing from his own prolonged illness, got the news in what he called the "public papers." Without delay he sent to Adams a heart-to-heart message, imparting warmth of sympathy with few, but well-chosen words. As he had done when Abby died, he reminded the newly made widower that to affliction of this kind he himself was not a stranger. "I know well," he wrote, "and feel what you have lost, are suffering, and have yet to endure." Long-drawn-out condolences would be worse than useless; they would open afresh the sluices of grief. It would suffice that both of them could find some comfort in the thought that while they would soon "deposit, in the same cerement" their suffering bodies, they would "ascend in essence to an ecstatic meeting" with those whom they had loved and lost. Moreover, they would still love them and never lose them again.[60]

These were not words of perfunctory piety. No professional dispenser of religious comfort, however honest and efficient, could have performed this duty better, within the limits of written language.

We have noted in this narrative that from the day the two men first met they had much in common, even throughout the years when they lived, in effect, in separate worlds, with few signals of communication between them. Now, for the remainder of their pilgrimage there was this additional bond. Each was compelled to travel that part of the road which lay ahead, as Jefferson had done for much of the way already traversed, without the companionship of the one with whom vows had been exchanged, in a long-ago time, at the marriage altar.

Jefferson never looked on the inscription composed with filial affection by John Quincy Adams and later chiseled on the sarcophagus wherein his parents' remains are entombed. If he had, he would have given hearty assent to its sentiments. The brief record of pertinent biographical facts is followed by this tribute: "During an union of

[60] Jefferson to Adams, November 13, 1818, *ibid.*, II, 529.

more than half a century they survived, in harmony of sentiment, principle, and affection, the tempests of civil commotion; meeting undaunted and surmounting the terrors of that Revolution which secured the Freedom of their Country, improved the conditions of their times, and brightened the prospects of Futurity of the race of man upon Earth."[61]

After their retirement to private life, both Adams and Jefferson made some use of their talents for public service. This was particularly true in the case of the Virginian.

At a time in life when many wither on the vine, he carried out a project which he considered, quite rightly, one of his most important services to future generations.

The decline of Charlottesville Academy and a consequent proposal to invigorate it appeared to him a propitious occasion for renewing his proposal for a "More General Diffusion of Knowledge" in Virginia. Included was a proposal for a state university. Convinced that a broad education for great numbers of youth was a safeguard for government of, for, and by the people, he set out to convert fellow Virginians to his view.

For many years he had noted with admiration the attention given in Massachusetts to public education. He was certain that long-continued emphasis in that commonwealth upon intellectual training had helped her to take a leading role in events leading up to the American Revolution. He regretted the fact that many people of his own state failed to realize that knowledge releases power and that individual and national weakness is often a by-product of ignorance.

It was natural, therefore, for this constructive schemer to seek suggestions for a state university from a region where training of the mind of youth was given relatively high priority. Perhaps he thought that his friend Adams was as well fitted as anyone in that area to give helpful ideas. At any rate, long before his university came into existence but while he was dreaming creatively about it, he let Adams know about his concern, and receptivity to ideas in this fashion:

[61] Adams, *Works*, I, 644.

"Have you ever turned your thoughts to the plan of such an institution? I mean to a specification of the particular sciences of real use in human affairs, and how they might be so grouped as to require so many professors only as might bring them within the views of a just but enlightened economy? I should be happy in a communication of your ideas on this problem, either loose or digested."[62]

Replying, Adams confessed, with "mortification," that he had never given as much attention as a parent should to the subject of education, and admitted that any hints he could give about subjects that should be taught in a university, how they should be grouped, and which ones should be emphasized in the making of a curriculum were "crude," "loose," and "indigested." It does not appear that he was of any help in this connection other than in the bestowal of his blessing. But it is worth noting that when the time came to choose professors for the university, another friendly difference of opinion developed between himself and Jefferson. With the latter, one guiding principle was to get the best, if possible, wherever they could be found. And he believed that in some fields of knowledge Europe had scholars outranking any that America could furnish. Adams had no objection to getting the best-qualified teachers available, but he maintained that there was no such shortage in America as to make necessary any importation from European centers of learning.

In 1816 the academy at Charlottesville was given the status of a college, a change which, it appears, gave Jefferson additional zest in promoting his scheme for a greater "Diffusion of Knowledge," especially on the higher levels of learning. The first fruits of those efforts were in the form of approval by the lawmakers at Richmond, in their 1818 session, of an appropriation of $15,000 for a state university. A year later legislation formally bringing it into existence—on paper—was enacted. Then came Jefferson's appointment as "Rector of the Board of Visitors"—equivalent to chairman of the board of trustees—a post of obligation and privilege which gave him a virtually new lease on life. For several years thereafter, he devoted much of

[62] Jefferson to Adams, July 5, 1814, *Adams-Jefferson Letters*, II, 434.

his attention to the building and staffing of this new creation in the educational field. Gradually the vision which provided him with this final major incentive approached full realization.

When it became apparent that the university would be established, Adams sent congratulations to the founder. They were tempered, however, with skepticism arising out of the writer's rather pessimistic view of human nature, an outlook which so often affected his thinking. "If it [the university] contains anything quite original, and very excellent," he wrote, "I fear the prejudices are too deeply rooted to suffer it to last long, though it may be accepted at first."[63] Adams did not lack vision, but it was not of the kind that engendered such an achievement as that which crowned Jefferson's public career.

His own civic services during the closing years of his life were confined to a relatively short period of time and were of minor importance in comparison with many others he had previously rendered. At the age of eighty-five he was honored by his fellow citizens of Massachusetts in being chosen as a presidential elector. He had basked in the sunshine of good feeling which spread over the country following Monroe's election, doing so all the more appreciatively, we may suppose, because of the invitation which came to John Quincy to enter the new cabinet. However, a little later he wrote to Jefferson about "Clouds" in the overarching skies which looked "Black and thick" and which, he feared, would produce throughout the country by some mysterious process an "effervescence." At the same time he predicted that Monroe and Tompkins would be re-elected and declared that they were entitled to that honor.

It turned out that the only "effervescence" which appeared bubbled up out of widespread satisfaction with the status quo. When the opportunity came, Adams himself cast his ballot for a Jeffersonian who, as the country soon learned, received the approval of every member of the electoral college save one New Hampshire dissident. That individual, so it was reported, did not want anyone to share with Washington the honor of being chosen unanimously as chief executive.

[63] Adams to Jefferson, May 26, 1817, *ibid.*, II, 518.

More noteworthy than the recognition given Adams during the presidential campaign of 1820 was that accorded him by his fellow townsmen when they chose him to represent them in a convention called to revise the state constitution. It was unusual for such a distinction to be bestowed upon a man halfway through the ninth decade of his life, and it was done very much in the spirit of pinning a medal on a veteran. When Jefferson heard of it, he added another to his list of congratulatory messages. It was good news indeed, so he wrote, that Adams' health and spirits were such as to enable him to take part in an important deliberative assembly.

When the convention sessions began, this older statesman actually seemed to feel better than he had felt several years before. At least he was willing at this time to sleep in a bed other than his own. He stayed in a home not far from the place of meeting, the State House in Boston. But he had no senile illusions about his value as a delegate. During the proceedings he spoke only a few times, and on those infrequent occasions, according to his own version of the experiences, he "boggled and blundered more than a young fellow just rising to speak at the bar."[64] The closest contemporary parallel to his appearance in this body is that provided by the aged Churchill in the British Parliament.

When Massachusetts voters registered disapproval of certain articles of the new constitution, Adams was slightly exasperated. With a trace of sarcasm he complained to Jefferson, "Our Sovereign Lords The People think themselves wiser than their Representatives."[65] He was candid enough to concede agreement with "their Lordships" in several matters, but his persisting attitude was that of one who had little faith in democratic processes. And while during the sessions he favored some forward-looking proposals, his voice, when heard, was usually like an echo out of the past.

Thereafter no further break in his retirement was desirable or possible. He submitted as gracefully as could be expected to the increasing limitations of old age. His public record was complete, and

[64] Adams to Jefferson, February 3, 1821, *ibid.*, II, 571–72.
[65] Adams to Jefferson, May 19, 1821, *ibid.*, II, 573.

it was one in which he never ceased to take pride, justifiable by any standards that make allowance for human frailty.

During this last decade of their lives, the attention of the two aged patriots was called, in a special way and without any initial volition on their part, to some questions relating to what actually happened while the American Revolution was in progress. This focusing of their memories was a result of the publication in 1819 of the so-called "Mecklenburg Resolutions."

This document, purporting to be a Declaration of Independence drawn up and adopted by a number of citizens of North Carolina in the spring of 1775, antedated, if genuine, Jefferson's masterpiece by more than a year. It appears that Jefferson had no knowledge of the appearance of these "Resolutions" until his attention was called to them by his correspondent in Quincy. The latter was puzzled, for the time being, not in respect to their genuineness, but to the manner in which they had been concealed from the public. Assuming, with a surprising naïveté, that they constituted a bona fide declaration of 1775, he wrote to another friend that Jefferson must have seen the document while he was a delegate to the Continental Congress. Following out the logic of this opinion, he added, "He has copied the spirit, the sense, and the expression of it *verbatim* into his Declaration of the 4th of July 1776."[66]

But the author of that Declaration dismissed, almost flatly, the North Carolina Resolutions as spurious. How, he very convincingly argued in a letter to Adams, could such an action, if really taken, have been kept secret for so long a time? "For the present," he insisted, "I must be an unbeliever in this apocryphal gospel." Adams, influenced by Jefferson's reasoning, joined him in his unbelief. But the mystery enveloping the affair appeared to him in a form as opaque as that in which it first confronted him. Writing to the man whom he hailed again as the "acknowledged draughtsman of the Declaration of Independence," he inquired, "Who can be the Demon to invent such a machine after five and forty years, and what could be his motive?"[67]

[66] Adams to William Bentley, July 15, 1919, *Works*, X, 381.
[67] Adams to Jefferson, July 21, 1819, *Adams-Jefferson Letters*, II, 545.

Having given some attention to this perplexing riddle and finding themselves unable to answer it, both men seemed willing to dismiss it as a curious footnote to actual history.

By the early 1820's nearly all the signers of the document of 1776, well authenticated by the testimonials of history, had passed away. When Adams heard that William Floyd was added to this number, his mood was similar to that in which he had written of the death of Paine and Gerry. He called Jefferson's attention to the fact that of the very few still surviving, he himself was the oldest. This unanticipated distinction gave him the hope, so he told his friend, that he would be the first to join Floyd and the others who had gone on. By the same token, Jefferson, who was the youngest, could look forward to be the last in bidding farewell to earth.

There was no evidence of enthusiasm in the response to this guess regarding the probable sequence of their respective exits from life. The youngest one of the survivors reiterated ideas previously conveyed to Adams about mere extension of earthly existence. The prospect of a tottery, doddering old age repelled him. To advance to the last stages of senility was to approach the life of a cabbage, and nothing could be farther from his desire than to deteriorate into a vegetable. He trusted that Providence would deliver him from any such anticlimax.

Fortunately, the boon of a sound mind in a weakening body was never withdrawn from either Adams or Jefferson. As mentally alert as ever, they kept up their interest in unfolding events and continued to share freely reflections induced by them.

From their separate posts of observation they watched closely a verbal conflict which at this time was attracting much more attention than the puzzle presented by the "Resolutions" credited to North Carolina patriots of 1775. The issue involved was the admission of the territory of Missouri as a free or slave state. It was the first such controversy to attain nation-wide proportions and become a matter of grave concern to citizens in every section. For a time Jefferson was genuinely alarmed. He likened the debate precipitated by Missouri's bid for statehood to a "firebell in the night." Far more pessimistic than he usually was, he could hear in this "firebell," the "knell of the union."[68]

Likewise, and very naturally, his friend Adams was not free from anxiety. To him this war of words was one of those thick, black "Clouds" threatening "thunder and Lightning," perhaps at no distant time an "effervescence." While the question was being argued in Congress, he showed his solicitude in a letter to Jefferson. "I am sometimes Cassandra enough," he admitted, "to dream that another Hamilton, another Burr might rend this mighty Fabric in twain, or perhaps into a leash, and a few more choice Spirits of the same Stamp, might produce as many Nations in North America as there are in Europe."[69]

Thus, halfway between the Revolution and the Civil War, the possibility of southern secession had a disturbing effect upon the two men to whom, more than any others still living, the Republic owed its existence. When the issue was resolved temporarily by compromise and dumped into the lap of the future for final settlement, they congratulated themselves that they would not be troubled much longer by mundane affairs. Soon they would be above all the commotions to which residents of this planet are subject. Adams reminded his correspondent, "What we are to see God knows," and added, "I leave it to him and his agents in posterity."[70] Jefferson also accepted willingly the necessity of leaving the problem to those who would inherit it, and to the Supreme Ruler of events.

But they were not yet through with this world, and neither wished to stop the flow of spicy comment about what was going on in it. They manifested keen interest in the fluctuating fortunes of Simón Bolívar in his South American campaigns, and were not very hopeful about the final results. While certain that Spain would lose control of Venezuela and neighboring colonies, they doubted that really free governments could emerge in the near future. Jefferson was not disturbed by the probability that independence, as he conceived it, for

---

[68] Jefferson to John Holmes, April 22, 1820, *Works*, XII, 158.
[69] Adams to Jefferson, December 21, 1819, *Adams-Jefferson Letters*, II, 551.
[70] Adams to Jefferson, February 3, 1821, *ibid.*, II, 571.

these peoples being "liberated" might be delayed. To his co-worker in the struggle for freedom of the thirteen North American colonies he wrote, "I do believe it would be better for them [Latin Americans] to obtain their freedom by degrees only; because that would by degrees bring on light and information and qualify them to take charge of themselves understandingly."[71]

This "dreamer" usually kept in touch with reality. Here he was giving another witness to his lifelong conviction that one of the most practical guarantees of the "inalienable" right of liberty is dissemination of knowledge.

It seemed to him, as to Adams, that the outlook for the near future of European states was even less rosy than that presented by South American colonies in the throes of revolution. The passing of their ancient foe, George III, and a little later of Napoleon, terminating in the one case a sorry, protracted death-in-life and in the other a period of inglorious exile, seemed to these two Americans to remove only the symbols of tyranny. In the spring of 1821, there being little in the world situation, as Adams viewed it, that appeared promising, he inquired of Jefferson, "Must We, before We take our departure from this grand and beautiful World, surrender all our pleasing hopes of the progress of Society? Of improvement of the intellectual and moral condition of the World? of the reformation of mankind?"[72]

As if it were an echo, there came back from the slopes of Monticello this response: "Are we to surrender the pleasing hopes of seeing improvement in the moral and intellectual condition of man?"[73] Two years later Adams, gloomily surveying the contemporary scene, addressed this query to his friend: "Can you perceive any rays of a returning dawn? Is the devil to be the 'Lord's anointed' over the whole globe?"[74] More hopeful than before, Jefferson replied, in effect, that he could see some signs of a new dawn, that while the

---

[71] Jefferson to Adams, May 17, 1818, *ibid.*, II, 524.
[72] Adams to Jefferson, May 19, 1821, *ibid.*, II, 572.
[73] Jefferson to Adams, September 12, 1821, *ibid.*, II, 574.
[74] Adams to Jefferson, August 15, 1823, *ibid.*, II, 594.

situations in Europe and South America were discouraging, they were not desperate.

It should be clearly understood that the hopes of both men were more persistent than their fears. One of Jefferson's basic beliefs that never cracked under the strains put upon it was that liberty, with its attendant blessings, would ultimately spread through both hemispheres. "I can not believe," he wrote to his colleague in the struggle for American freedom, "our labors are lost." They had helped start a conflagration with which he associated no "firebell" such as that which he seemed to hear when the debate over the extension of slavery was in progress. "The flames kindled on the 4th of July 1776 have spread over too much of the globe to be extinguished by the feeble engines of destruction."[75]

Nor did his companion in these reflections about the shape of things to come really think that the world would get worse rather than better. His dour comments, often repeated, about mankind are counterbalanced by many sanguine references to the future. In the realm of politics he was certain, at his best, that "rational systems of Government" would be more generally established; and when his view included other aspects of society, he frequently seconded Jefferson's motion of confidence in the improvability of the human race. In a frame of mind which was far from being rare, he wrote, "Thes[e] hopes are as well founded as our fears of the contrary evils; on the whole, the prospect is cheering."[76]

For most of the time hope continued to steer the bark, in Jefferson's figure, for these ancient mariners. And in a sense their separate courses, according to Adams' expressed wish, were closely parallel. They discerned, often simultaneously, rays of promise on the horizon that lay ahead.

By this time their friendship had matured into an affection strong enough to nullify the effect of a set of circumstances which otherwise could have jeopardized relations between them, and might even have resulted in another and more tragic rift.

[75] Jefferson to Adams, September 12, 1821, *ibid.*, II, 575.
[76] Adams to Jefferson, September 18, 1823, *ibid.*, II, 598.

In the fall of 1823 some letters written by Adams while he was still nursing wounds sustained in party strife were published. There is no doubt that the printing of those letters involved a violation of confidence. The use that was made of them, presumably for the purpose of putting a barrier between John Quincy Adams and the presidency, was on a par with that made, more than once, of Jefferson's private communications.

In what now came to light—and the publicity given was extensive—Adams had written, as he often did, without tactful restraint. Some of his statements were so far from being creditable to Democracy's patron saint that, had that individual been inclined to take offense, they would have been countered by open rebukes and recriminations. Instead, Jefferson straightway reacted with one of those fine expressions of charity which here and there grace his writings. The letter in which he revealed his attitude as clearly as he could with written words belongs to the great literature evoked by friendship. The writing and sending of this letter was, in the judgment of one of his biographers (also a biographer of Adams), "perhaps the noblest act of his entire career."[77]

It was an action taken, according to Jefferson, as something "due to a friendship co-eval" with the government under which they lived. The writer refreshed the reader's recollections of the circumstances surrounding them during the years in which the anti-Federalist movement was gaining momentum. As he had done before, he called attention to the fact that some men in each party were careless with the truth. Even "malignant falsehoods" were invented for the purpose of getting himself and Adams to harbor beliefs about each other the "most destitute of truth."

But all that belonged to a record long since closed. Passions usually subsided with the passing of the years. Certainly that had happened in their own experience. Most strange it would be now, if, old men as they were, they would allow anything out of the past "to disturb the repose of affections" that were "so sweetening" to the evening of their lives. Adams should not feel the slightest apprehension that this

[77] Gilbert Chinard, *Honest John Adams* (Boston, 1933), 342.

incident would make any difference in the writer's affection for him, which had been growing ever since their friendship was restored. The attempt that was made "to plant thorns on the pillow of age," as he described it, was wicked, and he was "incapable of receiving the slightest impression from the effort." With magnanimity of spirit, he called upon his long-time associate and colleague to put the matter out of his mind. "Throw it by," he urged, "among the things which have never happened."[78]

This letter was delivered to the addressee fairly early one morning while he was at the breakfast table. The scene as it was received, pictured for us by Adams himself, is impressive in this drama of friendship. He could not read the letter himself; the light available was not sufficient for his beclouded eyes, so that honor was given to a younger member of the family circle, "one of the misses." After the last word was pronounced, we are told that everyone in the little audience exclaimed that it was the best letter ever written. As if it were some rare, delectable dish, it was passed around the table; no one missed seeing with his own eyes the handwriting by which such generous sentiments were conveyed. All but one agreed that it should be printed; the man at the head of the table pointed out that such action should not be taken without consulting the writer. The most appropriate remark that he could make about its contents was this: "Just such a letter as I expected, only it was infinitely better expressed."[79] Nothing offered that morning on plates or in mugs delighted the partakers as much as the letter that had just arrived from Monticello.

Both men continued to revert in their exchange of letters to immemorial questions about man's origin and destiny and the meaning of his fleeting stay on earth. The average man wonders at times about the Power that made him and the reasons for his creation, and these above average men could not bypass such inquiries. Theology, of course, was not their prime concern, but while life lasted they never ceased thinking about the nature of the Deity, about man's place in

[78] Jefferson to Adams, October 12, 1823, *Adams-Jefferson Letters*, II, 600–601.

[79] Adams gives the details of this incident in his letter to Jefferson, November 10, 1823, *ibid.*, II, 601.

the comprehensive scheme of things, and about his ultimate destination. During the years in which Adams was a widower they shared, more intimately than ever, ideas forthcoming as they sought to probe the nature of Reality.

In this area there was no great change in the beliefs of either; however, on the emotional level, there was a growing inclination on the part of both, devout deists as they were, to let a simple trust in the Creator be their mainstay. This came about, in part, because of their deepening conviction that the way of earthly philosophies resembles a dead-end street. More than once Jefferson professed an unwillingness to indulge in "speculations and subtleties" beyond human understanding. In one of his later letters he wrote to Adams, "When I meet with a proposition beyond finite comprehension, I abandon it as I do a weight which human strength can not lift; and I think ignorance, in these cases, is truly the softest pillow on which I can lay my head."

Adams likewise affirmed that he was not disposed to bother himself very much about unanswerable questions. Once, as a part of his self-explanatory effort, he apostrophized some anonymous specimen of the human race in these words: "Vain Man! Mind your own Business! Do no wrong. Do all the good You can. . . . drink your burgundy, sleep your s[i]esta, when necessary, and *Trust in God.*" His response to Jefferson's remark about pillowing one's head on ignorance was in similar vein: "Oh delightful Ignorance! When I arrive at a certainty that I am Ignorant, and that I always must be ignorant, while I live, I am happy, for I know that I can no longer be responsible."[80]

We know, however, that the sentences just quoted do not, taken by themselves, give an accurate cross-section of the thinking of either man. It was impossible for Jefferson, throughout his life a penetrating student, to rest his head very long at a time on the pillow of ignorance. And even if Adams had desired to do so, he could never have hushed inner interrogations about the riddle of human existence.

[80] Adams to Jefferson, May 12, 1820, *ibid.*, II, 565. See also Adams to Jefferson, May 26, 1817, and Jefferson to Adams, March 14, 1820.

They did not find themselves in agreement at every point. The older man believed that there is a distinction, none the less definite because he was unable to explain it, between matter and spirit. Jefferson could not accept the idea of any such duality in the universe. He ruled out completely the conception of "immaterial existences." The notion that spirit exists apart from matter was to him heresy, even "masked atheism." Nothing in the teaching of the Founder of Christianity, he insisted, supported such a belief. He quoted Origen, Tertullian, and St. Justin Martyr—stating that others of the early Christian fathers were in agreement with these three—in support of his contention that matter is an element in spirit, even as spirit permeates highly organized matter.

When he had completed a moderate-sized essay on the subject, he dismissed it with the blunt statement that he rejected all organs of information except his senses; that is, he believed that if spirit with spirit can speak, it can do so only by way of matter.

Adams did not attempt any rebuttal to this argument, but subsequently he and Jefferson approached the area of religion and some of its subsidiary topics from other angles. Using as a pretext a passing reference which Adams had made to John Calvin, Jefferson vigorously set forth his ideas about that well-known ecclesiastic. He declared that if any man ever worshiped a false god, Calvin certainly did. In Jefferson's opinion, the religion of the Geneva theologian, who was so influential in shaping the course of the Reformation, was "Daemonism," in its essence blasphemy. The world, he maintained, would have been better off if Calvin's formulations had never been foisted upon it. Thinking not only of those who were preaching Calvinistic doctrines but also of many other leaders in "Christian" sects, he set down these words for Adams' perusal: "The truth is that the greatest enemies to the doctrines of Jesus are those calling themselves the expositors of them, who have perverted them for a system of fancy absolutely incomprehensible, and without any foundation in his genuine words."[81]

This was, of course, the restatement of an opinion, set forth this

[81] Jefferson to Adams, April 11, 1823, *ibid.*, II, 591, 594.

time, however, with greater emphasis than before. And frequently in this part of his correspondence he sketched in unmistakable outline articles of his personal credo. He believed that the Man of Nazareth could readily have mistaken the "coruscations of his own fine genius" for a unique and special revelation of the Creator. And he likened the doctrine of the Virgin Birth, accepted by the majority of Christians, to "artificial scaffolding," which would be removed when people were permitted and encouraged to think for themselves.

These convictions and similar ones were held honestly and grew out of many years of reflection in the light of his own reason. And on these points, and at this time, any differences between Adams and himself were negligible. The drift of Adams' thought about the "perversions" of Christianity had come to be parallel with that which may be traced in the writings of the younger man. In relation to the New England orthodoxy in which this son of "Deacon John" had been trained, he was unquestionably a nonconformist in his old age.

In one of the letters that went during those later years from his desk to Monticello, there are sentences elaborating views of religion, and particularly of abuses made of it, that might very well have been written by Jefferson himself. Laws such as some in force even at that time in Massachusetts constituted, Adams declared, "great obstructions to the improvement of the human mind" and should be repealed. He was thinking especially of a statute penalizing as blasphemy any investigation of the authenticity of the Scriptures. "I cannot enlarge upon this subject," he wrote, "though I have it much at heart." He summed up his opinions in these words: "The substance and essence of Christianity as I understand it is eternal and unchangeable and will bear examination forever but it has been mixed with extraneous ingredients which I think will not bear examination and they ought to be separated."[82]

With regard to what lies beyond the event of death, the views of both men continued in the main channel of Christian teaching. We have seen that in this matter, as in many others, neither of them had been a passive agnostic. As they came nearer the end of the earthly

[82] Adams to Jefferson, January 23, 1825, *ibid.*, II, 608.

journey, they witnessed to each other, more freely than ever, a personal belief in life everlasting. Frequently they dismissed with radiant confidence the dark alternative of annihilation. While they based their hope on evidence available to human reason rather than on divine oracles, they kept clinging to it without doubt of its validity. Once, having written to his friend at length about questions which neither of them, in common with all their fellow men, could answer, Adams concluded on this positive note: "We shall meet hereafter and laugh at all our present botherations."

A little later, in the same letter in which he paid his respects to Calvin, Jefferson said that he awaited "with more readiness than reluctance" the time and the will of the "God of Jesus." "May we meet there again," he went on—in reference to the world beyond— . . . with our antient Colleagues, and receive with them the seal of approbation, 'Well done, good and faithful servants.' "[83] In another context he told this one of his "Antient Colleagues" that in the "supermundane region" not only would old and cherished associations be renewed, but also a much more satisfactory post for observation of worldly happenings would be provided. In a manner comparable to that in which mortals look down upon ants and crawling creatures they would watch from above, in disembodied blessedness, the activities of those succeeding them on the stage of earthly life.[84]

In the next to last winter of his life, having just read what he called the most extraordinary of all books, Flourens' report of his experiments with functions of the nervous system of certain vertebrate animals, he was led to ponder once again the question of how the human body and the spirit that tenants it for a while are related. While occupied with these reflections, he added another assurance to others of this nature which had preceded: "All this you and I shall know, when we meet again, in another place, and at no distant period."

Soon there came to him, echo-like, this word from Adams: "We

[83] Jefferson to Adams, April 11, 1823, *ibid.*, II, 594.
[84] Jefferson's frequent witness to his belief in a personal immortality is worth noting in view of the statement sometimes made that he held no such belief.

shall meet again, so wishes and so believes your friend." On which spiritual morsel, however, he sprinkled this time a little pinch of salt: "If we are disappointed, we shall never know it."[85]

As the years continued to levy their toll on this remarkable pair, the physical labor of writing became increasingly difficult for them. In the year in which Abigail was taken from him Adams mildly complained of his inability to answer all the interesting letters he received. He explained that when he attempted to write, his fingers could manage only what he called "short scratches." Eventually he had to submit, almost invariably, to the necessity of dictating. Some of his grandchildren and other younger persons within reach became willing conscripts and wielded the pen which had become for him a cumbersome instrument. He did not take kindly to this unavoidable arrangement. "If I am not humble I ought to be, when I find myself under the necessity of borrowing a juvenile hand to acknowledge your kind favor."[86] So he admitted to Jefferson in words that he could not put on paper himself.

At the same time, the hand that wrote the Declaration of Independence had lost much of its agility. Adams sometimes overrated his friend's physical condition on the misleading evidence of his penmanship, not knowing what discomfort the elegant script had cost the writer. Once, thinking of his own crippling infirmity, he declared, "Had I your Eyes and Fingers, I should Scribble forever." But if Jefferson's eyes and fingers could, with some excuse, be coveted, not so the wrist which, dislocated years before, had stiffened with the advance of old age. That he wrote as many letters as he did in those closing years without "borrowing a juvenile hand" is evidence of a stoic determination to keep in touch with friends and of a persisting eagerness to put into such form his far-ranging observations.

Like most persons who advance well beyond the milestone marking threescore years and ten, both men had their good days and their bad ones, the latter recurring with greater frequency as the amount

[85] Adams to Jefferson, February 25, 1825, *Adams-Jefferson Letters*, II, 610. See also Jefferson to Adams, January 8, 1825, *ibid.*, II, 606.
[86] Adams to Jefferson, January 29, 1819, *ibid.*, II, 532.

of their "borrowed time" increased. In his eighty-seventh summer Adams boasted that on a recent day, evidently a good one for him, he had walked a distance of three miles over rugged terrain near his home. But with the next stroke of the pen—or the next breath of the dictation—he admitted this bitter and more immediate fact: "I feel when sitting in my chair, as if I could not rise out of it, and when risen, as if I could not walk across the room."[87]

Less infirm and dependent at this time than Adams, with his "quiverations," semiblindness, and muscular atrophy, the Virginia mountain-dweller was even more subject to temporary illness, sometimes alarming to his family. But he seems to have had better than average resilience. Upon recovery from rheumatic attacks or other ailments that for a time incapacitated him, he would ride, just as before, about the sloping fields of his estate or along the familiar winding roads of the neighborhood. He finally had to give up the comparatively long journey to Poplar Forest; but Charlottesville residents sometimes saw him—a figure which in the saddle gave little hint of the age to which its owner had attained—traveling, in one direction or the other, the few miles between his home and the site of the university which he had fathered. In his eightieth year he was still dreading a "doting old age," even though he could report to Adams that his health had been generally good, and continued to be good. Well on toward the time of his last bout with disease he kept up his habit, when the weather was favorable, of taking horseback trips, sometimes even beyond the boundaries of his plantation. Moreover, he was spared mental infirmity, the specter of which had often haunted him. Almost to his last day, the keenness of his intellect was not dulled.

The two friends often inquired about each other's health, with anxiety when the most recent report was not good, with gratification when it was more encouraging. In such context they kept reverting to the certainty that their lease on mortal life was running out rapidly. In one of his later letters Adams, more jaunty than usual when writing about the state of his health, incorporated this bit of prophecy:

[87] Adams to Jefferson, June 11, 1822, *ibid.*, II, 579.

"J. A. In the 89 year of his age still too fat to last much longer."[88] (Here again it is permissible to assume that Adams chuckled to himself, thinking of his bodily avoirdupois in connection with his imminent demise.)

For this former President, almost a nonagenarian now, who retained some of his former corpulence, life was, of necessity, fairly quiet. Peacefield became more peaceful than ever as the years of its owner lengthened. The big house, while never empty, was not overrun with visitors, as Monticello sometimes was. Even John Quincy got back only rarely to his birthplace to spend time with his father. The duties of his office, associated undoubtedly with the urges of his ambition, made it impossible for him, it seems, to take such a lengthy trip frequently.

But there was no lessening of the fatherly pride with which his career was followed. And down in Virginia the elder statesman whose acquaintance with the younger one had been of such long standing watched the unfolding of that career with an interest which may have been, at times, almost proprietary. While the issue of the 1824 presidential campaign was in doubt, Adams, writing to Jefferson, referred to his oldest son as "our John."[89] Gone entirely from the old man's memories was the incident involving what he regarded as unfair treatment of John Quincy by President Jefferson. He did remember well, however, that at a more remote time, when they lived in Paris, that same John Quincy had appeared to be almost as much Jefferson's son as his own.

The younger Adams was not Jefferson's first choice as Monroe's successor in the presidential office. His preference was for a southerner, William H. Crawford. But when the smoke of the quadrennial battle had lifted and John Quincy emerged victor, he sent one more message of congratulation to the father. "I sincerely congratulate you," he wrote, "on the high gratific[atio]n which the issue of the late election must have afforded you. It must excite ineffable feelings in the breast of a father to have lived to see a son to whose educ[atio]n

[88] Adams to Jefferson, November 10, 1823, *ibid.*, II, 602.
[89] Adams to Jefferson, January 22, 1825, *ibid.*, II, 606.

and happiness his life has been devoted so eminently distinguished by the voice of his country."[90]

Adams founded no university. On the other hand, the "visionary" who justly took pride in his paternal relationship to the University of Virginia did not have a son to follow in his footsteps to the post of highest eminence in the country. If between them the score of outward honors achieved was not precisely even, it was far from being one-sided.

In the record of those closing years there belongs the story of separate reunions with Lafayette. In the summer of 1824 the aged Frenchman came to visit the Republic with whose early struggles he had been conspicuously associated. One day, responding to a special invitation, he dined with Adams and other members of the Quincy household. Lafayette's secretary, who by virtue of his position shared in the entertainment, related afterwards that while the host joined in the conversation with fluency and evidences of good memory, he could scarcely get up from his chair and could not feed himself.[91] His tongue did not cleave to the roof of his mouth, but the "quiverations" of his hands were such as to make them almost useless.

A few weeks later the Marquis was received with open arms at Monticello. It is not unlikely that during his leisurely stay on the "little mountain" he had much to say to Jefferson about the bodily infirmity that masked the residual mental power of their common friend. At the time he left the Quincy home, he had said, according to one bystander, "That was not the John Adams I knew."[92] Perhaps he made a similar statement in the hearing of his Virginia host.

Toward the end of his pilgrimage in America, Lafayette went back to Monticello, as he did to Quincy, for one more visit. Again, in this special way memories of the Revolutionary years and those that shortly followed were quickened. And when the visitor, having spoken his final farewell, started homeward, Adams and Jefferson

[90] Jefferson to Adams, February 15, 1825, *ibid.*, II, 609.

[91] Edgar Ewing Brandon, *LaFayette, Guest of the Nation* (3 vols., Oxford, Ohio, 1950–57), I, 130.

[92] Smith, *John Adams*, II, 1133.

experienced anew and inevitably a loneliness for which there was, fortunately, the partial compensation of writing to, and hearing from, each other.

In the months that followed there came to Peacefield some other welcome visitors from a distance. Among them was Ellen Randolph Coolidge, recently married and accompanied by her husband, Joseph. Ellen, it may be recalled, was the second of the "sisterhood" which stood in granddaughter relationship to Jefferson, and the source of special attraction to two "Northern" travelers some years before. Abigail's eagerness to entertain her, expressed in a letter to her grandfather, had never been gratified. Now the days, all too few, which this daughter of Martha Jefferson spent in the "President's" house, along with her husband, were ones which could have been appropriately circled on Adams' calendar. Surely there was for Ellen, too, a thrill in the experience. How intently she must have listened to this man of whom she had heard so much, his mind still active and his tongue still ready. And it is likely that at intervals he gave her a chance to tell about life on the distant plantation, cupping his better ear to hear better what she had to say, either on her own initiative or in reply to his questions.

Ellen wrote a full account of this visit to her grandfather, who, we may be sure, read every word of it with great interest. "We found the old gentleman," she related, "just as he has been frequently described to you, afflicted with bodily infirmities, lame & almost blind, but as far as his mind is concerned as full of life as he could have been fifty years ago." She then wrote about her own and her husband's feelings as the visit ended. They were "penetrated with respect & admiration for the noble ruin which, time-worn and shattered, looks still so grand in comparison with what is offered to us by present times."[93]

About the time Ellen's letter was received there came to Jefferson's desk a brief report of this meeting from the "noble ruin" himself. He chose the adjective "delightful" as the best one to describe it. The

[93] Ellen W. Coolidge to Thomas Jefferson, December 26, 1825, *Collections of the Massachusetts Historical Society*, Vol. 61 (Boston, 1900), 366.

young bride's grandfather could be sure that she deserved all the high praise heaped upon her.

There was one more treat of the same kind in store for the failing patriarch of Quincy. Ellen's older brother, being on a visit to Boston, rode down the turnpike from that city and stayed for a little while with his grandfather's good friend, whom he had been very eager to see. Jefferson had written in a letter of introduction that this traveler would be greatly disappointed if he had to leave that part of the country without seeing Adams. Indeed, in such case he would think that he had "seen nothing." Turning a few of those deft phrases which still came naturally from his pen, the writer phrased his request in this manner: "Gratify his ambition then by receiving his best bow; and my solicitude for your health by enabling him to bring me a favorable account of it." The young man, he wrote, looked forward to recounting in the "winter nights of old age" his experiences in meeting a few of the "Argonauts" of the "Heroic age preceding his birth."[94]

This "Argonaut" looked upon the desire of anyone to see him in that capacity as most fitting and proper. Answering the letter containing Jefferson's request, he commented that it was one of the "most beautiful and delightful" he had ever received. Having been the target of criticism, much of it undeserved, during considerable portions of his active life, he was agreeably affected by any open recognition of his place of honor and eminence in history. And he reported that he was "very much gratified" with Mr. Randolph and his conversation.[95] To one whose contacts with the outer world had been narrowed by the restrictions of advanced age, these meetings with two of Jefferson's grandchildren were most interesting and helpful.

As they drew near to the inevitable end, there came to each of these veterans of the "Heroic age" a very special satisfaction. To the Virginian was given the great privilege of seeing in actual operation the university with which he claimed, indisputably, the tie of paternity.

[94] Jefferson to Adams, March 25, 1826, *Adams-Jefferson Letters*, II, 614.
[95] Adams to Jefferson, April 17, 1826, *ibid.*, II, 614.

Just one month before death called him, he wrote to his grandson-in-law in Massachusetts, "Our University is going on well."[96] To Adams a special pleasure and satisfaction never duplicated in American history was extended. As a former President, he lived to see the day on which his son was inaugurated as one of his successors. Beyond that, for more than a year he was permitted to follow, as well as he could from the seclusion forced upon him, but with unabated pride, that son's administration of his high office.

Since Abigail's death, her surviving partner and his good friend had "decanted" more than one additional "vintage." If the Master of the feast did not save for-them the best wine to the last, they could not complain much about the quality of what they were then permitted to enjoy. Along with many goodly favors bestowed was a privilege they had certainly earned—that of looking back upon careers of extraordinary usefulness. Each of them could have made his own an affirmation in Cicero's *De Senectute*, which Adams as an old man read, it is said, once a year: "I mean not to lament and deplore the lack of the pleasant and fresh time of my youth, as diverse and the same right well-learned men have done; neither do I repent that I have lived, because I have so lived and led my life that I may judge of myself that I was not born in vain, but rather for great utility and special consideration."[97]

As they had done from the time of their reconciliation, the two venerable men, leaders in a generation that had nearly vanished, kept in touch with each other by letter almost as long as they lived. We may well note, even if briefly, how they persisted in avowals of mutual respect and affection.

In one of his letters written in the summer of 1822, Adams, with a charming disregard of the long periods in which there was little or no communication between them, asserted that Jefferson was his friend

---

[96] Jefferson to Joseph Coolidge, Jr., June 4, 1826, *The Writings of Thomas Jefferson*, edited by Andrew A. Lipscomb and A. Ellery Bergh (20 vols., Washington, 1903), XVIII, 356.

[97] *Anthology of World Prose*, edited by Carl Van Doren (New York, 1935), 334.

"of forty seven Years Standing." Some months later, looking forward this time rather than backward, he wrote, "I . . . am your friend for this, and, I hope, and believe, for all future Worlds." Still later, as if the surface of their acquaintance had never been disturbed by the slightest ripple, he closed another of the Monticello-bound letters in this manner: "With my profound respects for your family and half a century's affection for yourself I am your humble servant."[98]

As he sought to match these sincere expressions, Jefferson kept drawing on the ample resources of his vocabulary. He rounded out one of the missives sent to Quincy with a statement that he might have made to some dear member of his own family: "I am sure that I really know many, many things, and none more surely than that I love you with all my heart, and pray for the continuance of your life until you shall be tired of it yourself." When he thought that he might be allowing events at home and abroad to disturb him too much, he suggested, as he had done in some previous letters, that they try to forget all human difficulties and wrap themselves in the "mantle of resignation" and of that friendship of which, he reiterated, "I tender to you the most sincere assurances." And as if there might be in Adams' mind some lingering doubt about the constancy of his own affectionate regard, he ended in this way a letter not far from the last of those belonging to the "great correspondence": "That it [Adams' health] may continue to the ultimate period of your wishes is the sincere prayer of usque ad aras amicissimi tui [ever at the altars of your dearest friend]."[99]

The tumults and shoutings of party rivalry, the misunderstandings and suspicions and resentment which came as tragic by-products of the history of their times—all these, if not entirely forgotten, had faded into a colorless haze. If it was part of the design of Providence that they be spared for many years to give to the world a convincing

---

[98] Adams to Jefferson, August 15, 1823, *Adams-Jefferson Letters*, II, 596. See also Adams to Jefferson, July 12, 1822, and Adams to Jefferson, February 10, 1823.

[99] Jefferson to Adams, December 18, 1825, *ibid.*, II, 612–13. See also Jefferson to Adams, August 15, 1820, and Jefferson to Adams, January 22, 1821.

demonstration of how friendship, even if broken by terrific pressures, may be re-established and strengthened, that purpose was now accomplished.

In their final exchange, the one initiated by Jefferson's introduction of his grandson, they once more gave evidence of a mutual affection rarely exhibited in the lives of great leaders. Jefferson, referring to his health, wrote, "Mine is but indifferent, but not so my friendship and respect for you." In Adams' reply these were the closing phrases, "My love to all your family and best wishes for your health."[100]

Then the curtain was drawn. A remarkable relationship, spanning more than half a century and acted out on the stage of history, with successive scenes of attraction, fusion, fission, and re-fusion, was at an end. Viewed in its entirety, it shows in bold relief greatness of spirit on the part of men who, in their several public capacities, served well their generation and belong now to the ages.

[100] Adams to Jefferson, April 17, 1826, *ibid.*, II, 614. See also Jefferson's letter to Adams, March 25, 1826.

CHAPTER VII

Ave Atque Vale

JULY 4, 1826

❧

THROUGHOUT THE SPRING and early summer of 1826 three famous Americans looked forward to July 4 with feelings that could not be paralleled in any other citizen. That day had a very special significance for John Adams, Thomas Jefferson, and Charles Carroll, the three surviving signers of the Declaration of Independence. There was left a remnant of other individuals who in some way had taken part in the Revolution, but they had not been as near as this venerable trio to the actual delivery of the infant nation. At Quincy, Monticello, and Doughoregan Manor memories that had no counterparts among the living were being renewed.

The infant had grown to the stage of robust young manhood. Twenty-four states belonged to the Union originally composed of thirteen. Six million people owed allegiance to a government which at its inception had claimed the loyalty of scarcely half that number. New York and Philadelphia had already made great strides toward becoming metropolitan centers, in the modern sense of that term, while scores of smaller cities and towns were steadily advancing in size and importance. Many of them were connected by turnpikes, on which lumbering stagecoaches and cumbersome freight wagons and oxcarts moved men and goods in slow but usually sure progression and in mounting numbers. Steamboats, having replaced to some extent sailing vessels on the Atlantic, were plying a few of the larger rivers and lakes. And canals connecting certain natural inland waterways were supplementing other means of transportation. In October, 1825, the "big ditch" that extended from Albany to Buffalo had been opened to public use with festive ceremonies appropriate to the completion of such an undertaking.

Moreover, as an augury of another mechanical wonder about to be realized for the benefit of travelers, in John Adams' home village grading was being done for a railroad, heralded locally as the first one in the country. Over it, before that year of national jubilee had run its course, a clumsy train of cars would transport granite boulders destined to be hewn into shape for use in the Bunker Hill monument.[1]

Along the seaboard, small industrial establishments were providing a means of livelihood for an increasing number of capitalists and laborers. West of the Mississippi, the more adventurous were pushing out toward new frontiers. In every section of the country society was being fashioned into more variegated patterns. Surveying the national scene in the first year of his administration, President John Quincy Adams commented in his diary that throughout the country there was "an unusual degree of prosperity, public and private."[2]

But in the over-all picture the colors were not all bright. In the newspapers and other contemporary records of life in the United States at half-century, modern readers can find stories of distressing experiences, similar in their main features to some of which they have first-hand knowledge. Great numbers of people were battling the forces of nature or confronting the ravages of disease. Along the upper reaches of the Mississippi and much of the course of the Missouri, fur traders, and Indians who had become farmers, watched helplessly as yellow torrents disrupted traffic and in many instances ended hopes of a summer harvest. At the same time, there were other distressing scenes, similarly caused, in parts of Virginia. In some states nature assumed a contrary, but equally unfriendly aspect; many fields and meadows lay parched because of long-continued drought. Here and there companies of the devout met to pray for the benison of rain.

In a few of the larger cities disaster struck in another and more terrifying form. With the coming of warmer weather, scores succumbed to the dread cholera morbus, infants being the favorite prey of this destroyer. On a smaller scale there were tragedies and near

[1] *Columbian Centinel* (Boston), October 11, 1826.
[2] *Memoirs of John Quincy Adams*, edited by Charles Francis Adams (12 vols., Philadelphia, 1874–77), VII, 98.

tragedies roughly resembling many of those reported with startling regularity in modern newspapers. As an example, just a few days before the Fourth of July of that year, a "dashing young fellow" driving a "gig" along a New York City street ran over a small boy, injuring him severely. This "speeder" evidently belonged to the same order of humanity as the hit-and-run driver of modern days, for, according to an enraged spectator as he hurried away from the scene of the accident, he "distanced everything but a bad conscience."[3]

Almost everyone, however, displayed keen interest in party politics. The vacuum created by Jefferson's withdrawal from public life had been filled by Andrew Jackson, widely acclaimed as the new champion of the rights of the common man. On this Fourth of July "Old Hickory" had a major interest unrelated to his duties as a cotton planter. His ability as a tactician was by no means confined to military campaigns; and he was now anticipating a supreme effort to achieve a political victory he had narrowly missed the year before. Many believed that only a deal between John Quincy Adams and Henry Clay had kept the General from winning in the recent presidential contest, formally decided in the House of Representatives. In nearly every city, hamlet, and countryside west of the Alleghenies and south of the Potomac and the Ohio there were men ready to rally under his banner as soon as it should be unfurled again.

As the natal day of the Republic drew near, Clay traveled from the federal capital toward his Kentucky home, not too well physically, but cherishing a strong hope that his own qualifications for the presidency would be more generally recognized. In all the region in which he and Jackson were the most prominent political figures, there was a yeasty bubbling of the human mass. The day of undisputed domination of the seaboard states in the government was over, never to return.

In southern Indiana, a seventeen-year-old lad was alternating as a breadwinner between the operation of a ferryboat and the performance of such farm duties as grubbing stumps and hoeing corn. In waking hours not spent in manual labor he could have been found at

[3] *New York Advertiser,* June 16, 1826.

the Gentryville store, spelling out the news in a Louisville paper and sharing neighborhood gossip, or at his cabin home reading Weems's *"Life of Washington"* or *"Aesop's Fables"* or some other book which he had probably begged or borrowed. We may well believe that whatever surface matters engaged his attention on this national holiday, he was at times thinking about his country's past and its future.

In the city of Washington, that Fourth of July was ushered in with salutes of artillery which echoed along the streets and on out to the wooded shores of the Potomac. At eleven in the forenoon, a spectacular procession moved on to Pennsylvania Avenue and headed toward the Capitol. Among other notables in the procession were President Adams and Vice-President Calhoun. At the Capitol, the government officials entered the chamber of the House of Representatives, followed by private citizens who had credentials entitling them to admittance. The Declaration of Independence was read by a veteran of the Revolution, and an "impressive and argumentative oration" was delivered by Walter Jones, Esq. Then two cabinet members, Barbour and Rush, in turn made earnest pleas in the interest of the author of the Declaration. The latter part of his long day of life had been clouded, they explained, by extreme financial difficulties. They pointed out that unless more aid were given to him, Monticello would be put up for sale. What a fate for a place "endeared to us as the long abode of philosophy, of patriotism, and of hospitality"! What a tragedy for its owner! Before the gathering was dismissed, Adams, Calhoun, and others walked to the clerk's desk and put their names, along with the amounts they were contributing to this relief, on a paper prepared for that purpose.[4]

In the capital city the anniversary was also featured by an "open house" at the Executive Mansion. There "all who hungered or thirsted" were admitted, "as usual, without distinction."[5]

Appropriately, Jefferson had been invited to share personally in the exercises at the seat of government. Responding to the invitation, he informed the committee on arrangements that the state of his

[4] *National Intelligencer* (Washington), July 6, 1826.
[5] *Ibid.*

health would not permit his attendance. Then with characteristic phrasing he gave expression to a hope which for many years had helped to sustain his spirit: "May it [the event of July 4, 1776] be to the world what I believe it will be (to some parts sooner, to others later, but finally to all), the signal of arousing men to burst the chains which monkish ignorance and superstition had persuaded them to bind themselves, and to assume the blessings and security of self-government."[6]

In New York City, for many of the residents and for a throng of visitors there was a special epicurean feature in the celebration. In the afternoon, at the Washington Parade Ground, the center of interest was a barbecue, prepared for and carried out in grand style. Roasted oxen had been "handsomely placed" upon tables which were "spread 500 feet in length" and were "decorated with flowers and greens of various kinds." By virtue of his office Governor Clinton had the privilege of being the first to help himself. Then a "general invitation was given to the citizens to approach the tables and join in the feast which they did, to a man, in good earnest." For the crowd of celebrants, numbering an estimated ten thousand, there was also provided a generous but not excessive supply of ale.[7] Before the day was over, there was neither a roasted nor a liquid remnant left.

But not all the attention of the local citizens and of outsiders who mingled with them was given to celebrating, by feasting or otherwise, the event that had taken place just fifty years before. Some of the auspicious possibilities of the future were formally recognized. In a public ceremony spokesmen pointed with pride to the completion of the Erie Canal, a symbol of a new era in inland navigation. During the exercises a gold medal was presented to a son of Robert Fulton, deceased, who had acquired some fame as the inventor of the steamboat.

In most places, however, there was no such extraneous item in the day's observance. In many communities, appropriate church services were held. Some ministers found for their discourses a fitting text in the levitical law: "Ye shall hallow the fiftieth year, and proclaim

[6] Jefferson to Roger C. Weightman, June 24, 1826, Jefferson, *Works*, XII, 477.
[7] *New York Advertiser*, July 6, 1826.

liberty throughout the land to all the inhabitants thereof; it shall be a jubilee unto you."[8]

There were many for whom noise of some kind was a favorite method of expression. A few of these fired cannon; others had to be content with whatever smaller detonations they could arrange. In Massachusetts, however, an act approved by the governor just two weeks before the Fourth prescribed penalties for anyone offering for sale "any cracker, squib, serpent, or rocket," or exploding such a device without first securing a permit to do so from local authorities.[9] Such legalized precautions, however, were not common, and one pessimistic commentator ventured the guess that on the anniversary day fifty people would be killed by the bursting of cannon or by the careless use of "crackers, squibs," etc. He overestimated the loss of life, but from various states there came, after the holiday, reports of fatalities caused by the explosives, forerunners of many others that would occur in subsequent years.

In the city in which the Declaration had been written and adopted and first proclaimed, there were, it seems, no rockets bursting in the air, no din of exploding crackers, no civic feasting. In that historical setting nothing more unusual than a parade and a program in Independence Hall marked the anniversary. According to one local observer, whose opinion was no doubt shared by others, the Sabbath-like tranquility was very much in order. This observer commented, "Groups of orderly persons of both sexes were seen in the streets." To this approval of the prevailing sobriety he added an indirect rebuke of the manner in which celebrations had been conducted in some other places: "Instead of boisterous and extravagant mirth, our country's glory formed a fruitful subject of serious contemplation."[10]

In the opinion of another resident who appraised the day's events there was one regrettable departure from the decorum generally observed. The formal oration in Independence Hall was, he reported, a political speech rather than a discourse appropriate to such a day and

[8] Leviticus 25 : 10.
[9] *Columbian Centinel*, June 28, 1826.
[10] *National Intelligencer*, July 8, 1826, quoting from *Freeman's Journal*.

in such a place. "It is a pity," he observed, "that we could not all meet and act, on this particular anniversary, simply as Americans."[11]

In New England, practically every city and civic center was the scene of ceremonies providing a greater variety of emotional outlets than the rather subdued one in the nation's birthplace. While there was a certain conformity in the observances, here and there were unique features suggesting some originality on the part of the planners. In the procession seen on the main street of Rutland there were thirteen young ladies dressed to represent the thirteen uniting colonies, and following them eleven younger feminine participants representing the additional states which had been admitted. In New Haven all debtors confined in the city jail were liberated. Awed spectators in Providence watched a procession featuring veterans of the Revolution. In an elegant barouche rode four men who had helped capture the King's armed schooner *Gaspé*. Back of them, in as comfortable carriages as could be found, were 106 others—a surprisingly large number—who had belonged to the patriotic troops engaged in the War for Independence.

As was natural, one of the most impressive of many ceremonies held on that July the Fourth was arranged for and carried out by citizens of Boston. Nowhere more than in the city which claimed Samuel Adams and John Hancock as its own and in which John Adams himself rose to local eminence had the revolutionary movement shown cohesion and determination. In it, as many of its people boasted, the "child Liberty" was cradled. Near it was fired the "shot heard round the world."

In the forenoon, as many prominent males of the community as were physically able, along with a number of visitors of distinction, marched in a parade which wound its way from the State House to historic Old South Church. There the galleries and the wall pews were filled with members of the "fair sex." According to a custom of sex segregation then common, most of the main floor pews were reserved for men.

About the time the exercises were scheduled to begin, the orderli-

[11] *National Gazette* (Philadelphia), July 8, 1826.

313

ness of the occasion was threatened by attempts of a number of persons who had not gained admittance to crash the doors. Still worse, there was excitement bordering on panic for a few moments as a cry was heard that the gallery supports were giving way, but in a short time the alarm was proved false and the outer doors were effectively barred. The capacity congregation, "squeezed to a hot jelly," according to one reporter,[12] nevertheless listened attentively to a carefully prepared program. There were musical numbers and an oration by Hon. Josiah Quincy, mayor of the city. Following this cultural feast, a "collation" near the State House provided ample refreshment for all comers. Many in the throng thought of it as the most wonderful holiday they had ever experienced.

At Cambridge an oratorical effort by Edward Everett highlighted the jubilee anniversary. This noted speaker managed to condense what he had to say into the space of two hours. For that length of time, we are told, Everett "enchained the the attention of a crowded and delighted auditory."[13] One in this "auditory" who wrote his impressions was the editor of the *Concord Yeoman*, who made this personal appraisal: "I never heard *Demosthenes*—I never heard *Cicero*—I never heard *Burke*, but I can say, I have heard Edward Everett, and am proud to say he is my countryman."[14]

The citizens of neighboring Quincy greeted the day with some emotions which in the nature of the circumstances were unique. They could claim a direct link with the event being celebrated, one that could not be duplicated elsewhere except at Charlottesville and at Carroll's Maryland home. Most of the men and women who appeared that day on the streets of the little New England city, dressed in their Sunday best, were comparatively near neighbors of a man who was actually present when the great decision was made. And there were few among them who did not know that his had been the most influential affirmative voice in the debate that preceded the final choice.

---

[12] *Boston Courier*, July 7, 1826.
[13] *Columbian Centinel*, July 15, 1826.
[14] Quoted in *Columbian Centinel*, July 12, 1826.

A few weeks before the great day, the committee responsible for the program extended a special invitation to Adams. Even if he could take part in the observance in no other way, would he at least dine with his neighbors and friends? Might it not be possible for him to be brought in a chair and to remain long enough to break bread with his admirers? It would be understood if he did not feel able to sit through the formal exercises that would follow.

But Adams, now well advanced in his ninety-first year, felt unequal even to that minimum effort. He dictated his refusal: "The present feeble state of my health will not permit me to indulge the hope of participating with more than my best wishes in the joys and festivities and solemn services of that day on which will be completed the *fiftieth year* from its birth of the *Independence of the United States.*" As Jefferson did in his communication to the similar committee in Washington, he restated his belief that the "birth" of this independence enhanced prospects for a "better condition of the human race." But he added a clear note of warning. Actually, what had happened on that other Fourth of July could, in his words, "form the brightest or the blackest page" in human history, depending upon whether the benefits flowing from it would be rightly cherished or shamefully left unguarded.

Along with the explanation of the reason for his absence and the expression of his qualified optimism was a felicitous statement of his feelings as a member of the local community: "I pray you, Sir, to tender in my behalf to your fellow-citizens my cordial thanks for their affectionate good wishes, and to be assured that I am very truly and affectionately yours and their friend and fellow-townsman."[15]

This Quincy observance was carried out according to the common pattern—a morning parade, a lengthy program in the "Meeting House," then a "collation," in which the public more generally shared, at a convenient center (in this case the town hall). Those gathered about the long festal boards that afternoon heard the greetings sent by their long-eminent neighbor. And when the toasts were proposed, these gestures of respect being regarded as no less impor-

[15] *Columbian Centinel*, July 22, 1826.

tant at such functions than the meat and drink, among them were these: "John Adams, the venerable sage of Quincy, the firm supporter of our independence, pure in patriotism, deathless in fame"; "A resplendent star, just setting below the horizon."[16]

Probably very few drinking to that latter toast realized how near it was to the literal truth.

One of the semirural celebrations was at Charlottesville, nestling at the foot of the mountain on whose summit Jefferson had lived so long. At the public exercises there no Demosthenes soared to the heights of oratory. A student of the university, a young man unknown to fame, delivered an appropriate discourse, and once again the townspeople and others present heard the familiar words of the Declaration. Among the circumstances attending this recognition of the nation's birthday was one strikingly similar to another overshadowing the Quincy celebration. On the neighboring summit one more star of the first magnitude was fading, if it had not already disappeared entirely, from mortal sight.

At the dawning of that day, watchers at Jefferson's bedside knew that unless some unforeseen reversal of the processes of nature took place, he would very soon finish his course. Likewise, as the clock in the distant Adams mansion ticked off the early daylight hours, those living there thought it very probable that the aged invalid was getting near to the end which he had so many times anticipated. But, of course, no one in either home or in the many throngs of celebrants throughout the country could know all that would happen before the summer day ended. We come now to a review of certain other circumstances leading up to, or immediately associated with, a remarkable conjuction of events.

The university which Jefferson founded presented to him in the final springtime of his career some problems for whose solution he felt himself to be principally responsible. A professor of law was to be secured. Requirements for proposed courses in botany were to be determined. Even such details as approving expenditures for materials to be used in laboratory experiments and ways of holding boisterous

[16] *Ibid.*

students in check were referred to him. These and other administrative duties were to him a labor of love, to which he was glad to give some of the remnants of energy left to him.

Also, it was necessary, as he thought, to spend hours in taking care of his correspondence, a task which irked him more than ever. In one of those later months of his life he wrote to Samuel Smith, "My memory gone, my mind d[itt]o, for over five months confined to the house by a painful complaint, which, permitting me neither to walk nor to sit, obliges me to constantly recline, and to write in that posture, when I write at all."[17] But as long as he could hold a pen he kept replying to correspondents who had some claim on him. He even responded to the request of an Ohio admirer that he write at least "two lines" which might, if two lines could do it, assure posterity of his real stand on the question of slavery. Reaffirming his opposition in principle to the buying and selling of human beings, Jefferson predicted, for the benefit of this questioner, that the traffic would in time be abolished. More hopeful than he had been a few years before, when the dispute over the extension of slavery affected him like a nocturnal firebell, he anticipated a gradual and peaceful eradication of the evil.

His financial predicament was actually worse than he realized. Like many Virginia planters of the time, he had found it difficult to make ends meet over a period of years. Eventually, when he became involved as endorser of a note in the financial downfall of Virginia's Governor Nicholas, it became impossible. In this emergency there was, after a time, partial relief. News of his plight spread over the country, and contributions came from personal friends and many others grateful for his long and varied services.

During those closing months, members of his family eased as much as they could this burden of anxiety which he had been forced to carry in his old age. The fact that the gifts already made were insufficient to meet his obligations was apparently kept from him. It seems certain, too, that he had no knowledge of the plan of some persons in

[17] Jefferson to Samuel Smith, October 22, 1825 (Massachusetts Historical Society, Jefferson Papers), quoted in Schachner, *Jefferson*, 1002.

high station at Washington to use the Fourth of July celebration there as an occasion for appeal to add to the relief earlier given.

Indeed, all his earthly concerns, of which there had been a great accumulation, were receding. From the middle of February on, there seems to have been little doubt in his mind about the imminence of his exit from life. In March he wrote a will, attaching to it a lengthy codicil. Later, as the weather became warmer, there were days when he appeared comparatively vigorous. On one such day he wrote to a friend that he felt better than he had in the preceding spring. But he did not expect to live through the summer, although he began to cling to the hope that he might be spared to see one more Fourth of July. By mid-June the horseback rides, the length of which had already been shortened, had to be given up entirely. On the twenty-ninth of the month a visitor, Henry Lee, called on business and found him, while able to converse, in a state of weakness which gave no promise of restoration.

Even before that date the members of his household understood the meaning of the accumulating symptoms and were trying to adjust themselves to it. The necessity of doing so soon became more apparent. On Sunday, July 2, Jefferson handed Martha a little box containing a token of affection in the form of appropriate quotations and a brief note of a personal nature. On the next day he slept, after the manner of many about to sink into the deepest sleep of all. Late in the evening he stirred, and out of a dulled sense of the passage of time but with enough consciousness left to understand that the day to which he had been looking forward hopefully was drawing very near, if not already present, asked one standing beside him, "Is this the Fourth?" The reply, a slight and pardonable deviation from exactness, was affirmative. Having heard it, the dying man went to sleep again with every appearance of contentment.[18]

Later in the night some stirring in subliminal depths manifested itself in the motions of writing. Unconsciously a feeble use—almost the last—was being made of the bodily machine. About the same time he remarked, as if he were living in the far past, but clearly and

[18] Randall, *Jefferson*, III, 546.

coherently enough to convey his meaning, that a warning should be given to the Committee on Safety. Then followed hours of deepening coma. Sometime during the forenoon of the Fourth, Nicholas Trist, husband of one of Jefferson's granddaughters, sat near the bed and recorded his observations in a letter. "He has not roused from his lethargy now for several hours," Trist wrote; "his pulse is scarcely susceptible to the slightest touch; and his extremities have the clamminess of death."[19] In little more than three hours after these words were written, the silver cord was broken. Thomas Jefferson in earthly form was no more.

John Adams still survived—but only through the brief hours of that summer afternoon.

For him, too, late winter or early spring had brought the beginning of the ultimate physical decline. Before April was over, relatives who cared for him suspected that his powers of resilience were almost exhausted. Very probably he had the same suspicion himself. Strange indeed it would have been if this man who so many times had mistakenly believed himself to be near the borderland of the next world did not realize it when he actually came within sight of it.

His correspondence, long since carried on only by dictation, was now reduced to a small fraction of its former volume. But in the writings of others his still active mind found interest and satisfaction like that which in the past had helped him through innumerable hours. Sitting in his chair, within easy reach of the cane upon which he was dependent in any attempt to move about, he followed at times the adventures of some of Scott's heroes and heroines, as younger members of the domestic circle read to him. At other times he listened to Cooper's sea stories. Occasionally the reading was from well-worn or recently acquired books of nonfiction. On sunny days in springtime and early summer he was taken on short carriage trips about the neighborhood, little outings which paralleled Jefferson's horseback rides. Apparently both of them were compelled to forego at about the same time the pleasure of getting out in the open.

In mid-June some Quincy citizens feared that this living link with

[19] *Ibid.*

the Revolution might be broken before the great commemorative occasion. But while it weakened perceptibly, on the last day of the month the chances against such a severance seemed good. At nine o'clock on the morning of that day the Reverend Mr. Whitney, who had been selected as the orator at the local exercises on the following Tuesday, called on the old statesman. During the short visit, Whitney asked for a toast which in Adams' absence might be presented in his behalf at the "collation." The two-word response was, "Independence Forever." The vigor with which this concise sentiment was delivered surprised the visitor. There was a familiar snap, too, in the rejoinder, "Not a word," when Adams was asked if he did not wish to add something to that brief phrase.[20]

As Whitney left, he may have thought that Quincy's first citizen would linger for a few weeks more. But on Monday, July 3, one of Adams' granddaughters wrote to her Uncle John Quincy that in the opinion of the attending physician their venerable kinsman could not live more than two weeks, and probably would not last out that number of days. On the next morning Thomas Adams penned a few lines to his brother, informing him that their father was rapidly sinking. Evidently there was a pronounced change in the invalid's condition during the week end just preceding the national jubilee.

But he lived long enough to greet the anniversary day, and he did so with a clearness of recognition that was not possible in the case of Jefferson. The morning light streamed into the New England mansion some time before it lightened the one on the southern hilltop. In the freshness of that dawn, John Adams stirred to wakefulness. A servant watching over him, asked, "Do you know, sir, what day this is?" There was little if any hesitation in the reply: "O yes, it is the glorious Fourth of July. God bless it. God bless you all."[21]

Then, lapsing into coma, he slept through the long morning. About one o'clock in the afternoon, not far, one way or the other, from the moment at which Jefferson expired, he roused again. One who was

[20] Adams, *Works*, I, 635.
[21] *Columbian Centinel*, July 12, 1826.

standing by his bedside heard him say, "Thomas Jefferson survives," the last of those words spoken indistinctly, but with sufficient clearness to be understood.[22] It is probable that no inkling of intelligence regarding Jefferson's serious condition had come to him in recent weeks, and on that day he had no way of knowing what was happening at distant Monticello. If the gift of ready speech which he normally possessed had remained with him to the end, he might have explained that final remark, one scarcely to be expected in such circumstances, by saying that the country would have yet for a while the benefit of Jefferson's living presence. If that was his hope, it was not to be realized. The assertion was false, or would be so before the day advanced much farther. But those three words, forced into speech in such extremity, may be construed as a parting tribute to his friend.

For several hours thereafter John Adams weakened more rapidly than he had during the morning. One narrator of the day's events, to whom we may attribute an exuberant imagination, reported that once Adams, partially roused by an artillery salute, was heard to say that every such gunshot added five minutes to his earthly existence. But the messenger whose arrival Adams had frequently expected was at last almost ready to issue his summons.

Meanwhile, the feasting and the program at the town hall proceeded. Fairly late in the afternoon the master of ceremonies introduced into the sequence of toasts the brief message which Adams had directed to be associated with his name. It was accompanied with even louder cheers than those heard when the earlier toasts directly honoring him were proposed.[23] Concurrence with the sentiment was, of course, inseparable from tribute to the man. About an hour later, not long before sunset, the one so honored, the nation's second President, ceased to breathe.[24]

As that Fourth of July passed into history, no human being knew

[22] *Memoirs of J. Q. Adams*, VII, 133.

[23] *Columbian Centinel*, July 22, 1826.

[24] Adams' grandson George, who was at his bedside at the time, wrote that he died "a few minutes before six in the evening." (*Memoirs of J. Q. Adams*, VII, 129.

what nearly all Americans would soon learn, that within the space of a few hours both of these men of towering eminence had joined the great majority. A relatively small number, men and women and younger people of Quincy, knew half of this truth. Scarcely had the banqueters returned to their homes when word leaped from house to house that Adams had passed away. We may be certain that hushed conversations followed in many of the little city's homes, and that a common feeling was frequently expressed in some such manner as this: "Since all men must die sometime, how appropriate that for this man, spared so long, the end came on the day it did."

Down in Virginia a still smaller number, we may believe, heard that afternoon or evening the news about Jefferson. It is natural to suppose that within little clusters of university personnel and of other Charlottesville residents, remarks similar to those spoken along the streets and in the homes of Quincy were made about the departed author of the great Declaration.

Several days passed before the majority of the country's population knew the whole truth, almost unbelievable. Modern Americans may find it difficult to realize that in that time news was carried no faster than a horse could run or a steamboat could make its way along a river-course. In most places, therefore, the festive mood of the day-light hours continued undisturbed throughout the evening. Here and there displays of *feu de joie*, under more or less careful super-vision, delighted spectators.

In one way or another, but not without many thankful and sober reflections, free men and women came to the close of a never-to-be-forgotten day. There are those who would not regard it as fanciful to picture John Adams and Thomas Jefferson looking down together from unseen heights upon prolonged jubilee celebrations and rejoic-ing in the view permitted to them.

When it became generally known that death had claimed both Adams and Jefferson on that day, many could not think of that fact as coincidence. Some in later generations have marveled at such a phenomenon in history.

If either of these former Presidents had died on any Fourth of July, there would have been comments on the singularity of timing, but the fact that both of them had received the final summons on the nation's fiftieth birthday aroused a general feeling of sheer awe.

Not long after the news spread throughout the country, one man with a flair for figures and the calculation of mathematical possibilities made this announcement: "Taking the age of Mr. Jefferson to have been 33 when he signed the declaration, and Mr. Adams to have been 40 years [at these points, at least, he was on safe mathematical ground], the chance of their both living fifty years longer, and dying at their expiration is only one in twelve hundred million."[25] He seems to have meant that these were the odds when figured in terms of *exactly* fifty years.

But there were factors involved independent of ordinary life expectancy figures. Nearly all school children and the great majority of adults knew about the leading part taken by each of these men in the beginnings and early development of the country. The irregular movements of the lines of their lives in reference to each other, paralleling, separating, crisscrossing, had been traced on pages of history with which many were familiar. There was no room in the average citizen's comprehension of the laws of probability for the phenomenon that these particular men would make their exits from life's stage on that particular day.

As if trying to add to the dimensions of the effect produced, one writer professed seeing mysterious significance in a few details which he twisted, evidently in ignorance, out of line with the facts. A few of those whose appetites for the bizarre had been whetted by the double visitation of death swallowed whole this writer's statement that the Great Designer timed the last summons for Jefferson and Adams with reference, not only to the day, but also to the hour, of special anniversary meaning. For, so it was stated, the Declaration was adopted between noon and one o'clock on July 4, 1776, and was proclaimed to the people around the State House about five o'clock

25 *Columbian Centinel*, July 15, 1826.

323

on that same afternoon. Therefore, in accordance with this reading of events, an extra touch of appropriateness was added as the two men finished their respective courses at those same hours of the day.[26]

But without any distortion of historical records, most newspaper writers did their best to put into writing what many were saying on the street corners, in village stores, in tradesmen's shops, and in city taverns, and what parents in many homes were seeking to impress upon their children. "Well is it repeated," a Boston newspaper declared, "by all who heard the tidings, that the deaths of two such distinguished men and associates as Adams and Jefferson, happening on that same day, and that day the completion of the fiftieth year of their connection, is a coincidence of events unexampled in ancient or modern annals, and would not be credited by posterity if not corroborated and confirmed by circumstantial evidence that can not lie."[27]

In the columns of a New York paper it was stated that the "like has never happened in the world, nor can it ever happen again, we may almost say with certainty."[28] Readers of the leading journal in the national capital were told, "No language can exaggerate it—no reason account for it. It is one of those events which have no example on record, and as a beauteous moral must forever stand alone on the page of history."[29] More picturesquely, another writer epitomized his comment in these words: "Two suns have set on this day of our jubilee."[30]

Naturally, the more devout portion of the population looked upon the simultaneous setting of these "suns" as a special dispensation of Omnipotence. It was argued in many pulpits, and even in other places having no special aura of reverence that here was a sign, as clear as if had appeared in the skies, that an Almighty Power rules in the affairs of men. A few of those whose belief in the supernatural evoked sensual images became almost lyrical as they expressed their reaction

---

[26] *Ibid.*, quoting a Philadelphia newspaper. Actually there was a much longer interval between the adoption of the Declaration and its public proclamation. See page 36 above.

[27] *Columbian Centinel*, July 12, 1826.

[28] *National Advocate* (New York), July 10, 1826.

[29] *National Intelligencer*, July 11, 1826.

[30] Quoted in *Columbian Centinel*, July 15, 1826.

to the double event. One of them claimed the thrill of imagining "two such spirits winging their way, at the same moment, through a boundless eternity to realms of light; raising at the same moment their voices, attuned to the melody of golden harps."[31]

The record inscribed on history's page by the "moving finger" under the date, July 4, 1826 helps to corroborate the old adage that truth is stranger than fiction. A creative genius of the first order might enrich the literature of imagination with a story of two such men as Adams and Jefferson and move them about in some such relationship to each other as that to which actual history witnesses; but he would scarcely venture to have both of them leave the earthly scene on the fiftieth anniversary of the day with which, above all others, both of their names were associated. Our own generation has many wonders to contemplate; very probably those to come will have just as many. But the chances are almost infinitely remote that we, or our descendants, will be confronted with a historical phenomenon similar to that which, on July 4, 1826, aroused wonder in the minds and spirits of millions of Americans.

Time never pauses in its onward march to recognize extraordinary events on our planet, but we human beings halt for a while our accustomed routines to memorialize our dead, especially the more illustrious among them. And in the days and weeks that followed the jubilee observance and the twin visitations that accompanied it, there were events that belong to the same pattern as those to which we have just given attention, and therefore have an appropriate place in this narrative.

At the expiration of a post mortem interval which seems almost irreverently short, the burial service for Thomas Jefferson was held. Only a few details filtered out into channels of public information. It appears that no general advance notice of the hour of interment was given. But it was late in the afternoon of the day following his death. Those who were present watched closely as under lowering skies the body was carried, without pomp or any special honors, a short distance down the mountain road to a grave made ready by the

---

[31] Quoted in *National Intelligencer*, July 18, 1826.

side of the wife of Jefferson's early manhood. There the Episcopal clergyman of the parish conducted the traditional rituals of the Christian church. There was, it seems, no eulogy, nor any funeral pageantry of the kind usually connected with the last rites for men and women of prominence. The minimum obsequies were in keeping with the legend, which had already taken form, of Jeffersonian simplicity.

Quite otherwise were the services at Quincy. After two full days of preparation, Adams' townspeople focused their interest on a funeral for which there had been no counterpart in Quincy's history. From various parts of the Old Bay State came persons who had known this man for many years. With them mingled visitors and residents belonging to a later generation, men and women who in childhood had been taught to associate the name of John Adams with highest patriotism. In the throng were some who in a distant time had not seen eye to eye with him in matters of public policy, but were eager to join with their fellow citizens in witness of their great esteem.

In the early part of the afternoon—it was Friday, July 7—a company of relatives and close friends gathered in the large mansion which was the heart of Peacefield. At the same time nearly all of Adams' male neighbors assembled in the hall where they had so recently been feasting and otherwise celebrating. Forming marching units, they proceeded to the shaded lawn of the home and presently formed the van of a long procession that moved slowly to the "meeting house." In the rear, separated as usual on such occasions from their husbands, brothers, and sons, members of the gentler sex, some of them relatives of the deceased, rode in the finest coaches the town could provide.

When as many as possible of the two thousand or more who sought admittance were seated in the church, the impressive rites began. There was no suggestion of haste. Those present were ready for much more than a fleeting pause when brought together to honor their dead in such manner. On this day especially, any sign of hurry would have been regarded as a mark of poor breeding. Along with music and prayer and scripture there was a standard-length discourse by Adams' minister, the Reverend Mr. Whitney. Beginning with words first applied to the Hebrew King David, "He died in a good old age, full of days, riches, and honor,"[32] he went on to extol the talents, services, and virtues of his friend and parishioner. Following the church solemnities, burial, which turned out to be temporary, took place in the town cemetery. In the multitude dispersing after the last words had been spoken were many who believed that John and Abigail were together again.

In Boston very little business was transacted on that day of commitment. Bells were tolled and flags on ships in the harbor and elsewhere hung at half-mast. In other New England centers of population, large and small, where the slow-moving news of the aged statesman's death had arrived, and with it information about the time set for final services, there was, for a little while, a general suspension of normal activity. In the ceremonies conducted on that Friday and in similar ones that took place in the weeks that followed, there was no such lack in tokens of respect as Adams had complained of in connection with the passing of some other leaders in the American Revolution. Even in that period of his life when, more than any other, he seemed to be obsessed with notions of earthly vanity, he could not have wished for a more fitting recognition of his removal by the hand of death.

Ignorant of all that was happening at home, John Quincy Adams spent that day performing his regular duties in Washington. It was not, however, without some reflections relating to human mortality that he went through the day's routine. He had already learned that Jefferson was no longer among the living. And on the next day came the letters from Quincy relatives. On Sunday morning, accompanied by his son John, he started on the long trip to his native place, clinging to the hope that he might get to his father's bedside before the end came. Slowly the carriage rolled on toward Baltimore, the travelers enduring as well as they could the merciless summer heat. Perhaps the older man recalled other lengthy, arduous journeys on which his companion had been, not his son, but his father. About eleven o'clock in the morning, while they were at Waterloo having a late

[32] I Chronicles 29 : 28.

breakfast, the innkeeper, who had just come out from Baltimore, brought the news which by that time was more than four days old.

A few days later President Adams was back in the home around which many recollections of his mature years centered. As he walked from one room to another, emotions welled up within him which presently found an outlet in his diary. The scene before him as he stepped, for the first time on this visit, into his father's bedchamber, struck him, in his own words, "as if it had been an arrow to the heart." By way of this diary he gave himself the admonition, "I feel it is time for me to begin to set my house in order, and to prepare for the churchyard myself."[33]

One day, not long afterward, he walked about the burying-ground, and for a time stood reverently and thoughtfully by a newly made grave and the older one next to it. In that day's diary entry he set down a few facts about some of his remote ancestors, laid away in that same churchyard; but fluent as he was with the pen, he wrote nothing about his feelings as he stood on that hallowed ground.

On Saturday, July 8, at some point approximately midway between Quincy and Monticello, no more than a few hours elapsed between the arrival of riders carrying northward the tidings of Jefferson's passing and that of other heralds carrying southward the news of Adams' decease. In New York City there were some who learned simultaneously that the country's second president and its third were dead. When the full story became generally known, the effect was stunning. One of the local journalists commented: "We have never seen New York exhibit such a feeling as it did day before yesterday. . . . The death of two such men on the same day, and so near to each other in point of time, was felt by the whole community. Friend stopped friend on the street and expressed in a few broken words their surprise and astonishment." It appeared to this observer that even those who might not have been expected, on account of their tender years, to share in the prevailing mood, actually did so. "The very children that play about the streets," he noted, "although they could

[33] *Memoirs of J. Q. Adams*, VII, 125.

form no adequate conception of the intelligence, yet seemed to feel out of sympathy for their parents and friends."[34]

The precedence which New York had over other large cities, except possibly Philadelphia, in getting the complete story of what had happened on the Fourth of July made possible a comparatively early expression, in an organized way, of the public feeling. Soon the details were arranged, and on the twelfth day of the month residents of the first federal capital gave their united tribute to the two men whose names were now, more than ever, strangely linked. Nearly all business places were closed. About every section, the factory districts, the shipping wharves, the shopping centers, and the residential areas, there was unaccustomed stillness, broken at intervals as minute guns at the Battery tolled off with reverberating salutes the combined ages of the two former Presidents. Spectators of and participants in a long procession which moved from the City Hall to the Middle Dutch church were in the grip of a mood very different from that which had prompted their recent revels on the nation's birthday. Those who secured entrance to the church heard a discourse which in substance was soon to be repeated in numerous cities, villages, and hamlets throughout the country.

Outstanding among the memorial services for the two departed statesmen was the one at Baltimore. The greatest possible use was made of funereal trappings and symbols. In the procession that preceded the outdoor services were several features attracting a morbid interest, among them two shrouded objects fashioned like coffins and mounted on a large vehicle. Back of these grim reminders of human mortality was a barouche in which rode Charles Carroll, now the sole survivor of the signers of the Declaration. Bowed down as he was with the weight of years, he provided a unique and somber reminder of his former associates whose memories were being honored.[35]

[34] *National Advocate*, July 10, 1826.

[35] Carroll died in Baltimore, November 14, 1832, at the age of of ninety-two, having lived for more than six years as the only survivor of the men who signed the Declaration of Independence.

The destination of the solemn procession was a vast natural amphitheater. There, sitting or standing in the shadows of encircling oaks, thousands of awed listeners heard all that they could, without the aid of loud speakers, as a lengthy program was presented.[36] The orator chosen for the occasion was Hon. Samuel Smith, United States senator from Maryland, locally distinguished for his service in that capacity and also for his record as a high-ranking officer in the War for Independence. He made a praiseworthy and fairly successful effort to reach the heights he was expected to attain. In a style considered suitable for such discourse, he apostrophized Adams and Jefferson, addressing them as "Holy Patriarchs of the Revolution," "Conscript Fathers of the Republic," "Twin sons of liberty." If permitted to look down on the world they had left, they would be witnesses, they were told, of the "outpourings of a nation's gratitude."[37]

The majority of New England citizens were not inclined to overlook or minimize Jefferson's contributions to the country, but it was natural for sectional pride to express itself in special emphasis upon Adams' virtues and accomplishments. In remote outposts of habitation as well as in the more populous centers, men, women, and youth came together to pay their tribute of respect to one whom they could claim as a "native son," and incidentally to do the same for his southern contemporary. In many villages local orators were called upon to put forth their best efforts. For those of greater fame the cities provided appropriate occasions. Caleb Cushing was heard at Newburyport. Edward Everett was heard at Charlestown, where he manifested again his "enchaining" abilities.

One of the most impressive of the memorial exercises held in Adams' home state took place in Boston on August 2. The scene was Faneuil Hall, which for years had been a shrine of more than local interest. It was packed to utmost capacity. Seated in places of special

[36] A full account of this event is given in *Niles' Weekly Register* (Baltimore), July 29, 1826.

[37] *A Selection of Eulogies in Honor of John Adams and Thomas Jefferson* (Hartford, 1826), 72.

honor, the President of the United States and others of the Adams clan shared in the proceedings. As in similar meetings throughout the country, a few who had lived through scenes of the Revolution were present. From the galleries ladies, row upon row of them, looked down upon the rest of the tense assembly. About them the terse fashion comment was that they were "suitably attired."

The speaker of the day was the "god-like Daniel." Seldom has such a stage been set for a public utterance by such a man. It was the platform of a hall whose very timbers were seasoned in an atmosphere which might be credited with providing special elements for the growth of human liberty.

As a master of assemblies, Daniel Webster had no superior, and few, if any equals, in his lifetime. In sheer personal magnetism, combined with a sonorous, spine-tingling resonance of voice, he can be compared, among Americans, only with William Jennings Bryan and Franklin D. Roosevelt. One can picture him on that day stepping to what served him as a kind of throne, tucking one hand beneath his coat lapel, as was his custom in public speech, transfixing the assembled throng with piercing eyes, then breaking the hush which his presence evoked with the simple statement: "This is an unaccustomed spectacle."

For more than two hours the torrent of his speech rolled on. At one point he dramatized the proceedings of the Continental Congress two days before the adoption of the Declaration. Referring to the members of that body, he said, "Let us open their doors and look in on their deliberations." During this exercise of imagination Adams, for a few moments at least, was not a dead man being honored; rather, he was a man very much alive, in full possession of mature powers, dedicated to a great cause. Impersonating him, the orator of the day uttered phrases which, as was reported, this sturdy advocate of independence had used in private conversation.[38] "Sink or swim," he thundered out, "live or die, survive or perish, I give my hand, and my heart, to this vote. . . . If we fail, it can be no worse for us. The

[38] See page 19 above.

cause will raise up armies; the cause will create navies. The people, the people, if we are true to them, will carry us, and will carry themselves, gloriously, through this struggle."[39]

Resuming the eulogy in his own character, Webster reminded his hearers of other public services which Adams had rendered. Interspersed between these narrative and laudatory paragraphs were others of a similar nature relating to Jefferson. By modern standards, the spokesman for the throng in Faneuil Hall was sometimes grandiloquent, but it all seemed appropriate in that time and place. And when the last word had been uttered, everyone felt that the two men linked in death so remarkably had been honored to the greatest extent possible within the limits of human speech.

However, John Quincy Adams shortly afterward made a candid entry in his diary which might appeal to those modern Americans who prefer brevity in memorial tributes. Having listened in recent weeks to several lengthy eulogies, he wrote, "I have received high though melancholy satisfaction from these performances, but found myself much, too much, overcome with fatigue."[40]

The formalized outpourings of praise reached a climax, so far as length is concerned, in the service held in the federal city. The date chosen for it, October 19, had at least an indirect anniversary significance.[41] The place was the hall of the House of Representatives. En route to it from Quincy, the President had come breakfastless from his lodging place on the previous night. Even though he may have anticipated fatigue, he was anxious not to miss any part of the proceedings. Seated with him on the main floor were other dignitaries of the government, accredited representatives of many foreign countries, and as many of the permanent city residents as could be accommodated. As was noted in reports of similar gatherings, the ladies were conspicuous by their presence in the galleries.

The anticipation of all these people had been raised to a high level. This was not an occasion for second-rate or short-winded speakers;

[39] Daniel Webster, *Discourse in Commemoration of the Lives and Services of John Adams and Thomas Jefferson* (Boston, 1826), 40.

[40] *Memoirs of J. Q. Adams*, VII, 140.

[41] It was John Adams' birthday, according to the Old Style calendar.

and William Wirt, attorney general of the United States, to whom the honor of voicing the common feelings had been delegated, was well qualified.

This statesman had looked upon the assignment as a "ticklish experiment" on account of his having known Adams only by reputation. Nevertheless, his praise of Jefferson's "friend of the North" was as detailed and glowing as Webster's references had been to Adams' friend of the South. The talents and virtues of the "Patriarch of Quincy" and of the "Sage of Monticello" were held up alike for universal approbation. And as Wirt neared his peroration, he remarked that "Heaven, itself," mingled visibly in the celebration of the "great Jubilee of the nation" in hallowing the anniversary day "by a double apotheosis."[42]

It took two hours and forty-five minutes for this orator to do what he regarded as justice to the occasion. A reporter who was present enthusiastically commented, "It did not seem to us half so long."[43]

The ceremony at the federal capital practically completed this form of public recognition. Nature itself places a limit upon such manifestations of sentiment. But there was a regrettable sequel. Having consigned, through participation in one or more of the long series of memorial observances, these "Fathers of the Republic" to the national pantheon, many Americans straightway disregarded, or forgot, some of the solemn injunctions laid upon them by the orators. There was another demonstration of the fickleness to which wayward humanity has always been prone.

Scarcely had the echoes of the eulogies died away when it became apparent to those most concerned that there would not be sufficient gifts of money to make it possible for the Jefferson family to keep the Monticello estate. In less than six months after the owner's death his furniture was sold to help pay off accumulated debts. Not long afterward both Monticello and Poplar Forest had to be given up. There came a time when grain was stored in some of the rooms of the

[42] William Wirt, *Discourse on the Lives and Characters of Thomas Jefferson and John Adams* (Washington, 1826), 67.

[43] *National Intelligencer*, October 21, 1826.

mansion which Jefferson had built and teams of horses were driven up and down the front steps.

Of course, many fellow citizens of the former President would have lamented this desecration had they known about it, but year after year went by without evidence of popular interest in the restoration of a home which in earlier times had been like a magnet to great numbers of people. A sharp thrust was made by a French writer, who may have had some royalist leanings, at this obvious lack of veneration. "The nobler emotions of democracy," he observed, "are of short duration; it soon forgets its most faithful servants."[44]

Adams' heirs were more fortunate in that there were no encumbrances upon the house which for almost four decades had been his home. His sons and other relatives received modest legacies, and in the final settlement a substantial sum was contributed, by Adams' direction, to the cost of a "granite temple," erected to replace the church building in which he had regularly worshiped.

Soon the country was involved in another hotly contested political battle, the most prominent victim of which was John Quincy Adams. Any claims he may have had to the honor of succeeding himself in the presidency were rejected by a majority decision, and for a time at least the name of Adams lost some of its former appeal. On a tidal wave that swept out of the South and the West and inundated parts of the East, Andrew Jackson was carried into executive power. The hero-worship which was now directed toward "Old Hickory" has rarely been paralleled in American history. Those who kept sacred the memory of the two men who had so recently received remarkable posthumous adulation were outnumbered by a new order of devotees, whose enthusiasm for the "Hero of New Orleans" left little room for any rival, living or dead.

Many of the eulogies delivered soon after July 4, 1826, were printed, and it appears that all of them, like the few especially noted here, were worthy of the occasion which brought them forth. In every case no words were spared, no rhetorical devices known to the

[44] Cornelis DeWitt, *Étude Historique sur la Démocratic Américaine*, quoted in Randolph, *Domestic Life*, 418.

speaker neglected, in the effort to extol properly the characters and the benefactions of the "Twin sons of Liberty" whose exits from earth had so strangely coincided. There were many lengthy reviews of their respective careers, the orators weaving as skillfully as possible the two strands into one pattern which all their hearers might admire and, as far as possible, follow. But about the personal relationships between these "Conscript Fathers of the Republic" very little was said.

Webster alluded briefly to the "difference and discord" that arose between them, stating that the occasion was not one "for entering into the grounds of that difference."[45] Wirt interjected the remark that the "cold cloud" which for a time was ominously suspended over their friendship "passed away with the conflict out of which it had grown, and the attachment of their early life returned in all its force."[46] And Everett took a few moments of the generous allotment of time he permitted himself to utter some words which, viewed solely in relation to their subject-matter, stand out like a tall, lone peak in the vast range of these eulogistic efforts. "I know not," he said, "whether, if we had it in our power to choose between the recollection of these revered men as they were, and what they would have been without their great struggle, we could wish them to have been other than they were, even in this respect. Twenty years of friendship succeeding ten of rivalry appear to me a more amiable and certainly a more instructive spectacle, even than a life of unbroken concert."[47]

But each of these spokesmen and the lesser orators of the time were too near to the subjects of their discourses, perhaps in some cases too little informed about certain details of their lives, to delineate them properly in the character of friends. The lapse of many years since the two statesmen passed away, along with the recent attention to publishing definitive volumes of their writings, makes possible a perspective which their early panegyrists did not have. From it may

[45] Webster, *Discourse*, 55.

[46] Wirt, *Discourse*, 63.

[47] Edward Everett, *Discourse in Commemoration of John Adams and Thomas Jefferson* (Boston, 1826), 31.

be viewed in clearer outline the times in which they lived, their part in them, and the results which followed in their mutual relations.

They were drawn together in early manhood, as if by magnetic attraction, because of a common militancy in the struggle for freedom of the American colonists. Each of them always remembered that in the early days of their acquaintance, a time when fateful choices were made, the other had been outspoken and resolute in defense of civil rights, while many of their associates were hesitant or submissive. For a few years after the climactic July 4, 1776, they were separated by the exigencies of public service, but there was no weakening of the bond forged in the crucible of a hazardous revolution.

Their subsequent meetings in foreign lands, and in connection therewith the convergence of other important lines of interest, brought them into a different, in some ways a closer relationship. There was a partial but very real merging of their respective families across the boundaries of age and sex. As they met, not only about conference tables but also in their own dining rooms, their friendship ripened. An adage already ancient in Cicero's time that "many bushels of salt must be eaten together" before fulfillment of friendship is possible seems applicable here.

Yet during that period of voluntary exile they were being subjected to influences analogous to those which were soon to work havoc with their friendship. Jefferson returned from France with a feeling approximating hatred toward the institution of monarchy; Adams, on the contrary, seemed to have had a fascinating spell cast over him by the British system of government. Many of his fellow citizens regarded it as most unfortunate, and a few of them deemed it to be almost demonic. In the first administrative period under the new constitution, political parties were born: "democrats" began to be pitted against "monocrats," "Gallomen" against "Anglomen." The same path along which the two men came, in turn, to the place of highest political preferment, took them farther and farther apart personally. Misunderstanding, suspicion, some jealousy perhaps, some chicanery certainly on the part of a few lesser men—indeed, the entire *milieu* of circumstances in which their lot was cast—made inevitable the temporary ruin of a friendship once highly prized by each.

For more than a decade after they met for the last time, no word passed between them. The man who carried the burdens of the highest office in the land did not receive, or seek, advice and encouragement from his predecessor, who in the formative years of the Republic had belonged to the inner circle of his companions. Even after both of them were permanently established, like Cincinnatus, in their rural retreats, having severed all relations with officialdom, the gulf between them seemed for a time to be as wide and unbridgeable as ever. Then the unpredictable happened. To the cautious approach of the older man there was an immediate and open-hearted response. Bygones became bygones in the sense that they were no longer divisive.

All of this, omitted or touched upon lightly by the men appointed to voice the nation's tribute after the "double apotheosis" of July 4, 1826, has been reviewed in the preceding pages. It should now be noted, as of course contemporaries of Adams and Jefferson could not do, that there has been an upward trend, especially over the course of our twentieth-century decades, in public recognition of the Homeric stature of these early Americans.

After years of neglect, Jefferson's mountain home was restored to its likeness during the years of his retirement, and has been purchased and dedicated as a national shrine. More recently, a memorial to him was erected on the south bank of Washington's Tidal Basin—a mute but impressive message in architecture to many visitors. His name is held in veneration by many belonging to the posterity which he so often envisaged.

Nor has there been any lack in these later generations of tokens of highest respect for Jefferson's great contemporary. Peacefield has become a National Historic Site. To it and to the church a few blocks away, where Adams' mortal part, with that of Abigail, rests, in the words of their epitaph, "until the trump shall sound," there come yearly a goodly number to pay homage. They and the pilgrims who make their way to Monticello and to the memorial structure in the capital city represent a still larger group of Americans who are mindful of the debt they owe to all those men who brought forth on this continent a "new nation, conceived in liberty and dedicated to the proposition that all men are created equal."

John Adams and Thomas Jefferson still survive. In addition to that personal, other-worldly immortality which they hopefully anticipated, they live in the transmitted memories of a great host of their fellow countrymen whom they antedated. Among those memories there will always be a rightful place for the story of a friendship that has few if any close parallels in the long history of mankind.

Index